DATE DUE

MAY 22 '89			

DEMCO 38-297

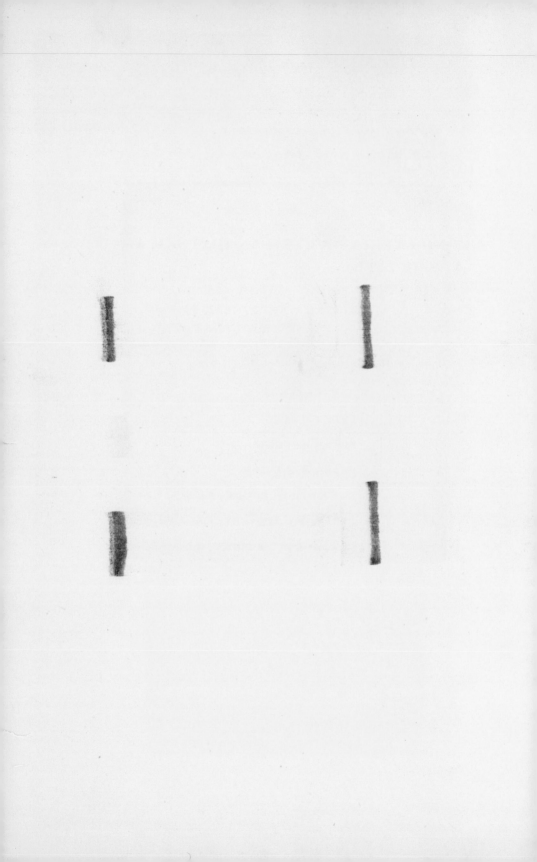

THE NORWEGIAN-AMERICAN HISTORICAL ASSOCIATION

NORWEGIAN-AMERICAN STUDIES

Volume 23

1967

The Norwegian-American Historical Association

NORTHFIELD · MINNESOTA

Preface

THE NORWEGIAN-AMERICAN HISTORICAL ASSOCIATION'S publications since its founding in 1925 now total over forty, including both special and serial publications. Volume twenty-three of *Norwegian-American Studies* adds eight essays, plus bibliographical material, to the association's principal series.

The volume opens with an appraisal of the role of the Lutheran churches in Norwegian emigrant life. This essay was read at an American Historical Association session in 1965 as part of a consideration of the religious experience of diverse immigrant groups: the Italian Catholics, the Jews, and the Norwegian Lutherans. It was clear that immigrant cultural traits were inextricably intertwined with the church experiences, that the experiences of each group differed from the others radically, and that it would be necessary to continue to study each group in terms of itself rather than a part of a merged consideration of immigrant church life in America. Eugene L. Fevold's revised essay is particularly useful in summarizing the key features of Norwegian Lutheranism in America.

The next four contributions comprise letters and memoirs. Millard Gieske has selected a few of Senator Knute Nelson's

Civil War letters from a larger collection that will ultimately appear in book form. Nora Solum has carefully translated a delightful memoir of a remarkable pioneer editor, now well in his nineties, concerning his experiences as an emigrant boy. C. A. Clausen has brought together important letters of the 1840's by the discerning and influential Gasmann brothers, Hans and Johan, in Wisconsin. The Knud Knudsen "Report" of 1840 which proved so significant when published in Norway is here presented by Beulah Folkedal in translation.

The three remaining essays are in the fields of social and literary history. Nina Draxten presents another installment of her study of that explosive reformer, Kristofer Janson. Arlow W. Andersen explores the period of Knut Hamsun's American residence. Marc L. Ratner contributes a critical study of Hjalmar Hjorth Boyesen's relationship to certain pervasive ideas in the United States of his times, especially those of Herbert Spencer. His essay supplements the biographical study by Clarence Glasrud published by the Norwegian-American Historical Association in 1963.

The efficient and persevering work of Beulah Folkedal and Lloyd Hustvedt in assembling and organizing the archives of the association, now located in the new wing of the Rølvaag Library of St. Olaf College, is regularly made evident in these volumes of *Norwegian-American Studies* by "From the Archives" and "Some Recent Publications."

Without the expert assistance of Mrs. Helen Thane Katz in editorial work, volume twenty-three of this series could not have been completed at this time. The association is deeply in debt to her for this and past services.

CARLTON C. QUALEY

Carleton College

Contents

NORWEGIAN-AMERICAN STUDIES

Volume 23

by EUGENE L. FEVOLD

1   *The Norwegian Immigrant and His Church**

DURING the century following 1825, sparsely settled Norway contributed more than three quarters of a million of her sons and daughters to the making of America. While that figure does not seem large compared with the numerical strength of other immigrant groups, Norway's proportional contribution was exceeded only by that of Ireland (in the post-Civil War period) and by Italy (from the 1890's on). The Upper Midwest was the destination of most of these Norwegian immigrants — northern Illinois, Wisconsin, northern Iowa, Minnesota, and the Dakotas. Then the line of settlement stretched westward across northern Montana and Idaho into Washington. There were enclaves of settlement in many other areas as well — in New York City and its environs, Texas, and California, for example.[1]

Nearly all of these Norwegian immigrants were Lutheran in background and upbringing. Norway has had an episcopally organized Lutheran state church, or folk church, since the time of the Reformation. Many who came to America had a

* A paper read at the triennial meeting of the Norwegian-American Historical Association in May, 1966. *Ed.*

[1] Studies of Norwegian immigration are: Carlton C. Qualey, *Norwegian Settlement in the United States* (Northfield, 1938); Theodore C. Blegen, *Norwegian Migration to America, 1825–1860* (Northfield, 1931); Ingrid Semmingsen, *Veien mot vest: Utvandringen fra Norge til Amerika* (Oslo, 1942, 1950).

deep affection for the faith, worship, and practice of the Lutheran Church; others did not. None, however, desired to duplicate on American soil the authoritarian organizational structure of the church of Norway.

The nineteenth century was for Norway an era of great change and progress on many fronts. It saw the establishment of a democratic form of government with the adoption of a liberal constitution in 1814, the emergence of a strong nationalistic spirit, and the development of a virile intellectual and cultural renaissance represented by such writers as Wergeland, Bjørnson, and Ibsen. More or less closely related to these phenomena were vigorous religious movements that profoundly influenced the immigrant and his relationship to his church. One of these is known as the Haugean revival, taking its name from the lay evangelist Hans Nielsen Hauge (1771–1824), who was imprisoned for his teachings, 1804–14. Haugeanism was a pietistic, grass-roots movement that brought new life and vitality into a church characterized by formalism and lethargy. It served as a leaven in all of Norwegian society, playing an important part in nurturing the democratic folk movement of the time, and stimulating the entrance into politics of representatives of the rural population. It increased tensions between the more privileged classes and the common people, as well as between the clergy and the laity. Some of these tensions were carried to the American frontier.

In the 1850's a second religious movement began in Norway, known as the Johnsonian awakening. It takes its name from Professor Gisle Johnson (1822–94) of the theological faculty of the Royal Fredrik University in Christiania. It resembled the earlier Haugean revival in many of its emphases, with the difference that in this instance leadership was provided by the theological faculty and the clergy trained by them. It added a theological dimension lacking in Haugeanism. Johnsonianism represented an emphasis on both piety and orthodoxy that has been typical of Norwegian

4

Lutheranism in both Norway and America. It gave a pietistic tone to all of Norwegian life. During the last quarter
of the nineteenth century, however, religious skepticism developed rapidly in Norwegian intellectual circles, and many
of Norway's cultural leaders became indifferent or hostile to
the church.

Both the Haugean and Johnsonian awakenings were powerful influences in shaping the views of both laymen and
pastors who migrated to the United States. Dean Theodore
C. Blegen, who has so effectively tapped the riches of com-
munications sent back to Norway by immigrants, says that
expressions of piety "flood the 'America letters.'" And he ob-
serves that large numbers of Norwegian immigrants brought
with them to America "a deep religious impulse." [2]

Religion, however, played a relatively minor role as a cause
of emigration. The basic motivation was a desire for material
betterment. Intertwined with this fundamental interest was
discontent with aspects of the Norwegian social and political
situation. The much publicized episode of the sloop "Restau-
rationen" (the "Norwegian Mayflower"), which brought a
small group of immigrants to New York in 1825, is not fully
representative of Norwegian immigration, for the passengers
included a few Norwegian Quakers and some of Quaker sym-
pathies who migrated for religious reasons. Economic factors,
however, were important with the "Sloopers" as well.

By and large, the attitude in Norway toward emigration,
of both government and church, was skeptical and unsympa-
thetic. Most leaders in public life looked upon it as a national catastrophe, practically a traitorous desertion of the
fatherland. For one illustration, as early as May, 1837,
Bishop Jacob Neumann of Bergen issued an episcopal letter
to the "emigration-smitten" farmers of his diocese. He ap-
pealed to their patriotism in urging them to remain in Nor-

[2] Theodore C. Blegen, "The Immigrant Image of America," in *Norwegian-
American Studies and Records*, 19:8 (Northfield, 1956); Blegen, *Norwegian Migration to America: The American Transition*, 100 (Northfield, 1940).

way and strongly emphasized the trials, disasters, and spiritual deprivation that were the lot of the emigrant. Toward the close of his epistle he made this dramatic appeal:

"Here in Norway rest the ashes of your fathers; here you first saw the light of day; here you enjoyed many childhood pleasures; here you received your first impressions of God and His love; here you are still surrounded by relatives and friends who share your joy and your sorrow, while there, when you are far away from all that has been dear to you, who shall close your eyes in the last hour of life? A stranger's hand! And who shall weep at your grave? Perhaps — no one!

"Give heed, then, to the advice David gave to his people: 'Stay in the land and support yourself honestly.'" [3]

Although the church of Norway, as an institution, did not take steps to provide spiritual leaders for the emigrants, many individual ministers followed them to America. Their numbers were insufficient, however, and the immigrant congregations soon realized that they would have to train their own ministers and in all other respects become completely self-sustaining.

Because the bulk of Norwegian immigrants who affiliated with churches in the United States remained Lutheran, the focus of this discussion is the Norwegian immigrant and the Lutheran Church.[4] This restriction is in no way intended to minimize the importance of other Norwegian-American denominational groups, but is dictated by the need for brevity.

In September, 1843, the first Norwegian-American Lutheran congregation was organized in the Muskego settlement, about twenty miles southwest of Milwaukee. Its first pastor was Claus L. Clausen, a Danish schoolteacher with

[3] Gunnar J. Malmin, tr. and ed., "Bishop Jacob Neumann's Word of Admonition to the Peasants," in Norwegian-American Historical Association, *Studies and Records*, 1:108 (Minneapolis, 1926). The quotation is from Psalms 37:3, as translated by Malmin from the Norwegian Bible used in Neumann's time.

[4] For a full discussion, see E. Clifford Nelson and Eugene L. Fevold, *The Lutheran Church among Norwegian-Americans* (Minneapolis, 1960); this work is in two volumes, the first by both authors, the second by Professor Nelson alone.

Haugean views. Within a few years many more congregations were organized in southern Wisconsin and northern Illinois, several under the leadership of the aggressive pastor, J. W. C. Dietrichson. Prior to 1843, church work had not been formally organized, and spiritual guidance was provided by Haugean laymen. Steps to establish a church body were then taken under the leadership of the ablest and most aggressive of these, Elling Eielsen, who at the urging of his followers was ordained that same year. The church formed in 1846, popularly referred to as the Eielsen Synod, underwent a reorganization a number of years later, when it became Hauge's Synod. Eielsen's group was radically Haugean, particularly in its early years, in its emphases — lay oriented, somewhat anticlerical, low-churchly, pietistic, and evangelistic.

A marked tendency toward divisiveness arose from the very start. As early as 1853 a second church body, destined to be much larger and more influential than Eielsen's group, was organized, popularly known as the Norwegian Synod. It was formed, and grew rapidly, under the leadership of young, aggressive, and well-educated pastors, including, in addition to Clausen, such men as Adolph C. Preus, Herman A. Preus, and Ulrik Vilhelm Koren, who successively served it as president. This group sought to perpetuate the worship, doctrine, and practice of the church of Norway. They were traditionalists in this respect. They stressed church order and organization and thus were critical of unsupervised lay preaching. Their concern for "pure doctrine" was increased and strengthened by the close ties which were early established with Missouri Synod Lutherans, a German body.

In the free environment of the American frontier, divergent views that held together in Norway under the broad umbrella of the state church were assuming separate institutional or synodical expression. Fortunately this decided tendency toward religious fragmentation was, in the course of time, chiefly in the twentieth century, to be counteracted and

7

largely overcome by a strong union movement among Norwegian-American Lutherans.

The process of fragmentation continued as many immigrants sought to occupy religious ground somewhere between
the options provided by Eielsen's type of Haugeanism and
by the Norwegian Synod. Two additional church bodies
emerged which aimed at an intermediate position, the very
small Norwegian Augustana Synod and the larger Norwegian-Danish Conference, of which Professors Georg Sverdrup
and Sven Oftedal were the best-known leaders. Despite the
tendencies toward fragmentation, there were strong factors
operating to overcome differences, the most forceful being a
mutual heritage. These Norwegian Lutherans were unified
by a common language, a common hymnody, the same form
of catechetical instruction, uniform devotional books, and
the like.

In 1890 the intermediate groups were consolidated, under
the presidency of Gjermund Hoyme, in the United Norwegian
Lutheran Church, which sought to hold in balance church
order and lay activity, pietism and orthodoxy, and other
divisive tendencies. This effort at union was not entirely successful, for in 1897 a minority in the United Church organized the Lutheran Free Church. The formation of the United
Church had been the first step on the way to a second merger
in 1917, which saw the reunion of the great majority of Norwegian-American Lutherans in the Norwegian Lutheran
Church of America, which was later called the Evangelical
Lutheran Church. The largest group not included in 1917
was the Lutheran Free Church; in 1963 it joined many
Norwegian-American Lutherans in the American Lutheran
Church, of which the Evangelical Lutheran Church had become a part. Unquestionably the 1917 merger was one of the
great events in the story of the Norwegian immigrant and his
church.

During the second half of the nineteenth century these
Lutheran churches were involved in a number of controver-

sies. The differences were rooted in deep religious convictions but probably were also an expression of individualism. Some were simply transplanted from Norway, such as the long dispute about the legitimacy or function of lay preaching. Others were provoked by the American environment, manifesting themselves in sharp debates about slavery and the American public school.[5] The most violent controversy of all, one centering in the difficult doctrine of predestination and related questions, came about through contacts with other American Lutherans (the Missouri Synod) and involved tensions transplanted from Norway.

The theological position of all these immigrant churches was a most conservative one, as their doctrinal debates and discussions revealed. As one brief illustration: In 1880–81 Bjørnstjerne Bjørnson, Norway's poet-patriot, visited the United States and during his stay made a lecture tour through the Midwest. He was greatly admired by the immigrants for his patriotism, his poetry and novels, and for his rather democratic political theories. But on his American tour he proceeded to air his liberal religious views. Since he denied many traditional Christian teachings, his discussions of religious subjects created a tremendous furor. His chief critics were clergymen, "the real leaders of the people," according to Arthur Paulson, who has studied the incident. A small group of Norwegian-American intelligentsia, led by Luth Jaeger, a Minneapolis editor, loyally defended and championed Bjørnson. Anything smacking strongly of theological innovation or liberalism was rejected by most of these immigrant people. The same treatment was accorded the

[5] The slavery question was discussed in the Norwegian Synod, an ironic situation inasmuch as Norwegian immigrants almost to a man were opposed to slavery and allied themselves with Lincoln's party. The controversy began after the Civil War was under way and climaxed in 1868. The central issue was one of Biblical interpretation: What did the Bible say about slavery and how was it to be interpreted? Some members of the clergy, although not proslavery, felt that their loyalty to Scripture demanded a distinction between slavery as an evil and slavery as a sin. The laity were not interested in what seemed to them a theoretical discussion of the problem. Nelson and Fevold, *The Lutheran Church*, 1:169–180.

9

Norwegian liberal pastor Kristofer Janson, who also made a lecture tour in America (1879–80), and spent a dozen years in Minneapolis in the 1880's and 1890's.[6]

The type of life inculcated by the Norwegian Lutheran churches was generally pietistic. The church, in seeking to strengthen the moral fiber of its people under rough frontier conditions which often tempted them to forget traditional morality, stressed strict standards, sometimes emphasizing prohibitions — for example, the rejection of many types of amusement, strict observance of the sabbath, abstinence from alcoholic beverages, and the like. William Warren Sweet, a historian of American churches, in writing about the role of religion on the frontier, has said that the many admirable qualities brought there and nurtured "would have gone for naught had there not been planted in the far flung communities of the west the seeds of moral, spiritual and cultural life. As Horace Bushnell stated long ago in referring to the American west, barbarism was the first danger."[7] The churches of the Norwegian immigrants, like other denominations, made their contributions to moral, spiritual, and cultural uplift on the frontier.

In a famous essay Professor Marcus L. Hansen has set forth the thesis that frontier churches are always inclined to be puritanical.[8] His proposition is undoubtedly sound. In the case of the Norwegian immigrants, however, it must be strongly underscored that a pietistic-puritanical orientation was part of the cargo brought across the Atlantic as a result of the impact of the Haugean and Johnsonian awakenings. While, generally speaking, the standards of conduct promoted by the church among Norwegian immigrants were rather austere, one is at the same time faced with extensive

[6] See Arthur Paulson, "Bjørnson and the Norwegian-Americans, 1880–81," in *Studies and Records*, 5:84–109 (1930). The words quoted are on page 87. See also Nina Draxten, "Kristofer Janson's Lecture Tour, 1879–80," in *Norwegian-American Studies*, 22:18–74 (1965).

[7] William Warren Sweet, *Religion in the Development of American Culture, 1765–1840*, 137 (New York, 1952).

[8] Marcus Lee Hansen, *The Immigrant in American History*, chapter 5 (New York, 1964).

evidence that drunkenness was an extremely serious problem in many Norwegian-American communities, as it was in Norway in the 1830's and 1840's. Nevertheless, many Norwegian Lutheran church people, following the exhortations of their pastors and other leaders, became promoters and supporters of the prohibition movement.

Undoubtedly one of the stupendous achievements recorded in our national history was the conquest and settlement of the westward-moving frontier. Norwegian immigrants played a significant part in this accomplishment, particularly in the Upper Midwest. From the mid-nineteenth century and on, much of the history of church work among Norwegian Americans is the story of what we would call "home missions" carried on under pioneer conditions. The various church bodies and individual congregations strove valiantly to follow the waves of immigrants to their places of settlement. In so doing they established hundreds of congregations, dotting prairies, valleys, and woodlands with churches. The constitution of a Norwegian Lutheran congregation in southern Wisconsin (Wiota), dating from 1851, includes a paragraph which begins: "This congregation's territory shall extend as far north, south, east, and west as there are Norwegian settlers who will accept this constitution." The Midwestern frontier provided an almost limitless mission challenge to congregations and pastors.

Group isolation and insularity characterized these immigrant churches. Generally speaking, they were suspicious of and poorly informed about American denominations. But, as probably could have been anticipated, from the very beginning many immigrants from Norway affiliated with a variety of American church bodies — sometimes for geographic reasons, sometimes in consequence of vigorous American mission activity, or, in other instances, for doctrinal reasons, or because Americanization proceeded too slowly in their own group. Usually it was a matter of an individual or family joining a non-Lutheran congregation, rather than group affiliation

11

by a community with an American denomination. Norwegian Baptists and Methodists, however, formed separate conferences, which were later absorbed into the mother denominations. One of the most interesting and successful stories of recruitment among the earliest Norwegian immigrants by an American denomination concerns the Mormons. In the 1840's, while headquartered at Nauvoo, Illinois, prior to their famous trek to Utah, the Mormons were conveniently located for proselyting work in Norwegian settlements. Some converts migrated to Utah. Subsequently some of them went to Scandinavia from Utah as Mormon missionaries, and although they were far more successful in Denmark than in Norway or Sweden, it is estimated that during the period 1850–1900 about 30,000 Scandinavians went to Mormon Utah.[9]

Not all Norwegian immigrants came under the religious-ethical influence of the church, but sizable numbers did. From the 1880's and on, the percentage of immigrants indifferent to religion increased. More were going to the cities, such as Brooklyn, Chicago, and Minneapolis, where social pressures leading to church membership were not so great as in rural areas. Some of the newcomers reflected the skeptical climate of opinion which was making headway in Norway, and the coolness toward religion that often accompanied the newer views. At the time of the merger of 1917 there were about half a million members in Norwegian-American Lutheran churches, about 30 per cent of all first- and second-generation Norwegians.[10] Many others, not formally affiliated, were within the sphere of the churches.

Students of the Norwegian immigrant group agree that the church was the most important social institution established in its midst. The comment of Professor Einar Haugen is rep-

[9] See P. Stiansen, *History of the Norwegian Baptists in America* (Wheaton, Illinois, 1939); Arlow W. Andersen, *The Salt of the Earth: A History of Norwegian-Danish Methodism in America* (Nashville, 1962); William Mulder, "Norwegian Forerunners among the Early Mormons," in *Studies and Records*, 19:61 (1956); Mulder, *Homeward to Zion: The Mormon Migration from Scandinavia* (Minneapolis, 1957); Kenneth O. Bjork, *West of the Great Divide: Norwegian Migration to the Pacific Coast, 1847–1893*, 76–131 (Northfield, 1958).

[10] Nelson, *The Lutheran Church*, 2:225, 245.

resentative: "The first and most persistent of the immigrant's institutions was the Lutheran Church," and in it the Norwegian pioneer found "a natural center for his social and religious cravings." Professor Laurence Larson, speaking of the Norwegian immigrant group of which he was a part, wrote, "In pioneer times the church was our greatest and most influential institution. . . . In the study of our history we shall never get far away from the church." The typical Norwegian community was located in the rural Upper Midwest, and in most such communities the church was the cohesive social force. And, notably in the early period, the homes of the clergy were the chief centers of culture in these communities, and the pastors were the intellectual leaders. The significant socio-cultural leaven provided by some pastors' wives is illustrated in the life of Mrs. Ulrik Vilhelm Koren in northeastern Iowa.[11]

Next to the church the immigrant press was one of the more influential social forces. One area where the church seems to have exerted little direct influence but where the press was powerful was in the shaping of political views. Rather typical of the attitude of the pioneer clergymen was that of Pastor J. W. C. Dietrichson. Before the election of 1848, he was approached by representatives of each of the three parties — Whigs, Democrats, and Free Soilers — asking him to influence Norwegians on their behalf, but, he wrote in a letter, "I considered it the correct thing to remain neutral." Some of the clergy, especially in the early years, exercised a good deal of influence upon the immigrant press, and not only upon religious periodicals. For example, when in 1852 the newspaper *Emigranten* began publication, among the early leaders in getting it under way was Pastor Claus L. Clausen. Throughout its history it maintained ecclesiastical interests and was friendly to the church. Dean Blegen says of *Emigranten* that

[11] On the church as a social institution, see Laurence M. Larson, "The Collection and Preservation of Sources," A. C. Paulson and Kenneth Bjørk, "A School and Language Controversy in 1858," and Einar Haugen, "Norwegian Migration to America," in *Norwegian-American Studies and Records*, 9: 98, 10: 77, 18: 19 (1936, 1938, 1954); David T. Nelson, tr. and ed., *The Diary of Elisabeth Koren, 1853–1855* (Northfield, 1955).

13

"it came to reflect, as no other pioneer Norwegian-American newspaper did, the life and position of the majority of the immigrants." [12] There were, of course, journals that were critical of the church, for among the four hundred or so Norwegian papers in existence at one time or another the whole political-social-religious spectrum was represented.

Since the school (in addition to church and press) was another influential social force among Norwegian immigrants, the church's relation to education must be briefly mentioned. As early as the 1840's the emerging American public school system was the object of much criticism from Norwegian Americans. Many pioneer congregations established parochial schools; these normally supplemented the public elementary institutions, but some of them also taught the three R's and other "secular" subjects.

Conservative pastors were among the leading critics of the common school. They had reservations about its efficiency as well as its nonreligious spirit and lack of discipline, but more fundamentally they feared that exposure to the public school would accelerate the Americanization process so rapidly that immigrant children would lose their cultural heritage and possibly their Lutheran faith as well. There were, however, numerous Norwegian-American defenders of the public schools, both lay and clerical, who presented their case in the press. During the time the controversy raged, the typical immigrant sent his children to public school, supplementing this with religious instruction in summer parochial school.

The most significant and enduring direct contribution which the church made to education was through the church colleges established by Norwegian-American Lutherans — Luther of Decorah, Iowa; Augsburg of Minneapolis; Augustana of Sioux Falls, South Dakota; St. Olaf of Northfield, Minnesota; Pacific Lutheran of Parkland, Washington; and Waldorf of Forest City, Iowa. No consideration of the Norwegian immigrant

[12] Theodore C. Blegen, ed., *Land of Their Choice: The Immigrants Write Home*, 151 (Minneapolis, 1955); Blegen, *Norwegian Migration: American Transition*, 303.

14

and his church would be complete without mention of the influence these colleges exerted upon his children. Maintaining close connections with the church, these institutions have been one of the major cultural forces in Norwegian-American life. Dr. G. H. Gerberding, a theological professor of another Lutheran synod, who knew the Norwegians of the Midwest rather well, wrote:

"And how they love education. How they will plan and how ready they are to sacrifice and to suffer that their children may have an education. I actually saw large families living in sod shacks on the open prairie sending a boy or girl to Concordia College."[13]

The whole sociological crisis of the Americanization of the immigrant churches was focused in the problem of the transition from the Norwegian language to English. In relation to this, the church was primarily a conservative force. Of the various factors which contributed to the preservation of Norse, the church was undoubtedly most significant. In fact, the linguistic rigidity of the church taxed the patience of many second-generation Norwegians who were embarrassed by the immigrant status of their parents. Out of respect for the older generation, for whom Norwegian was "the language of the heart," if not of the market place, a congregation often retained Norwegian beyond the time when the new generation, including young Americanized pastors, had begun to clamor for a change.

The transition from Norwegian to English was painful, involving as it did a psychological reorientation of which many first-generation immigrants were incapable. Novelist O. E. Rølvaag was probably unexcelled in his understanding of the poignancy of the Americanization process, particularly in his *Giants in the Earth*. World War I gave a powerful impetus to the linguistic transition, and by the time of World War II it had been completed. For our purposes this brief reference to

[13] G. H. Gerberding, *Reminiscent Reflections of a Youthful Octogenarian*, 150 (Minneapolis, 1928).

the transition in the language of the church is simply a symbolic reminder of the whole complex process of Americanization that the church experienced.

President Lars W. Boe of St. Olaf College, an outstanding religious and educational leader during the crucial period when the immigrant was in transition, wrote in the 1930's concerning the religious and cultural issues at stake in that experience:

"Ours is a mediating generation. By training and tradition we live in the spiritual and cultural land of the fathers. With our children we are steadily marching into the land of tomorrow. Ours is the riches of two cultures and often the poverty of the desert wanderer. We live between memory and reality. Ours is the agony of a divided loyalty and joy in the discovery of a new unity. Like Moses of old we see the new but cannot fully enter in. To us has been given the task of mediating a culture, of preserving and transferring to our children in a new land the cultural and spiritual values bound up in the character, art, music, literature, and Christian faith of a generation no longer found even in the land from which the fathers came." [14]

[14] See Boe's introduction, in P. M. Glasoe, *The Landstad-Lindeman Hymnbook*, 3 (Minneapolis, 1938).

edited by MILLARD L. GIESKE

2   *Some Civil War Letters of Knute Nelson*

K NUTE NELSON, for many years a leading and powerful Republican politician in Minnesota, was born, an illegitimate child, in 1842 at Evanger, district of Voss, Norway. His parents were Ingeborg Kvilekval and Helge Knutson Styve. He emigrated to the United States with his mother in 1849, reaching New York in July. The two lived briefly in Chicago at the home of John Haldorson Kvilekval, Ingeborg's brother. Then, in 1850, Nelson's mother married another Norwegian immigrant, Nils Olson Grøtland, who later took the surname Tangen and eventually changed that to Nelson. Soon after the marriage, the family went to Wisconsin to live, and in the spring of 1852 acquired a farm in the Norwegian Koshkonong settlement near Deerfield, in Dane County. At this time Knute took the surname of Nelson, though he was occasionally called Knute Tangen. Prior to his adoption by Nils Nelson he was known as Knute Helgeson: that is, the son of Helge Styve. In the Koshkonong settlement, young Knute experienced the trials and deprivations of frontier living. And although an aggressive youth, he was closely attached to his mother and stepfather and to William and Henry, his two half brothers, who were born in the mid-1850's.[1]

[1] Nelson believed that he was born February 2, 1843, but his baptismal certificate shows the correct year to be 1842; photocopies in the Nelson Papers,

Millard L. Gieske

The young Nelson was both typical and atypical of the emigrant frontiersman. He had a natural curiosity about the larger world about him, and this, wedded to a quick mind and a yearning for education and economic betterment, served as the foundation for the emergence of a personality strongly attracted to public life. Still, Nelson's first twenty years were difficult. In 1858 he entered Albion Academy, a Seventh-Day Baptist institution in Albion, Dane County, Wisconsin, and there worked for his schooling for three years.[2]

He was interrupted by the Civil War. Nelson eventually came to value the conflict as an integral element in his education. His military service proved useful to him after his entry into political contests, because of the normal popularity of the veteran. And he had an innate bluntness that he exuded to public and politician alike. He served three terms in the lower house of Congress, 1883–89; he was governor of Minnesota from 1893 until his resignation in 1895; and he was United States Senator from that time until his death in 1923. He was never defeated in an election.[3]

Nelson enlisted in the Fourth Wisconsin Volunteers late in May, 1861, one of nineteen Albion students, reflecting the intense patriotism that permeated their small campus, to join the armed forces. They began to train for military service at Racine, Wisconsin, and on July 15 left for Baltimore and the

Minnesota Historical Society, and the Norwegian-American Historical Association Archives. For his early life, see Brynjulf N. Hugaas to Laurits B. Swenson, December 25, 1924, Nelson Papers (box 261); Leiv Slinde, *Knute Nelson: Fra fattiggut til verdskjent statsmann* (Oslo, 1950). A sketch of Nelson is in *Dictionary of American Biography*, 13:418. See also K. A. Rene, *Historie om udvandringer fra Voss og vossingerne i Amerika*, 382, 502–506 (Madison, Wisconsin, 1930); Mary B. Dillon to Nelson, May 6, 1878, Nelson Papers. There is a story that Nelson's father was Ivar Nilson Evanger, in whose household Ingeborg was employed. Evanger's mother objected to her son's marriage to one beneath his station and hired Styve, a somewhat bibulous vagabond, to assume the responsibility of parenthood. See Knut A. Rene, "Min tur til Norge 1947," in *Vossingen: Tidsskrift for Vosselaget*, 49–54 (May, 1950).

[2] Nelson cut wood, built fires, and took care of the principal's horse. Every two weeks he walked fourteen miles home for provisions. After the war he returned to Albion, then entered a law office in Madison. A. R. Cornwall, principal of Albion Academy, to *Alexandria Post*, December 4, 1874. See also Martin W. Odland, *The Life of Knute Nelson*, 19–23 (Minneapolis, 1926).

[3] Millard L. Gieske, "The Politics of Knute Nelson, 1912–1920," chapter 1 (Ph.D. dissertation, University of Minnesota, 1965).

18

beginning of federal duty.[4] The letters that Nelson soon began writing home are valuable for several reasons. They mirror the experiences of a "man from the ranks" who reflected upon the progress of the conflict and his own commitment to it. As a chronicle of war activities, they are important. Finally, they comprise an early record of the ambitions of a future politician. These letters reveal hopes and frustrations, a yearning for genuine accomplishment, personal values ("Man is remembered by his deeds") , deep loyalties to family and friends, and a strong attachment to the national cause. They disclose much about Nelson's character and offer hints as to why he was attracted to political life.

Some fifty-six letters in the Nelson collection in the Minnesota Historical Society cover the Civil War period. A little less than half (twenty-three) were in Norwegian, most of these to his parents. The remainder, in English, were directed mainly to friends and to his half brothers. Fifteen are presented here.

Some mechanical changes have been made in editing the letters. Nelson did little paragraphing. Occasionally he ran sentences together or broke one off with a dash. Wherever the meaning and rhythm could be improved, these instances have been altered in the text. Nelson wrote Norwegian in a peculiar style, and the translated letters were subject to most of the changes. Miss Nora O. Solum and Mr. Andrew Davidson gave valuable aid in the translations. In the English letters, modifications have been limited to supplying punctuation and paragraph breaks. Nelson wrote well in English, but his spelling, which has not been altered here, reveals the youth whose education is still incomplete.

Nelson early showed a contentment with army life and a pride in his developing physical strength. He was exuberant over the warm receptions accorded the troops as they journeyed from Wisconsin to Baltimore. He became irritated with the "many disloyal at home." Soon he expounded on the war

[4] [Knute Nelson] to General F. C. Ainsworth, December 12, 1911, in *Minnesota History Bulletin*, 5:351 (February, 1924); *Dictionary of American Biography*, 13:418.

itself, stating that rebellion must be put down severely and treason ousted by force. The harshness of the conflict did not deter him, however, from giving a picturesque description of the Southern countryside. He commented dismally upon the treatment of the sick and the poor health of many comrades.

By June, 1862, Nelson was in a melancholy mood. He was concerned about the health of his parents and promised to return home (God willing) with new knowledge about the world and respect for his fellow creatures. He apparently enjoyed describing battles and skirmishes, and without visible remorse he told how the troops set a town afire as an example to other communities along the Mississippi River. He felt that he was seeing too little action. He told of the stoical spirit with which he viewed the dead and the dying. Later his wish for a real engagement in battle was fulfilled, and he lost blood in the encounter. He was wounded during the second assault upon Port Hudson, Louisiana, June 14, 1863, and taken prisoner, remaining in custody for almost a month. When Port Hudson was retaken, Nelson, who was walking with a crutch, was given a horse by a Negro so that he could ride to a hilltop and watch the surrender. Southern officers furnished their own horses, and this one had been stolen from a Confederate chaplain. Nelson became acquainted with a young Southerner named Arnold, beginning a friendship that was to be sustained for fifty years. Somewhat curiously, he proceeded to name his horse for Arnold's Negro slave, who had aided him at the battlefield.[5]

Nineteen months later, Nelson was offered a commission in a Negro regiment, and declined it. His enlistment period was almost up, and besides, he did not feel sufficiently sympathetic to "the black man" to accept. He was convinced, nevertheless, that the former slaves, with education now available to them, would at last begin to better themselves.

Nelson was something of a fatalist but held a rather prag-

[5] Nelson later wrote some anecdotes of his early days at the request of Simon Michelet; see item of September 6, 1919, Michelet Papers, Minnesota Historical Society. See also Nelson to D. B. Arnold, August 4, 1911, Nelson Papers.

matic view of the universe. Religious faith was not in itself enough, he wrote his parents. "You must not forget that you have been given worldly means to use and employ against human arrogance and wrong." Death among the very young was not always to be regretted, he told his brother; a longer life might be a sadder one. As it turned out, death of the young remained a plague upon his own house during his lifetime. Of his six children, five died early; the only survivor was the first-born, Ida, who married when she was in her fifties and had no offspring. One daughter succumbed as an infant, and, seven years later, three more within a week. Nelson's only son, Knute Henry (later Henry Knute) died of tuberculosis in 1908 at thirty-seven.

1. A SOLDIER'S LIFE
To G. Thompson, a friend at home, from Camp Utley, Racine, Wisconsin, June 24, 1861. (Translation)

Keeping a promise made before I left you folks, I will now take pen in hand for a little while and tell you about my experience of a soldier's life. We left Fort Atkinson by steam coach the fourteenth of this month and arrived in Racine late that evening. We were immediately marched to the camp, located half a mile south of the city. I do not believe a more beautiful place is to be found in the whole state. The camp lies on a twenty-five-foot-high level along the shores of the beautiful lake [*Michigan*] with a thick stand of trees around it and beautiful shade trees here and there in the middle of it.

Mess is fairly good. It is like what is found in American hotels except for cake and pie. Our utensils are all of tin except the knives and forks, which are part iron and part steel. At present about a thousand men are quartered here. It is a beautiful sight to see so many men together drilling. We are billeted in big canvas tents with six men living in each tent. One puts a little hay on the ground inside the tent and when we go to bed we wrap ourselves in big, thick woolen quilts or blankets. This is our bed. Our work for the day consists of the following: Morning: 4:30 reveille; 5:00–6:00 drill; 6:00 break-fast; 8:00–9:00 drill; 10:00–12:00 drill. Afternoon and evening: 12:30 dinner; 2:00–3:00 drill; 4:00–5:30 drill; 5:30 supper; 7:00–7:30 drill—hence, seven hours of drill every day. Great emphasis is placed on cleanliness, so we must wash our feet every morning and our whole bodies once a week. Forty men are stationed around the camp in the daytime as guards, and sixty at night. A certain number of men are drawn from each company for this purpose. Standing guard is the worst thing, particularly at night, but since the guard is off duty the following day this isn't so hard, and now that I am used to it, I don't mind it.

I already feel much stronger than I did two weeks ago. As for clothing (and other necessities), we have so far received only shoes and socks, towels and blankets [*towls og blankets*]. We expect to get the rest in about a week.

When we will leave here is as yet [un]known, but it is certain that it will be before long. As for myself, I can say that I have never felt healthier and happier than since I came here.

Excuse this awful scribbling, but when I tell you that I am writing on a board across my lap as I sit on the floor, or ground, you will not wonder at it.

2. HURRAHS TO THE TROOPS
The first letter to Nelson's parents after he left Wisconsin, from Camp Dix, Baltimore, July 28, 1861. (Translation)

Now, for the first time after going so far from home, I will take pen in hand and tell you about the journey from Wisconsin and how my health has been. On July 15 we left Racine at one o'clock in the afternoon. An enormous crowd of people had gathered to bid us farewell. So we left the city, and them, in a tremendous burst of hurrahs and immediately were traveling full speed toward Chicago. The steam coach was our horse and a speedy one it was. On our way we again passed the cities of Kenosha and Waukegan and in these places, as in

Racine, men waved their hats high in the air, shouting "Hurrah!" to us as we passed. The ladies did the same with their handkerchiefs. You may know how all this cheered the soldiers. At about four o'clock we were in Chicago, where we had to change trains. We marched from the north depot through the city, across the Clark Street Bridge, to the south depot. Here an enormous crowd of people had swarmed in to see the fine-looking regiment, the likes of which Illinois does not have in this war. While I was there I saw two people I know — Ragnvald Løhne and Stark Reque — but I didn't talk to either one. At sundown we left Chicago without having been given so much as a cup of water.

The steam carriage traveled all night and by six o'clock in the morning we were in Toledo, Ohio. Here the people had gathered together and prepared a wonderful breakfast for us. Great quantities of good coffee, cake, pie, eggs, sandwiches, and ham were consumed by all the soldiers. Everyone ate his fill, and that was not all. The ladies also filled our haversacks for the journey. At eight o'clock we finally left these friendly people, and having changed trains we moved on to the city of Cleveland, Ohio, which we reached at three o'clock that same afternoon. Here they gave us a wonderful dinner and they filled our canteens with coffee, the best we could have wished for.

At six o'clock we had to bid these good people good-by. And then we took the iron horse to Buffalo, New York, where we arrived at six o'clock the next morning. Here we marched through several streets of the city in full battle dress without having eaten anything since the evening before. And when they finally got us to morning mess we ate more like animals than human beings. It is unnecessary to say that we ate our fill, and had a good meal. At ten o'clock we left Buffalo and traveled south to Elmira, New York, arriving there at twelve midnight. Here we left the coaches and marched to the camp recently vacated by the New York troops. Here the ladies received us with a wonderful evening meal and filled our haversacks, and we slept through the night. Before five o'clock in the morning we were already on our feet. At seven we ate breakfast.

At nine o'clock we left Elmira and traveled southward. In some places this railroad cut through mountains, crossed trestles over valleys, and passed through thick woods. Though this was Pennsylvania, the country looked as if it were Norway. At three o'clock we came to the beautiful city of Williamsport in Pennsylvania. Here we were again given an excellent dinner and had our haversacks filled with all kinds of cake and good things. We left there by railroad at five o'clock in the afternoon and at twelve o'clock midnight arrived at Harrisburg, the capital of the state of Pennsylvania. There we marched from the coaches to a grassy field, where all of us, officers and everyone else, rolled into our blankets and slept well. I can say that I have never slept more sweetly than then. Next morning we were up early, and since we had to wait for our rifles we pitched our tents and got along comfortably enough. When a soldier has pitched his tent he is at home and feels that he is living well.

The morning after I got to Harrisburg, I felt a little dizzy and feverish. Actually, I was not very well. During the three days we spent there, I ate only once, but I was not sick abed. We left the town at four o'clock Monday afternoon, July 22, for Baltimore, where we arrived at four o'clock in the morning July 23. We have been here a few days, but we expect to leave soon and move southward to the combat theater. There are now about ten thousand soldiers here. There are a great many rebels in the city but they do not dare to say or do anything. I am not feeling much better than at Harrisburg, yet I am improving and expect soon to be well again. At present it is not much warmer here than it usually is in Wisconsin, but the water is not as good as there. However, I can say that we are standing it well. I can see that [you] think it strange that I did not write when I was in Racine. When you get this you must write to me.

24

3. ARMY LIFE

To Nelson's "Faraway parents," from Camp Randall, Mary-
land, September 12, 1861, concluding, "Yours for the duration of
the war." (Translation)

Only two hours ago I received your most welcome letter. I
am glad to hear that you are doing well and are in good health.
It seems to me that this year the Supervisor up above has
blessed you more abundantly than in years gone by. Maybe
that is because you were willing to give me up for service to
the country — laid your mite upon the country's altar.

I learn from your letter that a few of the young men at home
have enlisted. That is as it should be. But it surprises me very
much that so few of the ones who paraded every night last
fall in black coats, carrying torches high in the air on long
sticks and yelling like crazy, were willing. One sees only a very
few of them in the military ranks. They boasted that they
could lick those Southern fire-eaters, all right. Easy. No
trouble at all. But now the poor folk do not even dare come
out and look the enemy in the eyes. From this we learn much
that will be interesting in the future.

But enough of this. I see that that unfriendly (and often too
friendly) guest, Death, has been in the neighborhood, taking
away one of our dear old settlers. It brought sorrow to many.
But this is the lot of all the world and one ought to consider
it not as a matter for sorrow but as guidance and example.

I see that your old neighbor Brynjel has suffered an acci-
dent. Let him learn from this not to be so sure of himself. The
Lord gave, and the Lord hath taken away; blessed be the
name of the Lord, as the Scripture says. May he [*the Lord*]
take this into consideration and compensate for the hurt.

The health of the regiment is very good. Only thirty men
among us are on the sick list, and only two have died from
illness. We must consider this a good record in a body as large
as 1,100 men.

I have been very lucky this summer, compared to years
gone by. I feel so healthy and full of energy that a five-hour

drill is nothing—just a little fun. I cannot, like my fellow soldiers, everlastingly complain about the food. I'll tell you, I have eaten more pork and beef, coffee and sugar every day, than I ever did at [the] Tangen [farm]. Never before have I had such good food in my mouth, nor do I expect it to happen again in the future.

We are at the same place where we were the last time I wrote. We would like very much to enter Virginia, where we could attack the enemy immediately. But Major General [John A.] Dix wants us to stop here, not because it is his wish but because the natives who live around here want it. Tomorrow we are to move onto one of nature's more strongly fortified places. It is said that we have to carry up batteries and make our post as strong as possible in case an attack should take place. We have only half a mile to go on foot.

Finally, I will mention again that you are not to worry too much about me. I am quite able to take care of myself. Think rather of yourselves and your two little fellows. Tell them they must be diligent, and acquire understanding and wisdom. Then everything else will come to them.

4. BY SEA TO THE SOUTHERN FRONT
To Nelson's parents from Ship Island, Gulf of Mexico, March 31, 1862.[6] (Translated)

Little did I think a month ago that I would be so far away from you, but even though I well know it causes you anxiety I can say truthfully that it has meant great happiness and encouragement for me. First, because there is now more hope than ever before of being permitted to go into combat and meet the enemy in open battle and test our own quality as warriors. Second, we get to see and learn more of the world than by staying in one place all the time. We arrived here the twelfth of this month after a six-day sail from Fort Monroe. For me those six days were like so many months. Like the others, I was seasick; moreover, we were so jammed together that we could scarcely move from one end of the steamer to

[6] Ship Island is south of Biloxi, Mississippi, about ten miles offshore.

the other, so you can probably imagine what the trip was like. I have never valued ground so much as when I set my foot on this island. I'll take the solid land for mine; and let whoever will keep the sea. There are now about fifteen thousand troops here and General [Benjamin F.] Butler has arrived to take command. More troops are expected every day; our strength will reach twenty or twenty-five thousand.

The fleet, which up to now was anchored at this island, has recently left — no one knows for where. Wherever it goes we are sure to follow. We are now under marching orders, with forty-five rounds of ammunition and four-day rations, packed, to carry. Tomorrow we will be leaving this island and we are sure to be on the mainland of the cotton states within a couple of days. New Orleans and Mobile must be taken before we can expect peace, and that mission falls to this expedition. About the climate, the heat here is about like yours in midsummer; the nights, on the other hand, are chilly and require full winter blankets, as there is so much dampness that it penetrates an undergarment or coat. A bakery which has been set up and is run by soldiers supplies us with fresh bread every third day. The other day the gunboat "New London," with four hundred men on board, went across to the mainland, which is only ten miles from here. The men went on shore and found a lot of iguanas moving about in the open. They shot and killed a lot of them and came back with a good deal of fresh meat.

The health in the regiment is not as good as usual. In my company twelve are sick, but I am well and strong as a horse. I have never had a better appetite, and that is a good sign. Do not worry about me. Knute will get through the world all right. Tell my friends that I am still on my feet.

5. A PLEDGE
To Nelson's parents from the arsenal at Baton Rouge, June 10, 1862, with the conclusion, "Your reforming son." (English)

Though so far from home and seperated as it were by a wall of Rebells and blood-thirsty traiters, your favored token of parental affection and anxiety has not failed to reach me. How glad was I now to receive it! and although 3 weeks old, it caried me back to the old home to father and mother, yes if my bodily self was not there you may safly credit that my imagination and feelings were there.

It gave me *much* grief to hear that Father is slowly declining. I hope, sincerly hope that I am once more [to] be permitted to see *him* on this side of the grave. Should it be our fate never to meet again in this life of trouble and sorow tell him, tell him for *me* to burry in oblivion all trouble anxiety grief and disapointment that I have caused him; it has not been premeditated, but rather accidental. Let him gauge my conduct toward him by that toward mother and he will see that if I have treated him bad, I have mother eaqualy bad; and tell him not to have to much anxiety for william and Henry, if I should be permitted to return safe and sound from this war. Whatever is mine, is theirs; their cause is my cause. Tell him that this is a good school for his undutiful son. The careless reckless wild boy that left home a year ago will return home if Providence wills it, with more experience, and more thoughtful. He has at least learnt how to *associate* with his felow beings, he has learnt that the world is not the school house nor the narow limits of the litle farm. In short he has learnt to respect the rights of his felow-creatures and regard them as eaqual to his own. I know that I caused you much grief in leaving you as I did; but my heart dictated it and I could not otherwise. Forgive me. Forgiveness is the law of Heaven, and let it also be universaly acknowledged on earth.

You have not been able yet to secure help for the coming harvest; this is discouraging and I know that it worries you very much. What advice can I give (who can not assist) in this mater? Manifestly little or nothing, I might perhaps say, but you trust in Providence; but I know there is little consolation in this, under *such* circumstances, even to the most ardent professors of releigon. This only can I say: Let us hope that some of those of your neighbors who have neither con-

tributed man nor mite toward this mighty work now pro-
gressing will take in consideration your need and the cause of
my absence and lend you a helping hand. Would they prove
their loyality and patriotism? Would they prove that they
have a heart in the strugle? How could they better do it than
by such acts in their verry midts? For by aiding the needy and
dependant relatives of our Countrys soldiers, they aid the
country itself. This must be evident to the most selfish and
ignorant. I have confidence in some of our able neighbors at
least. They should bear in mind that the fortunate of today
may not be the fortunate of tomorow.

At ship island I wrote you tow letters, and if I mistake not
your last is the answer to my first at said place. I also sent you
a line while on board the Frigate Colorado in the S.W. pass of
the Mississppi. Three days after sending this communication
the Fts, were taken and the fleet steamed up to New Orleans.
We soon folowed it; and on the 1st of May the 4th Wisconsin
and 31st Meass. Regts. entered the city and took possesion of
the Coustom House and P. Ofice. The day folowing the remainder of the troops were landed. No one molested or insulted us save a few drunken Rowdies who at their own expense and our amusment would dub us "dam Yankees" or
"Abe Lincoln Monkies." But they were soon cured of this.
Gen. Butler has his iron grasp around them. Implicit obedi-
ence is required and enforced. No man dare now insult or
speak disrespecfuly of a U. S. soldier or his flag.

Ft. Jackson is to us here, what Ft. Lafayette is to you up
North. The traitorous Mayor who would not take councel or
advice from Butlers proclamation was sent to Ft. Jackson
and many other smaller lights with him. The 'Delta' the leading Rebell sheet of the city was confiscated, and sold with all
its appurtanances to a U.S. Officer. The old police has been
discharged and a new one of strictly loyal men organised. The
poor starving population has been feed and furnished imploy-
ment. The wealthy merchants have been compelled to open
their stores and shops and sell at a moderate rate and all

Contrabands ariving are received and provided for. In fine the city has been civilized. A Northern man can now do what would have been madness 2 years ago — pass trough any part of town safe and unmolested without arms even.

Let the country remember that no better man can be found for the Rebells of New Orleans. On the 9th of May our Regts together with the 6th Mich. starded up river escorted by a portion of the fleet. When oposite Lake Ponchartrain we landed on the left bank of the river and marched 6 mis, trough a Cypruss swamp ⅔ of that distance, and burnt 3 bridges tore up a large portion of the track and cut the Telegraph of [the] great Rail way betwen Beauregard and New Orleans.[7] This being done we proceeded up the river unmolested under the convoy of the Gunboats, to Vicksburg. The demand of the comander to surrender the town was refused in the most haughty and insulting language. "They had not yet learnt what it was to surender." "The meaning of that term was unknown to them." Now the Fleet could have taken the town emediately but the troops there were insufficient to occupy and hold it; for it is conected by R. R. with Memphis Corinth Jackson and other places. Hence we together with a portion of the fleet fell back to this place. Nor would we have occupied it had not the dastardly cowards fired on the crew (who were ashore) of a solitary Gun boat left here in our abscence up river. Our Regt and the 6th Mich occupied this place alone but we wer subsequently reinforced by 3 Regts and a Battery from N.O. Before their arival we were constantly on duty I did not sleep for 3 days and nights and was nearly gone [*done?*] up.

We are now living better again (once more like human beings are we treated). There are plenty yes more than I have ever before seen of blackberries at the outskirts of the town. Milk and vegatables we obtaine in any quantities in exchange for our beef Bacon coffee and bread. There are many who have

[7] Beauregard Parish, Louisiana, is on the Texas border northwest of New Orleans.

not seen Coffee or Flour for the last 6 months. For a pint of ground Cofee we get 6 quarts of milk notwithstanding the milk is worth 10 cents a quart. For a pound and a half of salt tough beef I have got ½ bushel Onions, and so on. Weel have the Rebells paid the penalty of this war, but none to much. A few Guerillas have been hovering near town, but doing no further damage than wounding the Col. of the 21ˢᵗ Indiana. We have captured a No. of them among them one of their Lieutenants whose plantation we burnt and destroyed, capturing him in bed.

The Sanitary [*health*] condition of our Regiment is very poor. But 500 of those 1100 able bodied men who left Wis. 1 year ago are now doing duty nor those over well, but this is not owing to the climate as much as to the bad treatment of both sick and well men. Understand this, I wil not relate particulars I reserve that for the fireside. My Co. No.ed [*numbered*] 112 men when we left home at Camp Utley. Now 45 do duty 35 on the sick book some slightly others severly. The ballance *Dead* or Discharged. I am in good health and tolerable tough I am reckoned one of the Kernels of the Co. in this respect. The climate agrees with me very well.

6. MONEY TALKS LOUDER THAN NEED
To Nelson's parents from Vicksburg, July 8, 1862. (Translation)

The mail came yesterday but there was *nothing* from you, *nothing* from anybody. I have been waiting for a letter for a whole month, and, as it happens, in vain. What can be the reason? So far as you are concerned, I don't know; but as for the others it is of course my own neglect about answering their letters. But if they only knew the circumstances they surely would excuse me.

You know them, but do not take time to consider that the scene of the war is not home in the house with table and chairs, and that ink and paper are not always to be had. Nor do you realize how much letters are appreciated in these areas

31

of the burning South. But never mind that— if you only will write I will not complain.

My last letter to you was written in Baton Rouge, the capital of the state of Louisiana. I was very concerned about you when I wrote that letter. Father was worse and there were no harvest hands to be got. All I could do was hear, not act. I suppose I gave a little advice, but of what use was that? I know that money speaks more loudly than need. Where need gets one person to help, money gets ten. We have had no pay since we left Baltimore; we are expecting money every day and after Vicksburg is captured they will have time to pay us. As soon as we are paid I will send you money and this you may depend on in August. Now then, you can promise whomever you will that if they will see you through the harvest they will be given money as soon as the work is done, and sound money too. Now what farmer is there in your vicinity who can do the same? Not one. I do not believe it even of Nils Bolstad. No, on other farms they will have to wait until winter, whereas at your place they will be paid as soon as the work is done. Use this method with a pious face and see if it doesn't succeed. But don't mention that I advised it.

June 13 we left Baton Rouge to go to Vicksburg, a brigade — four thousand of us. This was all that General Butler could spare from his small army. Two thousand men were left behind to protect the public buildings in Baton Rouge. On our way up, at a little town called Grand Gulf, the rebels fired on our transport boats.[8] We landed and took after the enemy immediately but they fled with their cannons in great haste. We pursued them, killed two, took ten prisoners. The rest got away, as they were faster on foot than we were. We set the town on fire and burned down every house as a warning to other small towns along the river.

The inhabitants had fled before we arrived. The town was about the size of Cambridge [Wisconsin]. We are now en-

[8] Grand Gulf, Mississippi, is on the Big Black River near where it joins the Mississippi.

camped outside the city of Vicksburg in full view of the rebels on one side and those [of the Union forces] on the other. Our fleet lies in the river above and below the city; [Admiral Andrew H.] Foote's fleet above and [Admiral David G.] Farragut's below have their iron vise around the city. They [*the rebels*] now have a large number of batteries and cannon and a force of sixty thousand men under General [Earl] Van Dorn of Arkansas. This is the only point of any consequence they have on the river. And this will be the scene of one of the great battles of the war. Although we have both fleets here, we have only a brigade of four thousand men, but every day we look to see a sizable addition from above [*the North*].

But it is neither cannon nor bayonet that will do the worst damage to this city. No, this place will remember the war against our government just as long as there are inhabitants here. Vicksburg lies on top of a bluff on the east side of a large tongue of land jutting out into the Mississippi. From a point five miles below the city it is only three fourths of a mile overland to a point ten miles above.[9] Along this line we are now at work digging a canal twelve feet wide and fifteen feet deep. As soon as this is opened, a swift stream will rush through; and since the earth is sandy and loose the canal will grow, and it is anticipated that eventually the big Mississippi with its whole family of tributaries will change its course and bypass Vicksburg.

This is the plan we are now working on and have nearly finished. We have been pretty busy for a couple of weeks. The canal runs through a wood. Here half of us have chopped and dug every day, though we have not been alone at it. We have taught slaveholders that we can make use of their slaves as well as their government can. We have picked out twelve hundred of their best slaves, who now do all the digging under our supervision. We give them the same food we have and twelve hours of work during the day. There was no trouble

[9] The winding course of the river would necessitate a fifteen-mile boat journey between the two points.

33

about our doing the digging as long as the canal was dry, but now it is deep and has two feet of water in it, so it is no fun standing in water and digging and digging with the hot sun above our heads. But now we have turned all the work over to the slaves and they like it very well. The health in the regiment is no better now than when I wrote before. One of my Albion comrades died the other day. He is the third of us [Albion students to die] and the fourth in the company. My health is excellent. I have the appetite of a horse.

7. THE WARRIOR LONGS FOR COMBAT

To Nelson's mother, from Plaquemine, Louisiana, February 18, 1863.[10] (Translation)

From the letter that you sent with William's, I know, of course, even though you have not said it, that you are unhappy because you have not heard from me for so long; also that you have heard that the Fourth Regiment has been in combat. To the first I can say that I have answered all letters that have come from home and that I feel certain that all letters from you have come here, as I have received the socks and *Fritiof's Saga*. I sent a letter to A. Gunderson from Baton Rouge, and in it one to William, which I believe you have already received. Concerning the other [worry], namely, that we have been in combat, I can tell you what you want to hear. We have not been in combat yet, nor do we know how soon we will be. This is not much to my liking. I would prefer being in a hard battle; however, I will be satisfied with whatever happens to me in this war, if only the country comes out of this peril safe and to the satisfaction of the finest and best government on earth. Do not grieve for me. God will surely take me under his protection, not for my own sake, but for yours and the country's. And what if I fall? I must of course die sometime and what does it matter whether I die today or tomorrow or twenty years from now? Isn't it the end of all of

[10] Plaquemine is on the Mississippi, about 150 miles south of Vicksburg as the crow flies.

us? What is best and most necessary usually happens. Let's be content with that.

8. MARCHING AND FIGHTING

To Nelson's brother William, from the field, May 22, 1863. The letter was interrupted by the first assault on Port Hudson, and finished June 3.[11] Eleven days later Nelson was wounded and captured. (English)

A week ago I received your letter enclosing lines from A. Gunderson and mother. I was glad to hear from you; endeed I can not hear from home to often. I have writen two letters since my return from the Port Hudson expidition which I hope have before now releived you of great anxiety concerning myself. I saw that you apprehended evil in advance and pictured to yourself Knute killed or wounded on the bloody battle field. Well the fault was mine — I should not have told you ere the thing was past. I simply intended to give you early news, insted of which it proved a bane of suspense and grief. I will be more carefull in future. I am glad to learn that you have paid so much of your Debts and that in these war times to. It is more than I could expect.

*

I had just scratched the above when we were ordered away in great haste. I will now resume and write what I can though I hardly think it will be but a little, for marching and fighting is the order of the Day. My last letter to you was sent from Opelousas in the begining of May; since I have received two letters from you. At Opelousas we were organized into mounted Infantry capturing our own horses in the country thereabouts. On the 3 of May [General Nathaniel P.] Banks left Opelousas with his whole force save a Regt. left to guard the place, and advanced to Alexandria on the Red river 100 miles distant, where he arived on the 7th. A portion of [Admiral David D.] Porters & [Admiral] Faraguts fleet had arived 10 hours previous. The Infantry remained and rested there;

[11] Port Hudson, Louisiana, is on the Mississippi River about seventeen miles in a straight line north of Baton Rouge.

while the Cavalry and Mounted Infantry advanced 35 miles up the Red river persuing and scatering Gen. [Richard] Taylors retreating force. The persuit of the enemy being of little importence we returned to Alexandria, and from thence the whole force marched to Simm's port on the Atchafalaya 10 miles from the Red river the mounted force and Baggage bringing up the rear.[12]

From this point a portion of the force were shiped on Steamers up the Atchafalaya down the Red and the Mississippi to Bayou Sara 12 miles above Port Hudson on the same side of the river: the ballance crossed the Atchafalaya * thence by land to Point[e] Coupee oposite Bayou Sara, crossing over to said place. We were with this part of the force having charge of the Baggage train. On the evening of the 25th ult. we crossed the Mississippi to Bayou Sara Bivouacking there over night. By this sudden movment from the Red river[,] Banks threw half of his entire Army to the north and rear of Port Hudson forming a junction with the other portion of his Army under Gen [Christopher C.] Augur from the south and below the enemy, thus investing Port Hudson completely by land from River to river. Augur had advanced from Baton Rouge on the 20th ult. and had advanced to and gained possesion of the Clinton road in the left rear of the enemy when the junction was affected. On the 25th the junction was complete. The country from Brashear city to Alexandria trough which Banks with his army had passed and defeated and driven the enemy was left without any troops or Garisons, thus showing that the *chief* object of the expidition was to throw a force on the rear and flank of the enemy at Port Hudson so that he could be captured or starved to a surender at all events.[13]

[12] Opelousas is in St. Landry Parish, west of Baton Rouge, and Simmesport is northeast of it. Alexandria is on the Red River about forty-five miles in a straight line northwest of Simmesport.

* "Pronounced/chaf-a-la-a accent on 1st syllable." (Nelson's note.)

[13] The Atchafalaya River runs parallel to the Mississippi and empties into Atchafalaya Bay in the Gulf of Mexico. Pointe Coupee Parish is along the west bank of the Mississippi above West Baton Rouge Parish. Brashear City is on the Atchafalaya about eighteen miles north of the Gulf.

Well, western La. is nearly cleared of the enemy and Port Hudson invested. But to the Regt. again; to comprehend the whole I can say but little and that a mere guess at best. On the 26th we left Bayou Sara and took up our position in the rear of [General Halbert E.] Paines Division behind Port Hudson with the rest of the mounted force. In the evening we were in ill humor supposing that being mounted we would have but little share in the fight. The moron [*morning*] pacified us when we were ordered to leave our horses and join in the fight as Infantry.

This was our element and we advanced as Wis Infantry. The day previous the enemy had in this portion of the field been driven to within a mile of his Earthworks and now the task was to drive him within completely. Being some distance in the rear we were not on the ground til the fight had begun. Two lines of troops had advanced ahead of us, we formed a portion of the third which emediately advanced. The ground was broken into small hills and ravines densely covered with heavy timber felled by the enemy to obstruct us. This kept our line broken, but reccompensed for this in now and then afording us shelter. Previous to the advance early in the morning this space of felled trees was held by the enemy. In advancing we unmasked him and gradualy drove him to his intrenchments. We advanced, the two lines ahead gradualy melting into killed wounded and an astonishing number of skulkers and cowards found laying on their faces hugging the ground shivering with fear. These we passed over kicking punching and damning them though a *very, very* small number of even our Regt showed the white feather much to our regret yet in this respect we were better than other Regts. When within 80 Rods of the Earthworks we found ourselves ahead of all steadily advancing encountering a storm of bullit, grape shell and canister yet hesitating not we came to within 30 Rods of their position of Breast works when order was given to halt. We halted dropped down among the fallen timber and were out of sight yet keeping up a fussilade of minies so that

37

few heads were seen above the parapet and several pieces of canon were silenced the Artillerists being picked off so that the guns could not be worked. Owing to the felled timber our Artillery had given us no assistance yet; but now it came thundering and whising over our heads. The Rebell Breast work soon became a dead mound with no visible occupants. This gave us rest we needed it for it was half a days hard work we had endured. The investment here was complete.

Looking back over the crests and gullies we saw our own and Rebell killed and wounded. The scene was not a happy one yet we looked upon it in the cold stoical spirit of a soldier — a slight chilling pang and then a return soul and body to the enemy before us. The wounded were soon picked up and taken care of, and before night most Dead were burried. We bivouacked among the graves of the Heroic Dead that night, but without camp fires. 8 companies of the Regt. were engaged — 308 in all. 65 were killed and wounded in the days engagement. Co. B lost 9 killed and wounded out of 44 in action. Thank God not a hair of mine was hurt. I am tough, healthy, and rugged as never before. We remained for six days holding our position; on the third of which our much beloved Col. [Sidney A. Bean] was killed by the sharpshooters of the enemy while going from our Co. to the next, giving orders.

Last night we were relieved and returned to our camp and horses. This morning we were ordered to report to Col. [Benjamin H.] Grierson Chief of cavalry seven miles in the rear of Port Hudson which we have already done. Our duty will now be in the rear and on the flanks not in the midts of the fray. This Col. Grierson made a raid with the 6th and 7th Ill. cavalry from west Tennesse to Baton Rouge trough the width of Jeff's confedracy thus giving Bank's a much needed cavalry reinforcement. John Shearer an Albion boy was killed the only one in the Company. Tell this to Pollock's Kenedys and J. H. Stewarts they were acquainted with him.

Night has now overtaken me. I must quit. I have no pen,

no Ink. I think you can hardly read it. If you cant[,]get some one to decipher it for you. Scribbled hastily.

9. NEW SOUTHERN FRIENDS

To William, an undated fragment of July, 1863. Nelson had been held prisoner for almost a month following his capture on June 14. (English)

This Negroe's name was "Pud." His master, the Mississippian Arnold by name, was a frank warm hearted generous young man of my own age nearly though a great deal taller. His Father was a wealth[y] Planter of North Mississippi who had reaped the full reward of his iniquitous rebellion. Being only 22 mis. from Memphis our army had overrun and devastated his Home and lands, leaving the rich Nabob and his Family without anything to eat save a few barrells of Apples hid in the Cellar; and a Major of an Ill[s] regiment had smashed up his Daughters Piano for refusing to play the "Star-Spangled Banner" on it when requested.

Young Arnold became an intimate friend of mine. We would read to and talk with one another a large share of the time. I came into the Fort nearly shirtless, —he furnished [me] with shirts; and I had no books to read— he got me Books. Whatever he had he divided with me.

The day before the Fort surendered he had a long conversation with me, when he told me that he had once taken pride in the Confederacy, its cause and in being its soldier, but this had now vanished. Could he but get home, he would never fight Uncle Sam any more, and would deport himself peacably under our government which after all is not so bad. He bid me goodby saying, "When the war is over come and see us in North Mi[ssissippi]. If the U.S. do not confiscate everything my Father owns we will have somthing still left to receive a Guest with." "You will be welcome. Come by all means." Poor man he was contrite and penitent. He had felt the war to the utmost having had three brothers killed, and

39

himself very near it in this unusual war. The *war* had made him respect the Union if not love it.

But to my Horse Pud. I called him so to remember both Master and Slave, as well as Port Hudson and the Chaplain.[14] Besides there is something odd and lugubrous in the comparison of Arnold's Pud and my Pud. His a Human being, mine a Brute. Yet both being eaqualy dear to and beloved by and holding nearly the same relations to their masters.

Last week I sent you a letter informing you that I had sent 80 dollars to Ft. Atkinson for Father. I write of it now if perhaps the other letter might not reach you. No military movements are at the present transpiring here. Having nothing more worthy of aluding to I close with my best wishes to you and all at home.

10. DEATH CANNOT INJURE

Nelson to his parents from Baton Rouge, September 3, 1863. He looked back to the eve of his wounding and his feelings of that time. (Translation)

Your welcome letter of August 18 came yesterday. I note with much joy that you are still alive and in pretty good health and also that everything has been settled about the harvesting of our usual good crop. That things are going so well with you now under this war's fearful swervings of fortune is of the greatest joy and satisfaction to me, particularly when I see almost daily how many rich become poor, how many have as good as nothing to live on. Remember now that, next to God, you have a good government to be thankful for — a country without its equal in the whole world. And teach the little ones to appreciate all this so that in the future they can become good, loyal citizens. It is with this as with religion — one usually believes what he has been taught.

The fellow who gave you such unnecessary grief was really a nitwit; I would call it reckless foolhardiness. Even if the scoundrel knew it to be true, it was still not his place, as a stranger, to go and report it to you. The newspaper had the

---

[14] For the incident of the chaplain's horse, see *ante*, p. 20.

true story. I was wounded and taken prisoner. You grieved four times as much for me as I did for myself.

The evening before the attack of June 14 we knew very well what the morning had in store for us, and that our regiment would lead the attack. We were not unaware of the dangers. We handed such of our little things as might have some value to a few who were sick and could not take part in the attack, and gave them the addresses of our parents and friends so they could write to them if we died and send them all the articles we had left. We did all of this as calmly as you eat your dinner. There is one thing I want to tell you about the soldier: He thinks less about eternity than about home, parents, and friends.

That evening, when I lay down to get some sleep before three o'clock in the morning, I could not go to sleep immediately. My thoughts kept going round and round about you and home, in concern about you and your future. As soon as my thoughts had collected themselves, I fell asleep. I compared your present situation with what it was when you came to Koshkonong and had nothing. Now you have a good little farm, nearly debt free, and as much if not more help. William is as old as I was at that time, and Henry is right on his heels. Now you have enough, even if it is not wealth, to live on, and with these thoughts it seemed to me that my death could not injure you and might be a help to my country. About the unknown future I did not allow my thoughts to soar. That death was near, I suppose I believed, but I saw it only as a rest after the day's work.

I recently wrote to William and now have no more news except that nearly all the troops around here have been sent to New Orleans. One expedition will soon be leaving for either Mobile or Texas. We do not know whether we will be going with them or not. Our health, on the whole, is good. I get your newspapers. Send them as often as you can. And you must also write to me — but not in Danish. With good health and courage.

11. NOT MUCH OF A CHRISTMAS

Nelson to his parents, from Baton Rouge, December 16, 1863.
(Translation)

Your welcome and very much appreciated letter came into my hands yesterday. It was just what I wished for, full of news and very interesting. I am overwhelmed to hear how well you are getting along. In the midst of these hard times it is our good health and good sleep that are enjoyable. But we have many other things of a worldly nature and activity. I cannot report anything else except what is good. But also, that articles for sale here are sold at high prices. However, you in Wisconsin are luckier in one thing. The war has not devaluated your paper money. Greenbacks are to be used as money, not devaluated.

War reports of any setbacks are not in the news at the moment. Part of the army has captured the southwestern part of Texas around the Rio Grande River, the dividing line between Mexico and the United States. It is a very important location. Throughout this area the rebels had gathered great quantities of war materials, provisions, and clothing. It was the only supply depot the enemy had established anywhere inside Union territory. The expedition which went overland toward Texas has returned. They had a few slight skirmishes with the enemy, of very small consequence, and really no loss. The aim of the expedition evidently was just to scare enemy power away from the protected part of Texas while one detachment made an invasion. As a result of this, our troops met very little resistance.

It is reported that we are organizing a regiment of Negroes. There are now over twenty regiments, of five hundred men each, of these black and white units, manned by white officers. Officers in the Negro regiments hold the same rank as officers in the white regiments. Many in our regiment have acquired commissions in these black corps. The same examination is required for all candidates who make application for officer's rank. I could acquire a commission in one of these

42

regiments if I wanted to fill out one of those application blanks. Officers of my regiment have recommended it. But as my enlistment time will soon be over, I have no desire to secure this officer rank. It would take my enlistment time beyond the end of the war, and I do not like the black man well enough for that.

The troops' health is good at this time of the year. The weather is mild, very warm some days. November was cold and rainy. December is much milder. The ground hasn't frozen yet and about a hundred recruits have arrived for this regiment. Christmas is just a little way off, but not much of a Christmas for me because we have no steak, no big can of beer, no gathering of friends or elaborate meals, no dance, no church service, not even a Jule buk [*Christmas goat*]. Christmas Day for us is just December 25, no more, no less. This doesn't cause us any sorrow. We are just as happy and cheerful — maybe on account of this we are better off.

About three months ago I wrote to Gullick Saue. I have not received an answer. Ask him to give his opinion about the war. Is he against it or for it? How does he behave from day to day?[15] No more. Now greet all my friends and relatives.

12. SCHOOL FOR NEGROES
To William, with a note added for Henry, from Baton Rouge, March 25, 1864. (English)

Your very well writen letter of the 25th of last month has come also one from Henry and Mother. I am glad to hear from each and all of you as often as you can write. I only miss Father; he never sends any word in your letters. Next time, you write a few words for him just as he will tell you.

I hope Father and Mother may be better by the time you get this. Help them all you can with deeds and kind words.

[15] Gullick Thompson (Saue) had become rich during the California gold rush, and he acquired about two hundred acres in the Koshkonong area. The Nelson farm was near his home, and the school attended by Knute Nelson, called the Thompson School, was on his property. Thompson ruled the neighborhood. Odland, *Life of Knute Nelson*, 19.

God will reward you for it. My time is out July 2nd and then I will come home as soon as I can. I hope to be home by the 15ᵗʰ or 20ᵗʰ of that month, though I might be delayed until the first of August but not beyond that time I think. If you can hire anyone do so, to make sure for an early harvest and to make hay befor that time. How many acres of Wheat and Oats are you going to have this year? Sow thick and drag it in well and good so that you may have a good Crop. Sow and plant all the Onions Carrots Turnips Rota Beggas Cabbage and Vegatables of all kinds that you can. I shall want a plenty of them you may depend upon since I have been so long without them. You must not forget Water Melons or Musk Melons either. Have a good Garden when I get home if you can.

Those who have reinlisted are going home on Furlough — that is with permission, next week to stay a month. The remainder of the old soldiers and the Recruits are going to New Orleans to drill, so it is said. We surely need this for wee have had scarcely no time to drill hitherto.

A Fort on the Red river was captured two weeks ago and 315 prisoners and several pieces of Artillery. Banks is moving with a large army in western Louisiana and up the Red river driving the Rebells into Texas where he will no doubt follow them. I think the Rebel army beyond the Mississippi will be defeated and scattered this summer and Fall. No movment against Mobile is intended by Banks at present as all the troops are withdrawn from that direction. Sherman has crossed the river into west Louisiana where he will probably unite with Banks. It was a portion of his force that captured that Fort on the Red river.

Gen. Banks has issued an order for the instruction of Negro children. Schoolhouses are to be built or rented and Teachers hired for this purpose, and the farmers and planters are to pay the Taxes in support of this. Thus these Negro children who 3 years ago dared not be seen with books in their hands are now to have their education at the expense of their old masters who formerly treated them like so many Dogs. These young Negroes will learn too. Many of them learn faster than many White children I have seen. And all both young and old are very anxious to learn. They have not had the opportunity before, but now they have. We shall soon see how they will improve it. If I mistake not they will astonish us.

There has been a few cases of Small Pox and Measels in the regiment, confined mostly to recruits. With this exception the health of the regiment has been good. Send Emigranten when you have read it, every Week if possible. I will send you some Stamps as soon as I can get them, for that purpose. Yours fat and hearty.

To Henry: Dear brother I read your letter you sent me. It is very good. Write more and better next time. Be a good boy to Father Mother and brother William mind them and God will like you. If you are a good boy I will come and see you next summer.

13. HUMAN ARROGANCE
To Nelson's parents, from Baton Rouge, March 30, 1864. *(Translation)*

I received your letter of the eighth of this month a couple of days ago. It makes me very happy to know that you are still alive and in tolerably good health, and that you can look calmly upon matters of worldly concern. You say that your hope is in God, and he will, I am sure, stand by you. But you must not forget that you have been given worldly means to use and employ against human arrogance and wrong—it is necessary to see such things with a broad mind in order to oppose them. Nothing is ever so bad that no good comes of it, says the proverb, and that can be said about Gullick's conduct toward you.[16] You had many kindhearted neighbors whom you pushed aside at a hint from Gullick, just to please him, and in this you made a mistake by placing too much

[16] See *ante*, note 15.

45

confidence in a mortal being and he a most unjust one. Your blind reliance on him and your fear of him drove you too far.

But now the veil is lifted. You can now see and observe Gullick as he really is. You can now see that a man has not gotten on bad terms with his whole neighborhood without blame and reason. I suppose you will say that Gullick helped you a great deal when you needed it badly. True enough. But for what reason? That is the question. The answer is short. In order to enrich himself. Why did he buy the east forty? In order to get his stock to the creek. Why was he so ready to help in getting the road over the creek laid on our land? So that no road southward from Hollingen [?] would run across his own land, and to satisfy his hatred of some of his small neighbors. And many lesser affairs can be brought up against him in the same way, but it isn't necessary. You can think them over yourselves. The short of the matter is this, that Gullick was good to you as long as he could use you either for his own pocket or for his revenge on the neighbors. Do not deceive yourselves — it was for these reasons you were once used. I do not say this to censure you, but that you may be more careful in the future. As I have said before, let the matter rest where it is until I come home. My health is good. I am fat, strong, and hopeful. I wrote to William a few days ago and so have no news to report at this time.

Enclosed I am sending you forty-one dollars to use and employ as seems best to you. Write as soon as you receive [it].

14. REFLECTIONS ON DEATH
To William, from Baton Rouge, May 15, 1864. (English)

Your letter of the 23ᵈ of last month came yesterday evening. I had long and anxiously awaited it, for your letter of the 11ᵗʰ of Apr. gave me a very gloomy and discouraging account from home. I can hardy tell you how glad it made me, to hear that Father was up and well again. It has allways been my hope and wish that if I am permitted to return home again I may see all of those that I left there when this terrible war broke out. It would be but a half home should either Father or Mother die before I could see them once more.

I am glad, yes truly glad, that the Death Angel has passed you by untouched this time, though he has not gone far from you for a victim. "Caroline T[hompso]n is dead and Thomas her brother sick and near the point of death." [17] This is very severe on Thompsons family, and yet it may be for the best. The longer we live on this earth the further we go astray and depart from the way of the Almighty, and the more difficult to reform and return. While young, though we may be very anxious to live, our hearts have not become hardened our faults and frailities are not so many and we die repentant sinners rather than doubting fearing unpardoned reprobates. On the whole I can say I am never sorry that a very young person dies for if any enter gods kingdom it is those who die young; and even were I to wish them a longer life and were that wish to be fulfiled I can not help thinking that the wish would be far oftener for the worse than the better. Not only may it be better for Thomas and Caroline to die in their youth, but what good may it not do that hardened hardhearted man —their father. It may make him a better man, maybe a Christian, You say G[ullick] has become a little softened towards you. I am glad of that. I think he will be more reasonable hereafter. I hope so at the least.

I am very glad that you had plenty of Hay and thereby got help enough to put all your grain into the soil. How many acres of Wheat have you? You ask me to send you a couple of Rifles. I dont know how to get any without paying double what they would be worth up north. When we were changed into Cavalry we turned our Rifles over to the Quarter Master. Our arms are now, a Sabre or Sword, a Carbine (a short breechloding Rifle) and a large Six shooting Pistol or Revolver. These arms belong to Government. And as long as the war last it has need of these arms, so that if I wanted to buy any I could not get them on this account.

[17] Caroline and Thomas were Gullick Thompson's children.

47

I would like to take home a Pistol but see I cant do it. Besides you don't want a Rifle. A good little Shot-gun is just the article you need, and that you can get much cheaper up north. — You must tell Lewis the same too.

Henry must be a smart boy to have been draging so much this Spring. It is to bad that old Tom is used up. Havent you got some big Steers to break in that you can use in his place.

I am pleased to learn that you are to have School this summer. You must attend every day possible. Give my compliments to your teacher. She has recited many lesons with me before our former Lutheran ministers. I cant help thinking of school days once in a while yet.

On the 3^d of this month the Regt. went out some 25 miles in the country. 1000 infantry and 4 pieces of Artillery went with us. We came up on the enemy fought them and drove them four miles, when they crossed a creek tore up the Bridge and laid in ambush on the creek bank in thick brush and timber. We came up supposing the Rebbs kept on retreating, but on coming to the bridge, we found we could not cross for the planks were torn up. — Here they emediately opened a heavy fire on us killing the Colonel [*Lieutenant Colonel Frederick A. Boardman*], and a man in Co. C, and wounding one man and killing 3 horses in Co. B. The Col. rode at the head, and Co. B just behind him. Hadnt the Rebells fired too high every one of our Co. would probably been killed or wounded. We stood their fire for a few minutes but as we could not advance right away, we had to fall back. With the Infantry we could have crossed but we got orders to go no further. We captured 1 officer and 3 men and killed or wounded about a dozen. Yesterday we went out on another scout[,] about 100 of us[.] 20 miles out we came up on 600 Rebs fired a few shots at them, took 3 prisoners, and came back.

15. IN GOOD HEALTH AND FULL OF HOPE

*Nelson's second to last letter home, to his stepfather, from
Baton Rouge, June 16, 1864. He was mustered out July 13, 1864.
(Translation)*

Your letter of the thirtieth of last month came yesterday.
It is good to hear that all goes well at home — that you have
seeded and planted as much as you wish to. Last month the
weather was pretty dry here too, but during these last days it
has rained almost continuously. A part of the day it rains and
then again the sun shines extremely hot. The cotton and corn
are growing fast, and garden produce and small plants are
ripe and ready to eat. But everything is so extremely expensive that a dollar here is no more than ten cents among you.
Butter is sixty cents a pound, eggs are sixty cents a dozen, and
it's that way all down the line.

There is a little sickness in the regiment, mostly among the
recruits or latest arrivals. The army now lies inactive and will
continue to do so until the start of autumn days; for it is now
too hot to do anything in this line of work. It is in Virginia
and Georgia that the war now rages and where it will continue;
for at these points — Richmond and Atlanta — the enemy's
main strength is concentrated. If we take these places we take
the head and heart of the whole rebellion, and this we will
certainly do in the course of the summer. Up to now all has
gone well with our armies in these places. Great battles have
been fought but always with victory for our side.

As for news of any interest to you, I have none to report.
Yesterday I had a letter from Knute Quitne. He is in good
health and spirits, but he says he wishes he hadn't re-enlisted.
His regiment is in northern Alabama. Those who re-enlisted
and were home on furlough came back the thirtieth of last
month — Asbjorn's Nels was one of them but he stayed and
hasn't returned yet and no one expects that he will. He promised me when he went home that he would go to see you, but
evidently he has not done this, since you say nothing about it.

You would much like to know when I am coming home.

Millard L. Gieske

That I cannot tell you exactly — more than that, you must not begin to expect me before July 10 and then it might perhaps be still better not to look for me before the twentieth. It is not known yet whether we will be mustered out here or will be sent to Madison. If we are mustered out in Madison we will get home sooner. I would advise you to hire a worker for the harvest if it is possible, as it is uncertain how I will stand the change of climate and of food and water. If only I could come home half a month before the harvest, it would be better. Yours in good health and full of hope.

by SIMON JOHNSON [1]
translated with an
introduction by
NORA O. SOLUM

3   *An Immigrant Boy on the Frontier*

S IMON (formerly Simen) Johnson tells in his memoirs the story of his Americanization, from boyhood to young manhood, on the prairies of Dakota Territory. His account takes us back to the early 1880's, when the Johannes Bergumshagen family were natives of Gudbrandsdal, Norway, and owned a small farm there. The incentives for their emigration to America are familiar; namely, the difficulty of supporting a family in the homeland, and the lure of more opportunities in the new.[2]

To eke out the lean living afforded by the farm, Johannes, a man of considerable grit and brawn, undertook to work at improving roadways in the parish, a job which few of his

[1] Simon Johnson, well-known journalist and novelist, was born in Gudbrandsdal, Norway, in 1874. At the age of eight he came to the United States with his parents. He edited *Normanden* (Grand Forks, North Dakota) for four years, and was a member of the staff of *Decorah-Posten* for fifteen years. He has published the following books: *Et geni* (1907), *Lonea* (1909), *I et nyt rige* (1914), *Fire fortellinger* (1917), *Falliten paa Braastad* (1922), *Frihetens hjem* (1925).

[2] The selections translated here form parts of chapter 2 of Simon Johnson's unpublished memoirs entitled "Opplevd: Noen minner, funderinger, og skildringer — og livsoppsjør tilslutt" (Experiences: Some Memories, Reflections, and Sketches — and a Casting of Accounts). The original manuscript is in the possession of the Norwegian-American Historical Association.

51

fellow parishioners would attempt because of the difficult hill-and-vale terrain. This undertaking earned him some repute among his neighbors.

A severe winter set in, paralyzing the area under snowdrifts and putting an end to road work. After weeks of layoff Johannes took to the mountains, hoping to return with a bagful of ptarmigan to bolster the family board. Late one night he returned unexpectedly, almost empty-handed, hungry, and worn-out. He resolved to leave for America as soon as possible. During these years the parish was abuzz with stories of the land of abundance across the Atlantic, given credence by the return of successful adventurers who had been there. The son, Simon, remembers the incredibly stony look on his father's face and the pitifully distraught stare of helplessness on his mother's at the announcement. Johannes would go alone; Mother Anne and the children would follow later.

Arrangements for their trip and a heavy burden of responsibility during the period of separation fell to Mother Anne. The uprooting was difficult — this had been the family home for hundreds of years. But the full realization of what it meant came to Simon only long afterward.

The family was reunited after a couple of years. Johannes had rented some acreage and started building a sod house; a neighbor brought Anne and the children from the railway station to his own home, where they awaited the arrival of Johannes, who had been there every day to see if they had come. Anne and the children — Simon, Mathias, and Vesla (Little Girl) — had been given a room for themselves. The following scene moves directly into chapter 2 of Simon's memoirs.

SIMON JOHNSON'S NARRATIVE

Mother was busying herself with the family's clothing. Suddenly she drew up and stood stock-still, a rapt expression on her face. The garment she held in her hand fell limp.

The door opened and a man stood there. His clothes resembled those of the man of the house, but his beard was darker. It was hard for him to fix his eyes on what was directly in front of him; he stared blankly ahead.

"Johannes!" Mother cried out as she opened her arms to him. He choked out something which sounded like, "Welcome!" Questions began. Had they stood the trip pretty well? Vesla, too? Oh, yes, but Vesla hadn't paid much attention; there had been too many menfolk around. And Mathias? The youngster only looked bewildered; he couldn't figure out who this bearded man was who was making such a to-do about Mother. And what about Big Boy Simon, the family heir?

Questions and answers went on and on between the two grown-ups — the journey, the old valley, Lillehammer, Christiania, the ship, seasickness, arrival in this country, New York, canals, trains. And from the other direction: What about work over here, pay, food, clothing, houses, ways of doing things, knowledge of Christianity in this new land?

Time lengthened. Not even the stalwart housewife's appearance with a pot of coffee and a tray of goodies could stem this questioning. And Big Boy could scarcely get a hearing for his story about a closed shanty door in Christiania, which had aroused his curiosity when he went exploring near the hotel where they were staying, waiting for the time to board the ship. Nor for his tale of those shining streetcar horses he had seen in New York, and the Garden of Eden he had glimpsed when the train crossed a high bridge over a valley. Finally, between opening and closing his eyes, he fell to wondering whether the man sitting before him was actually the same one he had awakened to see and hear on the night which ended the ptarmigan hunts in Gudbrandsdal and brought on the decision to try life in America.

*

A few days later the lad from the valley couldn't understand why tears came so readily into Mother's eyes, nor what made her sink down so despairingly on the immigrant chest the first time she entered the house in which they were to live.

It didn't bother Simon in the least that the house had only board outside walls and naked studdings inside. What he noticed was that all the studdings were alike and all exactly the same distance apart. The same was true of the roof supports. It was fun to look at such things and speculate how they had been done and where they were from.

Not only was it fun to guess how these things had happened but also to become a part of what was going on. One day he discovered that a man was plowing right outside the house. Now, that must be some plow! And drawn by beautiful horses! Presently the man took his sights and plowed a furrow straight as a line. At the turn he repeated the process. Finally a wide dark swath was cut into the green prairie vastness.

Before leaving, the man stopped a few moments to talk to Father and tell him that this was the best kind of sod, terribly tough, no danger of its crumbling. There should be no difficulty with the thickness either because there were wheels on the plow. After a last look at the walls, he started for home.

That very afternoon the reason for this phenomenon revealed itself, for Father immediately went to work cutting the turned-up sod into lengths that could be handled and carried to the house or carted off in a wheelbarrow. Yes, the board walls of the entire house were to be covered with peat sod, and for this job everyone except Vesla could lend a hand. Mother was shocked to see how deep-set the windows and doors would be, but Father assured her that now the prairie winter could rage all it liked and that wouldn't faze them in the least. She nodded her satisfaction immediately.

When it came right down to it, the prairie could really exhibit a variety of interesting things. It even proved to have underground beings, not the kind one reads about in fairy tales, to be sure, but underground beings all the same. They lived a good way down under the surface, but every now and then they would pop up into the daylight, rear up on their haunches, turn their heads this way and that, and peer around in every direction with curious eyes. If a person stood stock-still and only looked at them, they would begin to sniff about in the grass for something to gnaw at. When they sat upright and looked about like this the boy often remembered a squirrel he and Grandfather had seen by the roadside the morning the old man had walked with them on the way to Lillehammer, except that the valley squirrel frolicked in the trees, whereas the gopher of the prairie had to content himself with digging in the earth, because he lived underground.

There was, however, one thing about these creatures which few folks had seen. The neighbors called them pocket gophers. As they burrowed deeper into the ground they carried what they dug loose up to the surface in pockets — ingenious devices, located on either side of the face. The boy had never seen this, although he had seen the mounds made from emptying the pockets. A couple of times he had noticed that something had been added to a little mound already there — a sure sign of life down below. And he promised himself that in good time he would see one of these things too.

That's how it was with the underground creatures of the prairie. As for water beings, could there possibly be any such? Now and then someone would mention fishing. But in the thing that passed for a river over here — never. Not for one who had been along the River Laagen in Gudbrandsdal, had here seen it placid and glittering with the sky in it, and there running a brisk current, and had even tried its fishing holes. No, what people called a river here was no more than a thin stream in a so-called valley with some leaf trees along its banks and muddy water coursing drearily past wide bends. Let others cast their shining American fishhooks into such slop, and to tell the truth it must be admitted that such extranice hooks deserved a better fate.

The prairie had more to offer seeing eyes and listening ears, however, than muddy, spiritless rivers. When there was a far-reaching, quiet light over it, one might hear a whirring sound rising somewhere in the distance. It didn't seem to mean much to some people. "Nothing but prairie chickens," they would say in superior tones. But to the boy's ears the sound carried a peculiarly questioning note, or again it seemed to mutter something no one could understand.

There were unforgettable moments, such as when the big, faintly bluish eye of the sun 'way out there in the west seemed suddenly to regret that it couldn't stay longer and tried to make up for that by turning to gold, edging the clouds with its glory and radiating through the heavens far upward and outward. If then a meadow lark would glide into the evening and take to singing from some hillock or fence post, the golden luster of the sky would fill with warblings at once delightful and melancholy. Then the fledgling prairie lad had to hold his breath in an awareness of something infinite.

But the prairie could give him moments of another kind, especially when busy menfolk, having finished some job they had been struggling with, took time for a relaxing smoke. Then it would happen that those who were out in the open air wearing long overcoats or fur coats would occasionally glance in the direction of the north wind. The time for speculation came quickly to an end; for if one so much as stuck his nose out the door, the roar of winter would be upon him. Then the sturdy sod hut was absolutely tops as a refuge. Time and again Father was to see it proved that he was right in what he said when the sod walls were being built layer upon layer from the ground up.

Well, enough of this. The boy from the valley was here, and here to all appearances he would remain. Of what had belonged to the old valley he remembered only one thing for long and that was the River Laagen. The "Catechism," the "Bible History," and the "Reader" used here were identical with those they had brought with them. Now there was talk of its being time to study the "Explanation" (*Forklaring*). Of this he had no fear. As for the English public school — just let it come. They couldn't cut off his fingers on account of that funny language. Word had also begun to go around that they would soon be having a month of Norwegian church school out here on the prairie — during midsummer most likely, when students at the theological seminaries were having vacation and could serve as teachers.

What, aside from such things, was there for a boy from a simple sod hut to occupy himself with?

Fishing was of course out of the question; the dirty gray river had eliminated that. Perhaps his zeal for the sport had fallen off a little, anyway, that day back in Norway when Grandfather's fishhook had stuck in his finger instead of in the fish. The pain was gone now, of course. Even the scar was scarcely visible, and Mother had assured him that in a few months it would be gone altogether.

But there were disadvantages in being a newcomer with only a sod hut for a home. He knew at least three boys who were more fortunate. Take Paul, for instance — he had a beautiful rifle. One had a nice shotgun, and Albert, the shiniest revolver on the prairie. All three had gunpowder, bullets, and shot. Could anything be more perfect for a prairie boy?

There were many things to be heard when bewhiskered men sat drinking punch or coffee or just smoking pipes. They often talked about a certain war — the Civil War. Some of the men who had eventually come to the prairie had been in it, had worn uniforms, had marched from place to place, had shot with long rifles, which were bought and sold. Now almost every prairie home had at least one hanging on the wall, an object of high esteem.

Things other than slavery and the Civil War brought men to think about guns. The Indians — half-naked, painted, gruesome, yelling wild men — had something to do with it. When they were bent on violence they really couldn't leave decent people alone. In some places in Minnesota they had carried on like possessed, had shot down little children or thrown them against walls, carried off pretty young girls, set fire to houses which settlers had nearly worked themselves to death to build. Among their victims were several Norwegians. The name of Guri Endreson, for instance, lives on the prairies to this day.

It was unbelievable how this Norwegian backwoods woman had managed to save herself and help others too, during the period when the redskins raged at their worst. It was said that Guri Endreson would never be forgotten in Minnesota — a distinction which hundreds of fine Minnesota ladies had never attained. And to imagine that anything like that could happen to a person with a name like Guri!

For the boy from a sod hut — one without a Civil War rifle on the wall — such talk was rather depressing. He didn't even have a shining revolver to show anyone, like Albert, who was just his age — not to mention Paul's rifle and Ole's shotgun.

Things began to look better when the promise of Norwegian church school became a reality that summer. The "Explanation" would certainly have to be taken up now. As for the "Bible History," there would never be an end to that so long as much of what was in it continued to be quoted by the minister himself. And the "Reader" had a series of sections in it, each more demanding than the one preceding it. Simon brightened considerably when church school began.

The teacher, Bernt Haugland, had much to do with this. He was tall and well built and had a bright face, a brown mustache, and wavy hair the same color. It was good for any boy to see this kind of person. He could, no doubt, be strict as any grownup, but the pupils chose to avoid doing anything to make that necessary. A disappointed glance from the teacher was usually sufficient. And his face glowed with warmth when recitations went well and everything else in the schoolroom was pleasant.

He was well dressed, although not in such a way as to make one afraid to go near him. He wore a watch the like of which must have been unknown on the prairie. It was so large that its shape showed on the outside of his vest pocket, and its double case of shining silver clicked so loud when he closed it that everyone, even those at the back of the schoolroom, heard it, especially when it signaled that recess was at hand.

With Haugland as a teacher, mastering the "Explanation"

and the "Bible History" was no problem at all. He was good natured in almost everything he undertook, not least when the day's recitations were over and he asked all to rise and join in singing, "Lord, Bestow on Us Thy Blessing." Every voice in the schoolroom responded:

> Lord, bestow on us Thy blessing
> Let Thy face upon us shine;
> May we all, Thy grace possessing
> Walk within Thy light divine.
> Come and visit every heart
> And Thy peace to us impart.
> Father, Son, and Spirit hear us
> Be Thou now and ever near us.

Even at the end of the school day, no one, no matter how lively, could start any tomfoolery for a good while after he had joined in this hymn.

*

The boy often observed that his mother was especially happy about the Norwegian school and Haugland's teaching. It came out distinctly on one occasion when a neighbor stopped by and had coffee. As the conversation touched on such things as the Norwegian church school and the public school, the man took a deep puff on his pipe and remarked, "That Bernt Haugland is a born teacher if ever there was one." It was Mother who then brightened, nodded a vigorous assent, and hastened to bring the coffee. This visitor was most welcome to that extra drop, even though of late she had been anxiously watching the dwindling supply in the jar.

After Haugland had left and a breath of fall now and then came in the air, a considerable stir arose in the house because of what Mother called the "English" school. "You will need warm clothes," she said, and sat up late at night struggling to finish stockings, mittens, and the like. But she didn't show the eager happiness that she had when Haugland was expected.

It was with a sad look that she saw the boy off, that first day of school.

The "English school," the public school of the prairie, was different in many respects from Haugland's summer classes. The attractive mustache was no more to be seen, for it was a woman who took over. The big, shining silver watch with the case that clicked gave way to a little golden thing that dangled from a chain around her neck. And though the lady was different from most of the prairie women, her geniality seemed somewhat short of that which had radiated so naturally from Haugland. But she was pretty, and she had a pretty name — Mildred Steen on paper, Miss Steen when you had a question to ask. And bearded fellows who were acquainted with such matters did not hesitate to assert that she knew a thing or two.

Almost twice as many children came to this school as to Haugland's, attendance being drawn from a district, not a congregation. There were no empty seats in the wooden schoolhouse. One got to hear and see a good many things not mentioned when Haugland was in charge. On the back wall hung a large map with state and territorial boundaries distinctly marked, and to one side of the blackboard was something called a "chart." It had pages of letters which were to be combined into words, and then pictures of the things the words stood for. This contraption was in frequent use, especially during the first few days, and Miss Steen was an expert in turning up the shining bright pages.

Among the Halling folk on the prairie was a boy whose name was Ole, but because he was spindly and a head taller than the other boys his age, he got the nickname "Lanky." His learning ability was not up to the level of his tousle.[3] But Miss Steen applied herself with patience and diligence to Ole's slowness.

Finally a day came when she hoped that Ole could combine letters into words and thus join the class of boys his own age.

[3] I.e., tousled head.

She deftly turned the pages of the chart until she came to one with more difficult words than Ole had so far encountered.

It didn't work. Through word after word Ole stood silent, Miss Steen's grimaces and suggestive lip movements notwithstanding. The sound of pencils scratching on slates became less audible; the attention of every pupil in the room was being distracted by what was going on at the chart. When nothing helped, the now impatient and disappointed teacher turned back to the simpler words, picked the word "cow" with the matching picture of a sturdy bovine, doing as before her facial best to force recognition and remind Ole that here was something he had seen many times. "Name this one — hurry up now and name it!" she prodded.

A light broke in Lanky's face, and straightening to his full height, he burst out fast and triumphantly in broad Norwegian dialect, "Eit kjyr!"

Like a flash a boy ducked behind his desk and tried in vain to suppress his giggling, whereupon a good many others let go, and shrieking laughter soon drowned out everything else in the schoolroom. Miss Steen, helpless to resist, had to join in, in spite of wanting to control her irritation and maintain discipline.

And Lanky? Well, he seemed not to know what it was all about.

*

In time much was learned within those rough board walls. The globe on the teacher's desk in the front of the room showed the entire world, but it was a poor competitor to the more diligently used map of the United States on the back wall. It was about America that the schoolbooks had the most to say, and a good part of what was to be learned had to do with that country. Furthermore, this information was about men and women — principally about men who had done, said, or written something glorious in America.

The only trouble was that there were too many such heroes

for one to remember them all offhand. Names like George Washington, Abraham Lincoln, Ulysses S. Grant, and Robert E. Lee were the exceptions, but if one racked his brains ever so little he could add Benjamin Franklin, John Adams, Thomas Jefferson, and James Madison. As for writers, such men as Franklin, Bryant, Longfellow, Whittier, and Poe might be included, although one who came from a sod hut would hardly know much about these fellows. On the other hand, the wild midnight ride of Paul Revere, and how he felt as he sped across the countryside warning people that British troops were on the march, bent on taking possession of everything and everyone—this was something that one could live oneself. What a man this Paul Revere must have been! And the horse he had! It could well be that that splendid animal sensed that he bore something more than an ordinary rider that night.

In the new schoolbooks on his desk the boy could read about this and a great deal more. There was as much to be heard as read, for the teacher talked about the same things, putting them in her own words. For example, she told how the brave people who came over in the "Mayflower" had to clear patches in the dense forest for places to raise food. This meant not only the never-ending toil of felling trees and digging up roots for spots of tillable ground, but also always carrying a musket to guard against attacks by savage redskins who lurked behind tree trunks and in the bushes round about. The prairie farmer ought to remember this, for he needed only to ride out with a plow and, with no trouble at all, he could turn up the richest soil.

Who should have the credit for making all this possible? Yes, it was these pioneers who in spite of hardships not only persevered but also had the vision to see what the new land could become for oppressed and unfortunate human beings the world over. "We, too, secure within these four walls, should be thankful," said Miss Steen. Every now and then she mentioned George Washington's boyhood years and the incident of the cherry tree. This was a fine and useful tree and the father was furious to discover that it had been chopped down. During the investigation which followed among the family and slaves, George confessed that he was the sinner. He stood remorsefully before his father and explained that he had been unable to resist trying his new hatchet on that very tree, and then when he began to think of his misdeed he didn't dare to tell a lie. That's the kind of boy George Washington was, said Miss Steen. This inborn honesty later shaped his career and earned him such esteem among his countrymen that they finally honored him with the title "Father of His Country." She added, "Of course none of you boys in this room can become the father of his country, for only one can be that. But that kind of honesty can be just as useful to you as it was to him."

Oh, there was much to be heard in this community. One day the boy Simon listened to a rather inquisitive fellow who seemed bent on finding out about the battlefield exploits of the neighborhood's only Civil War veteran. No matter what he hit upon to ask, he got nowhere. Perhaps this uncommunicative fellow was no veteran at all? Finally the silent, harried man rose to his feet, straightened to his full height, and said, "I have seen General Grant ride before his ranks, swinging his saber. Then it was easy to follow." And he turned and walked away, leaving the inquisitive one looking dashed. The sod-hut boy sat stock-still for awhile, staring.

General Grant rode before his ranks swinging a saber.

*

The pupil from the sod hut couldn't help wondering a little naïvely what manner of person this Miss Steen really was. She always spoke English, wouldn't tolerate a Norwegian word, either in or out of the schoolroom, and yet seemed pretty well acquainted with the "Explanation of the Catechism" and the "Bible History." During the Christmas holidays that year something entirely unexpected happened.

On the third day after Christmas a sleigh, nicer than the

usual kind seen in the neighborhood, drew up in front of the
sod hut. In the back seat, all bundled up and wearing a hat,
sat Miss Steen. After a couple of short words to the driver she
stepped out holding a package in both hands. In she came, just
as if she had been invited, and the sleigh drove on. Once inside, she put down what she was holding and began immediately to remove her wraps and hat. There, where distaff
visitors had been farmers' wives in plain attire, she was something! She seemed a phantom. Had she come to show off and
put the sod-hut folk to shame? It was possible. It hurt to be
made to feel that way — now of all times on the third day of
Christmas.

But the unkind thought was short-lived. It quickly became
clear that what the phantom held in her hands was a thump-
ing big pie as beautifully wrapped as if it were intended for a
wedding. It must have taken half a morning to make it, to say
nothing of what it cost. Moreover, it was the kind of pastry
that newcomer women never attempted. "It should by rights
have been here on Christmas Day, but I didn't manage it,"
she explained as offhandedly as if such a pie was a normal part
of the Christmas festivities in this sod hut. A faint aura of
delicate perfume surrounded her as she went from one person
to the next with a special greeting for each — all in the Val-
ders dialect, with now and then an English word. The school-
boy went hot to the roots of his hair when his turn came and
she said, "And here is my bright pupil." Before long she managed a low-voiced conversation with Mother, behind the bed
curtain in the corner — an action that in turn caused anxiety
because of the neglected treats. But without more ado she
glanced at her watch, which today as always hung on a gold
chain around her neck. "No, no, don't even mention it." Any
such thing was out of the question. The sleigh would be here
any moment. And it was. A shout came almost on the instant,
leaving her only enough time to put on her coat and hat and
offer a last Christmas greeting from the half-open door.

The real occasion for the visit came to light only later.

64

And it got to be worrying Mother, who finally brought it up. Ever since starting for America she had been plagued with anxiety because the American school system did not permit instruction in religion. The short conversation with the teacher and the visit itself had given her a good deal to think about. Her mind had been relieved of a great worry, she said, half apologetically but in her own forthright way. From now on she would encourage the children to attend both the English school and the Norwegian church school. Miss Steen had showed herself to be a real Christian. And as for son Simon, surely he hadn't forgotten how the fine old schoolmaster in Norway had taken the trouble to pay a visit just before they left and speak an encouraging word.

What Mother said about Miss Steen and the schoolmaster in the old country was greeted with approving nods and brightening faces. Later she confided to Father that there were signs that a little American could be expected — the family's first native-born child.

*

The family name was to undergo a typical American change. The place name "Bergumshagen" had seldom been used in the Norwegian valley; "Svensen" was more common because it was a patronymic. Among settlers from that same community in Norway, this, changed to Swenson, was usually adopted in this country. When, however, Father became a farm owner in Dakota Territory he ordered the name "Johannes S. Bergumshagen" registered in the deed of conveyance—a name unpronounceable among Americans. Hence it happened that when the children began going to the public school, Father's given name was rewritten "John," a usable name, and the children's family name became "Johnson." The eldest, Simen, immediately became Simon. Among the neighbors the names Bergumshagen, Swenson, and Johnson were used interchangeably, but as the immigrants were accustomed to such variations, this caused no difficulty.

65

The passing years allowed Simon little opportunity to further his education. There were, to be sure, the regular annual
terms of public school and as a rule a few weeks of Norwegian
church school, but that was all. To learn to handle farm im-
plements, to lead a pair of oxen, to steer a plow, to rein horses
properly (after they replaced oxen) — these were more important than going to school. And after a few years, when the
machines came, they were the most wonderful of all, except
for school and books. Yes, the machines!

*

During the winter Mother had an almost fatal illness, and
recovery was very slow. When therefore it became known that
Dr. Eduard Boeckmann of St. Paul was going to hold a clinic
for a few days in one of the near-by prairie towns, it went
without saying that this was an opportunity not to be passed
by.

Throughout the Dakota prairies the opinion prevailed that
competent doctors treated the settlers like stepchildren. The
best doctors preferred locations where "shillings" were more
plentiful and distances shorter. Moreover, among Scandinavian frontier folk it was said that the American doctor was not
as well trained as the European. These did not apply to Dr.
Boeckmann. He had passed an examination brilliantly in Norway; more than that, he had decided to use his skills for the
benefit of his countrymen in the Northwest. In the third place,
he was so Norwegian that his origin enveloped him like spring
weather wherever he went. During a few years in America he
had built up an extensive practice in Minneapolis and St.
Paul, and his name was familiar everywhere in the prairie
settlements to the west.

Mother must by no means miss the chance to see him,
which seemed to be an answer to prayer. Because the drive
would be fairly long and horses were still only a dream to
Father, he seriously considered hiring a horse and buggy.
Mother opposed this vigorously. On the way over and back

they could make use of the cool night hours for driving, when oxen were at their best. A little hay in the wagon box and something to wrap up in would be fine.

So far as Mother was concerned Dr. Boeckmann lived up to his reputation. Because she was the simply attired housewife, Anne from a sod hut, she expected a curtly superior manner and a quick disposal of her case on the part of the celebrated physician. But never think it! She could not have been treated more courteously had she appeared in silk. And the examination? Hm, hm, she certainly had had a serious ordeal, according to the doctor. This sort of thing happened again and again when one was torn up by the roots and transplanted. "Your one lung, Mrs. Swenson, has become more than a little troublesome and must be treated accordingly. Much fresh air; fortunately there is an abundance of it on the prairie. And as many regular rest periods as possible every day. And you will not leave without bottles. I will see to it that such bottles are available at the pharmacist's in the town nearest you. And now then, a safe return home!"

That is what it was like to be received by Dr. Boeckmann, even though a tentful of people sat waiting anxiously for the white-clad attendants to record their names, addresses, and other information in a huge book. And the ride home in the rattling wagon box, after the cool of the night had set in, was much less worrisome.

As the years passed Dr. Boeckmann's diagnosis, so far as the lungs were concerned, proved not to have been exaggerated. But the years were also to prove that having less than two lungs did not stand in the way of becoming the mother of more children — American girls with corresponding citizenship privileges.

The years also saw to it that little boys became bigger boys. And what the big boys — and in-between ones too — could think up to do increased with the years.

Whenever, for example, Nils Coffee-Toddy was mentioned the sport would be on. This Nils Coffee-Toddy was, so to speak, an in-between specimen of a human being. He could not read, much less write, but he could speak up at times in a way that stung. He had emigrated to America because, in all likelihood, some poor-relief officer in Norway wanted to get rid of him. It was said that at one time he had just barely kept out of jail. He was married, but that didn't keep him from being acquainted with women of questionable repute in this land of the free. His nickname derived from the fact that nothing could put him in such good spirits as a mixture of coffee and alcohol.

Strange to say, Nils Coffee-Toddy was fond of children, and children understood and were instinctively attracted to him. They unhesitatingly climbed up into his lap, to be bounced up and down on his knee and hear something the like of which they never heard from other lips:

> Biam, biam-bipp
> biam, biam-bipp!

Which presently went over into:

> Biappam bare, bia appam bire
> bi appam bipp!
> Biappam bare, bi appam bire,
> bi appam bipp!
> Bi appam bipp.

A singsong jingle like this could be repeated indefinitely. What was needed by way of melody came naturally, with the children bouncing to the rhythm of the syllables as soon as the text was learned. But it wasn't only when he had a child on his lap that Nils Coffee-Toddy would burst out in this way. It was known to happen when he was simply in a good mood.

*

In these years many things began to change for the sod-hut family. Their status was enhanced by the exchange of the oxen for a pair of horses, and good-looking ones they were. One of the pair, a shapely, gentle animal and a little tricky, was said to have a strain of Morgan blood. When Father had caught on to him he told, smiling in his beard, how the horse, when hitched in a certain way, could find a place of support for his end of the doubletree so as to make his pull easier than that of his less cunning partner. American smartness in a horse's head! But what Simon thought about most of all was how friendly this Morgan crossbreed could be — at times almost amusingly so.

With the years the family got rid of the sod hut and the rented acreage on which it stood and acquired a farm with a white dwelling house on it. The moving took place in stages, with delays and confusion between times. While this was going on, the industrious Simon caught a severe cold and had to crawl into bed for several days among the chattels which had been moved over from the sod hut.

When some order was established in the new place and Simon could get into his clothes again, Mons, the cat, was not to be found. During the turmoil none of the adults had remembered to bring him. Even Mother could not claim having seen the cat when the door to the sod hut was locked. Originally a vagrant, was he to become one again? It might well be. But that did not eliminate the possibility that he was still in the hut and would die of neglect, which was an unthinkable possibility. It certainly wasn't necessary to prod Simon into finding out, even less now that they had something resembling a cart to hitch that likeable Morgan-featured fellow to.

Simon started out the next day. The fall weather was bracing but sunny, with now and then a breeze from the south. But the cart was only soso; it had only a board for a seat. Wheels and shafts, however, were in order and they mattered the most. The Morgan crossbreed was, as usual, pleasant to handle. He made his way as if he knew both the road and the destination. The chills in Simon's body went away. Nothing remained of them but the memory.

It was almost eerie to stand once more in the now empty sod hut and see the naked walls and supports, pasted over in some places with yellowed pages of *Decorah-Posten* and *Skandinaven*. But in the light of his errand this didn't bother Simon much. For all his whistling and calling, "Mons! Mons! Mons!" there was no answer to be heard, nor movement seen, only dull silence within the walls. Nor was there anything to indicate that the cat had been there when the sod hut was locked.

There was still the low grain shed and the sod barn. In the grain shed he met with the same dead silence. Only the smell differed. Nothing suggested that the cat had been locked in there either.

In the barn, which had served both cows and horses, the situation must be more promising, for besides hay and straw a lot of stuff had been thrown in there that wasn't worth moving. It still smelled like a cow and horse barn. So the whistling and calling began again, "Mons! Mons! Mons!" with still no answer and no sign of a living thing. Would he have to do something for which he had no stomach, drive to neighbor Eng's, the cat's original home, to see if Mons had found his way back there? That could of course only be interpreted as showing that the gift hadn't been sufficiently prized.

As Simon hesitantly approached the exit he thought he detected something stirring up on a shelf. He crawled up into a crib to get a closer look, and caught a gleam. It was the cat! It was Mons! And he tried to purr, immediately making it clear that he had no objection to meeting his old friend. Had Mons suffered since the sod-hut folk moved away? That had to be determined first. A single look in the daylight was enough. The cat was as plump and healthy-looking as the last time Simon saw it. It was delightful to sit out in the sunny fall weather, to stroke the soft fur, and to hear that cozy purring. But this was no time for lingering. They must be on their way to that new and grander place which was to be Mons's home from now on.

Translated and edited by C. A. CLAUSEN

4   *The Gasmann Brothers Write Home*

AMERICA LETTERS have been called "the lifeblood of the emigration story." Among the most influential writers of such letters were the Gasmann brothers, Hans and Johan.[1] Hans, a well-to-do *bonde* who had twice been elected to the Norwegian Storting (parliament), caused considerable surprise when he sold his holdings near Gjerpen and in 1843 left for America. A contemporary writer, Pavels Hielm, wrote a long farewell poem to Hans in which he vainly tried to solve the riddle of why a man of such standing should want to abandon his native land. Gasmann himself undoubtedly offered the solution in one of his early letters: "I believe I have achieved what I desired: a better life for all my children" — of which he was to have thirteen. He joined a Scandinavian colony on the Ashipun River in Pine Lake, Waukesha County, Wisconsin, founded two years earlier by the famous Swedish emigrant leader, Gustaf Unonius. There Gasmann took out a claim to a quarter section and soon bought an extra tract of 1,000 acres near by. In the letters here presented he gives an

[1] For information about the Gasmann brothers, see Theodore C. Blegen, *Norwegian Migration to America, 1825–1860*, 135, 138, 151, 178, 206–208, 228n (Northfield, 1931); Ingrid Semmingsen, *Veien mot vest: Utvandringen fra Norge til Amerika 1825–1865*, 93–95, 267–269 (Oslo, 1942).

account of his experiences on the frontier and of his reactions to American life.[2]

Hans Gasmann and his family sailed on the emigrant ship "Salvator," whose captain was Johan Gasmann. Johan won an enviable reputation in emigration history for the care he took of his passengers and for his recommendations for improving conditions aboard the ships which plied the Atlantic in those days.[3] Apparently the captain was not at first enthusiastic about emigrating; but in 1844 he had an opportunity to visit his brother in Wisconsin. This firsthand introduction to conditions on the frontier changed his thinking radically. Not only did he write enthusiastic reports about Wisconsin as a land of promise for prospective emigrants, but in 1847 he himself yielded to its allurements. The letters here translated indicate, however, that despite the many advantages he found in his new home, he — like so many other emigrants — could never forget the old country. To the end of his days he was haunted by loneliness and by longings "for old friends and for dear old Norway."

1. THE LAND IS EASY TO WORK

An extract from a letter written by Hans Gasmann from Pine Lake, Wisconsin, July 27, 1844, to a relative in Norway; it appeared in Morgenbladet *(Christiania), December 19, 1844.*[4]

My whole family and I are doing well, thank God — better than I could have expected. I believe I have achieved what I desired: a better life for all my children. As for myself, I must,

---

[2] Gjerpen is in Telemark County, southern Norway. Hielm's poem, translated with an introduction, is in Theodore C. Blegen and Martin B. Ruud, eds., *Norwegian Emigrant Songs and Ballads*, 52–63 (Minneapolis, 1936). Gustaf Unonius' *Minnen* has been translated and edited by J. O. Backlund and Nils W. Olsson under the title *A Pioneer in Northwest America, 1841–1858: The Memoirs of Gustaf Unonius* (Minneapolis, 1950, 1960).

[3] These recommendations were made in a letter to Consul J. Gasmann, a third brother, who served on a special commission appointed to draft laws pertaining to the emigrant traffic. A translation of the letter is in Theodore C. Blegen, *Land of Their Choice: The Immigrants Write Home*, 99–102 (Minneapolis, 1955).

[4] Transcripts of letters 1 and 2 are in the archives of the Norwegian-American Historical Association, part of a collection of America letters gathered by Theodore C. Blegen in 1928–29 from newspapers in the library of the University of Oslo. Pine Lake is in Waukesha County, twenty-six miles west of Milwaukee. Ex-

of course, be satisfied so long as I can live free of worries about the necessities of life. And I hope that, with God's help, I shall be able to do this. My greatest enjoyment in Norway, namely, to mix with educated and noted people — which, as you know, not infrequently fell to my lot — has been decreased, of course. But I have pleasures here, too; because, thank God, I am not entirely deprived of companionship in this country that some people have called a desert. Besides some good Norwegian families, we have in this neighborhood several refined Swedish and Danish families, among whom are some educated men. Furthermore, I have the pleasure of knowing that if I am permitted to live awhile I can work up one of the most beautiful landholdings imaginable. You know that I have always greatly valued such property. People can say and write whatever they please about this country, but I assure you that it is both scenic and fertile. I believe that both my family and I will be able to live quite pleasantly here and, with God's help, free from anxiety about our livelihood. But even though we believe that we can get along here, this would not necessarily be true of everybody. A person must have either labor power within his family corresponding to its size, or enough money [for hiring it]. I pity those who arrive lacking both these factors. This ought to be plain to anyone who realizes that he comes to a land largely uncultivated and partly covered by the densest forests.

There is, however, a great deal of land in Wisconsin already cultivated, and it presents to the eye the most luxurious fields and meadows. But if you want to buy such land it costs lots of money. A quarter section, . . . if under the plow and supplied with proper buildings, will not sell for less than five or six thousand dollars.[5] If a person has enough money to buy cultivated land, the size of the area [needed] will, of course, depend on the size of the family. They say here that a small fam-

cerpts from the captain's account of his visit are translated by Carlton C. Qualey in Norwegian-American Historical Association, *Studies and Records*, 5:30–49 (1930).

[5] Elision marks indicate lacunae in the transcripts.

ily can get along on 40 acres and a very large one on 160; and very little additional capital or labor will be needed. Once the land has been cultivated, it is extremely easy to work. And since many even maintain that a person can live very well off one acre, it is obvious that the necessary money can be raised when he sells the surplus produced by the rich harvest. However, if a person hasn't enough capital to buy cultivated land, then he must have ample labor help, besides enough money to defray his living expenses for one or two years until crops can be harvested.

Bringing new land under cultivation is done as follows: Openings [*aabningsland*], as they are called — that is, land on which there are only a few trees, as in an orchard, or even fewer — can be plowed without further ado, since the few trees will not harm the crop. To keep the leaves from casting too much shade, it is customary to cut a circle through the bark around the trunk of the tree, causing it to die. Later it can be cut down at a person's leisure. To break this kind of land, four or five yoke of oxen are needed — horses are not used for this type of work, as they are not suited to it — and a man to steer the plow, besides a boy to drive the oxen. About an acre or an acre and a half can thus be broken in a day.

If a person breaks this kind of land in June or early July and seeds it in August or early September, he can be certain of a pretty good crop — but not so large a crop the first year as later, because it [*the land*] increases in productivity each year without being fertilized. I have been told that there are farmers who, without using any manure, have had the most bountiful crops for twenty successive years, simply by sowing and harvesting. Ditches or water furrows are not used here, and are unnecessary. Wheat and everything else grows very well in the deepest marshland and on the most level plain without being harmed in the least by water.

If a person does not himself own oxen or a plow, he can get such land plowed, or "broken," as it is called, for three dollars per acre. Once the land has been broken, it is very easy to work — much easier than in Norway. The soil is so light and loamy that it resembles a well-worked garden more than a field.

The wooded land is cleared in the following manner: The trees are cut down and those parts which are not saved for some use are piled up and set on fire. When everything has been burned, the ground is harrowed and seeded to either wheat, turnips, beets, beans, or peas, or planted to potatoes or corn. Since the soil in such areas is much looser than in the openings, a person can raise exceptional crops for two or three years without plowing — merely by harrowing. People here claim that wooded land is of better quality and produces good yields much longer than the openings. But also, it costs much more to get it broken. If you have to hire labor, you must usually pay four or five dollars per acre to get the wood cut and two or three dollars extra to get it burned. Anyone who cannot do such work himself, but has to hire help, must have money. The process is easier, however, than at first thought it would seem to be. When a piece of land has been put under cultivation, it soon yields so much that the owner can sell part of the crop and pay the laborers; and thenceforth, step by step, it becomes easier.

I know that people in Norway wonder — as I did myself — how a farmer over here can sustain himself, seeing that labor costs are so high and the market price for his produce is so low. When a person becomes familiar with conditions in this country, however, it is easily understood. If as much help were needed to cultivate the soil here as in Norway and if the yields were as small, it would be impossible to make ends meet. But we must bear in mind that over here, once the soil has been broken, very little help will be required. In this region there is no work connected with fertilizing, ditch digging, or clearing away of rocks, because there are no mountains. Neither is much help needed to care for the cattle, because they forage richly for themselves outdoors most of the year. In short, there is so much less work than in Norway.

Furthermore, a person is free of so many other expenses that you have in Norway. The taxes are negligible. Local [civic] expenses are practically nonexistent, poor rates absolutely unheard of, as are fees for drawing up documents and salaries for the officials. When we consider the rich crops and the little work connected with harvesting them — crops of which the farmers can sell a large part instead of buying extra, as most of them must do in Norway — then I believe we can understand why a person gets along better here than over there.

From this you will get a fair understanding of what is needed by those who wish to settle here. If a person does not have money corresponding to the size of his family or if he has little capital and little labor power, then I would not advise him to come.

One class of people I do, however, believe can come, even though they have little money: free and single working men and ordinary, industrious servant girls. They never have any trouble finding jobs. And I think the time is far off when the need for such people will decrease. You might suppose that with the great influx of immigrants the demand for help of this kind would decline, but I do not think this need be feared. We must note that conditions are different from those in Norway. When a young, vigorous man has worked for others a couple of years he will be so well established that he can buy land of his own, and thus he needs [hired] help instead of further employment. A laborer — a good worker — has no difficulty getting ten to twelve dollars per month plus good board during the summer, and from six to ten dollars during the winter. A good maidservant will get from four to six dollars per month.

From the foregoing it will be easily understood that there cannot be many paupers or beggars here. There is not only always opportunity for employment for those who can and will work, but food supplies are very cheap. And if it happens that a couple have more children than they can care for —

which was the case with one Norwegian family that came over with me — the Yankees (Americans) are immediately willing to receive such children and bring them up as their own without any expense to the community. You can imagine what a joy it is for a sensitive person not to be aware of any poverty or any beggars. I can assure you that I have not seen a beggar since I touched American soil.

Report has it that, unfortunately, poor people are to be found; but to the best of my knowledge these are all Norwegians — I am sorry to say — and so far as I know they are located in one region, namely, a place here in Wisconsin called Muskego. And this is not surprising, because in that area — where at first there were only a few and, I believe, less industrious Norwegians — several hundred of our countrymen have congregated. Most of them had little or no capital and there was no one in the settlement who could give them work. Furthermore, they were stowed together in the few small houses found there. This caused severe sickness and many deaths. Anyone will realize that the result had to be poverty and misery. Also, the area is swampy and flat with very poor water — factors which always cause sickness over here.[6]

It was there that the carpenter Anders Brynildsen settled, the one who has given such an unfavorable account of America. I am not at all surprised that he found conditions bad — a man like him who is a good carpenter, but can do no other type of work, settles in a place where a whole crowd of miserable, sick, poverty-stricken and partly unemployed people have packed themselves together like bees; people who have not the wherewithal to sustain life, let alone give employment and income to a good carpenter! It seems to me that if he had had a bit of common sense he should have realized what the result would be. As far as I know he did not visit any other

[6] Muskego, in southeastern Wisconsin, was the first Norwegian settlement in that state and became, despite its drawbacks, one of the most influential communities founded by Norwegians in the Middle West. See Blegen, *Norwegian Migration, 1825–1860*, 118, 146, 202, 268; Carlton C. Qualey, *Norwegian Settlement in the United States*, 47–52 (Northfield, 1938).

part of this country. Consequently it does not surprise me when he states that a settler here must buy all his food grain the first three or four years. This undoubtedly holds good for the area where he stayed. According to what I have been told by reliable people — in fact by one of the first Norwegians to arrive there, a man with money aplenty — the settlers there hardly worked at all on their land. Very likely Brynildsen clung to those fantasies which we sometimes met with in Norway, that over here everything should rain down upon us and roast doves fly into our mouths, thus making work unnecessary. Any reasonable person will certainly admit that blame for this state of mind cannot be ascribed to the country or its institutions but solely to the notions of naïve individuals.[7]

I have not enough experience or sufficient knowledge of the country and its institutions to give you or anyone else complete information; it will be late, or probably never, before I will be in a position to do this. My letters are based on what I have observed in my community and during my travels in the country at large — which have been rather extensive. My own impressions have been supplemented by other reliable observers. However, I cannot, at least not immediately, give either my countrymen or the Norwegian government the desired evaluation. But I believe that everyone has or soon will get an opportunity to secure a far more complete account than I could ever hope to give — the account by Mr. Reiersen of Kristiansand. Last fall he traveled through a large part of this country. He spent several days with me, and before he left for home he sent me the account he had written about the United States. On the whole I found it to agree so completely with my own observations that I had no reservations whatsoever in endorsing it.[8]

[7] Brynildsen's letter is quoted in Blegen, *Norwegian Migration: 1825–1860*, 205.

[8] Johan R. Reiersen was one of the most famous Norwegian proponents of emigration. His controversial *Veiviser for norske emigranter til de Forenede Nordamerikanske Stater og Texas* (Pathfinder for Norwegian Emigrants to the United North American States and Texas) was published in Christiania in 1844. For a discussion, see Blegen, *Norwegian Migration: 1825–1860*, 243–248. See also

I still live near Pine Lake where, as you know, I claimed a piece of land and built a house. You probably know, too, that later I bought a thousand-acre tract five and a half English miles from here. This land is covered largely with fine woods, that is, all sorts of deciduous trees such as oaks, elms, lindens, poplars, walnut, apple, and plum trees, gooseberry bushes, and many other varieties. Furthermore, there are numerous maple trees which in spring yield sap, from which sugar is made. This is very profitable, for from one tree alone as much as twenty pounds of sugar can be obtained annually. We also have lots of grapes. Through this property of mine runs a beautiful river where I have set up a sawmill, because I have plenty of timber. As soon as possible I will also set up a flour mill. As yet I have only one saw, but we still cut some six or eight dollars' worth every day. We do not work at night. As we have trees in abundance right around the saw, I make pretty good money. I do not believe there will be any market shortage, because a great number of people have settled in my neighborhood and I suppose more will come. All of these are going to build houses and consequently will need lumber. I believe the demand will be lasting because at present all the settlers are merely building modest log houses. When the land is partly under cultivation, however, and people have more time and money, it is customary in this country to build more elegant dwelling houses — which, of course, demands still more lumber.

My land is about twenty-eight English miles from Milwaukee, or about four Norwegian miles. Communication with the city is by land, but construction of a canal from Milwaukee has been started. It was supposed to pass close to our place. But God knows whether it will ever be completed, because the company which has the contract has already stopped digging and is now involved in a legal battle with the government. But I hope we will soon have towns closer at hand. One

Reiersen, "Norwegians in the West in 1844: A Contemporary Account," translated and edited by Theodore C. Blegen, in Norwegian-American Historical Association, *Studies and Records*, 1: 110–125 (Minneapolis, 1926).

by the name of Pinevill [*sic*] is already growing up twelve miles south of us and another called Watertown eight miles to the west. I wish I could have lived closer to Milwaukee, but I came five or six years too late, because all the land clear up to here was already bought. In my neighborhood there is still unclaimed land and I believe that many of my countrymen who are coming this year will settle here. Some of the Norwegians who came with me located near Pine Lake — among them Bellerud from Kongsberg. The highly respected landowner from Hitterdal, Ellef Bjørnson Tungen, also lives close by.

I am now building a house on my new tract and hope to move in sometime next fall. Before my eldest son left for Norway I partitioned my land between my four grown-up sons.[9] But I retained 260 acres for my own use. When this is under cultivation I will have a beautiful farm. My son-in-law, besides, received eighty acres from me, on which he has built a house.

2. REIERSEN'S "PATHFINDER" IS RELIABLE

Hans Gasmann wrote to friends and relatives in Norway from Pine Lake, March 20, 1846. The letter appeared in Bratsberg-Amts Correspondent *(Skien), June 16, 1846.*

I had the pleasure of receiving your letter of September 15 last, but not the copy of Reiersen's work, "Pathfinder," mentioned. I suppose the reason is that both items were sent to America by ship and they couldn't forward the book from the port by mail. Fortunately, however, I received the book through my son, who was in Norway last year. Therefore it doesn't matter whether or not I get the copy you sent me; but it is very unfortunate that I do not have access to the issues of *Morgenbladet* in which Pastor Dietrichson's letters were published. This prevents me from commenting as fully as I

[9] The following footnote was found in the newspaper version of the letter: "Hans Gasmann's oldest son, Niels E. Gasmann, who brought this letter from his father, has arrived in Porsgrund on family business. He will return to Wisconsin with the first available ship."

might wish on these most remarkable utterances. I assume, however, that I am in a position to say something in this connection, since people who have read them have, to the best of their recollections, relayed the contents of the letters to me.[10]

I suppose you have been expecting an answer from me for a long time; but as I did not receive your letter until the sixth of this month, you will realize that I must be excused. It provokes me very much, however, that I did not get it earlier, because my comments might possibly — under prevailing circumstances — have had some value to those of my countrymen who were thinking of coming over this spring. Now, I assume, it will be too late for them. I have carefully read and considered Reiersen's "Pathfinder." I am unable to find much in it which does not agree with my convictions and my bit of experience. My knowledge of the country is, to be sure, rather limited. It does, however, extend to a large part of Wisconsin; and I dare assert with absolute confidence that what he says about this area is accurate. Furthermore, it shows that he has, with the greatest competence, acquainted himself with every detail and given such complete descriptions as could be expected only from a man of Reiersen's ability and determination. Since he has sensed and learned the truth about conditions in one part of the country, I assume that he cannot be so far off in his description of the rest of it. This conviction has been reinforced by information I have gathered from talking with reliable men who live in the regions where I am not acquainted. Their statements coincide with Reiersen's quite well. I do believe, therefore, that I can safely recommend Reiersen's book for guidance to my respected countrymen if they read it with common sense and understanding. I merely want to make the following observations:

[10] The Reverend J. W. C. Dietrichson was the first pastor ordained in Norway to work among his countrymen in the United States. He served congregations in Wisconsin in 1844–45 and again from 1846 until 1850. Always a "storm center of theological controversy," he denounced "the entire emigration movement with almost fanatical fervor" in letters to Norway and in a book, *Reise blandt de norske emigranter i "De Forende Nordamerikanske Fristater"* (Stavanger, Norway, 1846). See Blegen, *Norwegian Migration: 1825–1860*, 251–253.

1. About the calculation or estimate he made on pages 40–46 concerning the management of a farm and the economic progress an able landowner can make if industrious and well informed — it should be noticed that this estimate is based exclusively on the tillage of prairie land and cannot be applied to woodland. Since, however, not everyone may have either the opportunity or desire to settle on prairie land but may choose either openings or woodland, it follows that not everyone can expect to make such rapid strides toward affluence. I have examined the estimate carefully and find it to be reliable — or possibly too conservative. I believe that if no mishaps occur the estimate may be put higher. But calamities may strike, among them, sickness. Wisconsin is, to be sure, a rather healthful region; still, a large proportion of the immigrants fall prey to the climate fever or ague. Last summer it was more general than in previous years. The reason is said to have been the very hot and dry summer we had. That malady caused a serious setback for numerous people. There are many, however, who escape sickness, and the ague is seldom fatal — never, if a doctor is consulted.

Prairie land has both advantages and disadvantages. It provides no wood for fuel or other everyday necessities, and it does not yield as good crops the first years as woodland. A man who lacks money to buy four or five yoke of oxen and a breaking plow will do far better on woodland where, with his own strength alone, he can soon put enough under cultivation to make a living. Therefore I do not agree with Reiersen that poor people ought to settle on the prairie rather than in wooded areas. I do not believe, on the other hand, that a man who has the necessary capital can become rich in any quicker way than by owning and cultivating prairie land.

2. I agree entirely with Reiersen that emigrants will not gain much by coming through New Orleans rather than through New York or Boston. It must be emphasized, as Reiersen does, that if they choose the former route they should make certain to arrive in New Orleans by April at the latest. Later

in the summer it is impossible for Norwegians, fresh from the sea, to endure the heat. Many would assuredly pay with their lives. I am unable to say whether — as Reiersen asserts — a person is more likely to escape being cheated by following this route. If emigrants take ship directly from Norway to New York or Boston and are fortunate enough to come with a good captain who knows how to draw up a correct contract for his passengers with the transportation companies, I believe they are less exposed to cheating than if they go by way of Havre, unless they have an able man along with them who knows the language. One warning, however, I want to give my countrymen who intend to come with either a Norwegian or a Swedish ship: Investigate carefully before leaving whether or not it is too heavily loaded. This was the case with the vessel my brother, Johan Gasmann, commanded last summer. During a storm they had to cast a lot of iron overboard, and it was a God's wonder that the ship and so many passengers were saved. It is deplorable that the despicable greediness of one man [*the shipowner*] should expose so many to the possible loss of life.

I really have no other observations to make concerning Reiersen's book. Furthermore, I suppose it is futile for me or anyone else to write things that are commendatory about America or may inform the Norwegians that they might possibly do better here than in Norway. There is a class of people over there who do not hesitate to stamp as lies anything from here written in that vein; and they declare that we are motivated partly by a false feeling of shame and partly by greedy self-interest.

This particular judgment has been passed on Reiersen. They have tried to tell people that the signatures of Pastor Unonius, myself, and several respected men from this community are forged — signatures we attached to a letter Reiersen sent me; this, despite the fact that the printer, Malling, has testified that the original manuscript was followed. This strikes me as a particularly stupid accusation and I hope some friend of

Reiersen will expose it. This can easily be done. An examination of the manuscript will reveal that the signature is in my own handwriting — I know that many are familiar with it. Furthermore, I made a copy of Reiersen's above-mentioned letter to me, including the signatures; and since I have his book, "Pathfinder," where the letter is inserted, I can testify — if they will believe me — that it is copied verbatim. I therefore declare those who accuse Reiersen of forgery in this matter to be slanderers and liars.

A certain official in Norway is also said to have accused the Norwegian farmer, Ellef Bjørnson Tungen (who now lives in this community), of being absolutely unreliable, despite the fact that this man, both at home and now here, is respected as a very dependable, intelligent, and honorable person. But cases like this are matters of course in Norway.

Pastor Dietrichson's writings, on the contrary, are esteemed as oracles. And why should not people believe that all utterances by such a man of God are pure and unadulterated truth? But may God forgive me my gross sins! I cannot trust him. When he tries to tell our countrymen that the accounts we give our own relatives and friends are not trustworthy, but are motivated by a false feeling of shame or greedy self-interest, then I do declare in plain Norwegian that he is not telling the truth.[11] If anyone regrets that he came over, he is surely someone who is not much troubled by a sense of shame. And I cannot understand how self-interest could play a part. Presumably it would be the hope of getting cheaper labor if a great number of people came across, or possibly someone who wanted to sell part of his land expected to get a better price. But it does not seem to me that there is real substance to either of these suspicions. Few, if any, of the Norwegians who settled here have more land than they themselves need.

---

[11] The newspaper in which the letter appeared ran a footnote: "In the original a stronger expression is used"; *Bratsberg-Amts Correspondent* (Skien, Norway), June 16, 1846. The same paper stated that *Morgenbladet* (Norway's leading newspaper at the time) had declined to publish the letter. Its editor, Adolph Stabell, attacked Reiersen and other advocates of emigration.

Most of them have too little, and consequently nothing to sell. And I cannot understand why anyone should go ahead and buy at a high price as long as there is God's plenty of land available at the customary low price. Since everyone has small tracts, there are few or practically no Norwegian farmers here who hire laborers; and I am certain that as yet hardly any have made such headway that they can afford to hire help.

Furthermore, even if some people should be inspired by such ignoble motives, it ought to be plain that not all and every one of us would urge our relatives and friends to come over. I have advised many of my friends to come and will continue to do so. I therefore beg Pastor Dietrichson to be good enough not to frighten them by making them believe that I intend to use them as beasts of burden. Some "big shot" in Norway has told his people that Gasmann will hitch them to the plow when they come here. Pastor Dietrichson also says that "the lovers of truth" among those who have lived a longer time in America admit that they would go back immediately if it were possible for them to get the very same jobs that they had before. Yes, there are some, he tells us, who with bitter tears of regret have begged him to petition the king to let them return. Their houses here are poorer than their barns were back home, we are told, and their condition, on the whole, is much worse in America than it was in Norway. Well and good—even though I have once committed the gross sin of accusing the pastor of falsehood, I will not persist in this error but assume that some grains of truth are found in his reports. Undoubtedly he is correct in saying that there are some who wish themselves back home again. But, I must ask him, what kind of people are they? If he had said that these "lovers of truth" were drunkards or lazy, worthless people who came with the idea that they could live without working, then he would have told the truth. I assure you that industrious, decent people who have been here some time are not the ones he classifies as "lovers of truth."

About fifty or sixty Norwegian families live in my community. Some of them came the same year I did, some later. I dare maintain that I know only one person who regrets that he came over and probably would like to return home; and this man has several grown-up children who under no circumstances would go with him, they are so very well satisfied here. All the others whom I ask how they like it here smile and reply: "Where would we be satisfied if not here?"

It is true that many of our people have poor houses, but even in this connection I believe the good pastor has used the notoriously poor Muskego as evidence. As far as I know, his knowledge of America does not extend much beyond that community and another settlement called Koshkonong. In an earlier letter to Norway, which has appeared in the public press, I described Muskego and I do not want to bother repeating myself. That some of the houses there are poor is understandable, but it is not true that this is generally the case. At least, practically all the above-mentioned families who live in my neighborhood have built good and beautiful houses — about like good farm homes in Norway. To be sure, there are many excellent barns in Norway and if the pastor has them in mind he is, of course, correct. To my way of thinking, the pastor reaps little honor from telling how Mrs. Hansen met him with a stub of a candle when he came to their house in the middle of the night. Mr. Hansen is a respectable man in very good circumstances, so it was not poverty which caused that bit of candle to be used, contrary to what the anecdote presumably meant to imply. I am tempted to believe that Mrs. Hansen had in mind the Norwegian saying: "Two lights on the table for a hammersmith and a tallow dip for a peasant."

It is a wonder that Pastor Dietrichson wishes to come back to this miserable land and live among so many cheats and liars. But I can imagine it is brotherly love which drives this man of God to sacrifice himself — certainly it cannot be self-interest. Still, he has assured himself no mean remuneration for his self-denial. The Norwegian settlers at Koshkonong have been obliged to enter into a written contract with him

wherein they bind themselves to pay him five hundred dollars
per year besides special fees for all such services as weddings,
baptisms, and burials. Furthermore, he is to have a forty-acre
farm with a parsonage on it. Many of the settlers are poor folk,
a fair number of whom have no land, just mere claims which
they may be forced to abandon. Consequently the pastor has
been discreet enough to make his parishioners sign, one for
all and all for one.

In that settlement there is also a Swede who is quite well
fixed. The Swede thought he was shrewder than the Norwegians and figured that this [contract] might become a dev-
ilish affair for those with some means. Therefore he refused to
enter the agreement. But what happened! The Swede has a
daughter whom he asked the pastor to confirm, offering to
pay him properly. The pastor refused, however, since he did
not belong to the parish. Then the silly Swede went about
claiming that this was paltry vindictiveness on the part of
the pastor because he refused to sign the contract. He cannot understand that the pastor acts out of pure altruism and a
stern sense of duty. In this manner he hoped to compel the
Swede to join the church and thus save him from becoming
an accursed heathen — of whom there are supposed to be so
many in this country, as the pastor, no doubt, has heard in
Norway. With the same aim in view the good pastor has
barred very respectable persons from being sponsors at baptisms if they were not members of his church. And people
here are so benighted that they also criticize him for this.
But that's the way of the world: A man is misunderstood
even when he acts out of the noblest and purest motives.

Thus it came to pass that the parson brought a lawsuit on
himself before he left for home last year, simply because he
wanted to introduce the good old practice of excommunica-
tion. The situation was, namely, that among his parishioners
was a man addicted to drink. The pastor therefore ordained
that on Sundays this individual should seat himself near the
church door. The man was so callous, however, that he would

not submit to this well-meant chastisement. Proud and arrogant, exactly as if he were not under the ban, he strode up the church aisle and sat down among the other people. It was, of course, impossible for a Norwegian minister, aware of his rights and obligations, to tolerate such behavior. He therefore ordered his assistants to throw the man out. But can you imagine how confused people become when they get over here! The excommunicate did not consider it a sin at all to sue the man of God. And as evidence of what our judges are like, I am correct, I believe, in reporting that a fine was slapped on the pastor, while the excommunicate goes about freely both to church and other places.

I assure you solemnly that what I have written is by no means inspired by either personal hate or friendship, because I am not well acquainted with either Pastor Dietrichson or Mr. Reiersen. But when I learn that a man has been very diligent in searching out the real truth and has published a most competent account of his observations (as Reiersen has) in the hope that it may further the welfare of his countrymen — and when I then discover that others who have no information whatsoever about the localities concerned undertake to belittle such a deserving work, even to the extent of branding it a concoction of lies and chicanery, then my obligation to both Reiersen and many of my countrymen is to sift facts from falsehoods so far as my abilities permit. Pastor Dietrichson and many others picture America as a desert region so miserable that people are even in danger of starving to death. But I believe that everyone who is slightly acquainted with this country and knows how productive it is, how great the opportunities are for those who can and will work, and how low the cost of living is — I believe every such person, if sane and rational, will realize that tales like Dietrichson's are distorted; and I hope all those who want to be convinced of this will have the opportunity. Whether the authors believe that their gloomy sketches tally with the facts, and whether they are inspired by brotherly love — or, by chance, that self-interest which they ascribe to those of differing opinions plays a part in their calculations — this I will leave to them to decide.

In my previous letters to Norway I have always advised every industrious and reputable person to come over; and this I still do. But I have also indicated that it is not easy for those who come here with absolutely empty hands. It should be plain that a person cannot expect jobs and earnings to be waiting for him, so long as he does not know the language or at least understand it somewhat. Furthermore, many of those who come over are at first subject to the climate fever or ague and may thus be exposed to want. I dare affirm, however, that none of the Norwegians who settled in my community have suffered want in any form. They got along well on their own, even though many had little money and some of them, perhaps, not any at all. Among the Norwegians in this settlement we have had only two paupers, an old couple who came here without money. The husband became sick and the wife had to beg. But as this situation was most unusual among the Americans, she was helped so liberally that they got along very well — better than many a farmer in Norway. When the husband recovered they took care of themselves and are now doing fine.

If this letter can reassure those of my countrymen who would like to believe that Reiersen's book "Pathfinder," is reliable and that he is not an impostor, then I will be extremely pleased.

P. S. I almost forgot to report that one of Pastor Dietrichson's "lovers of truth" has returned home, namely, a man from eastern Norway — from Ringerike, I believe — by the name of Gubberud. He had quite a bit of money when he came here but spent every penny on liquor. Then he got married to a Norwegian girl from Telemark who had a farm in this community. Shortly after the marriage, however, he left her and returned to Norway. This was about the time that the pastor left, but I do not know whether they went together.

3. I DO NOT EXPECT TO HARVEST GOLD

Johan Gasmann wrote from Kristiansand, January 10, 1847, shortly before leaving for America, to Captain Rye, his brother-in-law, in Bø, Telemark.[12]

I did not have time to write you before my departure, which happened at a breathless pace. I must ask you to excuse me, but still more I beg you not to be angry with me for failing to redeem the 100-specie-dollar bond which you have endorsed. I will not resort to any subterfuges to excuse myself but simply tell you that it was impossible at the time. Jacob Müller promised me that it would be redeemed by the time I returned from my last voyage and I set aside 10 specie dollars per month from my salary for this purpose. But Mr. Müller had found it more convenient, now as formerly, to deliver his warehouse trash to my wife at high prices, thereby liquidating my monthly salary so that nothing was paid [me] after I set out last year. Now, God be praised, my embroilments with those honorable Norwegian shipowners or merchants have ended. As soon as possible I shall send you successive installments on this debt. I hope it will not take very long, if I obtain the shipbuilding job I expect to get in Milwaukee. You may feel assured that, far or near, I shall not forget what I owe you; and I know full well that you too, dear Rye, are in need of money.

If I get the shipbuilding work in Milwaukee I will be on top because then I can earn from $500 to $600 per year; and I have 360 acres of good land on Round Lake. Here "mutter" and the boys can work — so I hope we will be able to get along. I expect to get sixty to eighty *tønder* of wheat or rye there in the fall because I have seeded twenty acres; and the boys already have a fine bunch of pigs, two oxen, and sheep and hens.[13] If I get there early enough in the spring — as I hope to — I will plant some more plots to corn, potatoes, etc.

[12] Transcripts of this and the following letters are in the NAHA archives. They were furnished by Ingrid Semmingsen, professor of American history in the University of Oslo.

[13] A *tønde* equals four bushels.

I wish I had some more money to start with, because I must get four to six cows and two more oxen. Well, some way may be found. I have paid for the land and the house — that's the main thing. But, enough of this. I must chat a bit with you and sister Christiane.[14]

First I wish you a happy new year. May every blessing come your way! Next I congratulate you on Mr. Mathias' recent examination, which, I understand, he passed with all possible honors. And no less do I congratulate you on Dick becoming a cadet. Now he will receive free instruction — and *ankerknapper* and *smørstikker* besides.[15] I can imagine your joy; and a hard pull you have had, my dear Rye. I suppose you will still feel the pressure for awhile, but the future must appear brighter for you now than formerly, and this is a great blessing. Man lives more in the hope of a better future than in the enjoyment of the present. I hope your sons will be good boys and appreciate what you have done for them.

I received a brief letter from you, dear Christiane, before I left, but I have not had time to reply. You say that we have been together too little in this world. Yes, God knows we have; but that is fate, and soon the little play is ended, dear sister. I am now fifty, and you are older. Gladly would I have ended my days closer to my relatives and friends and on the soil of the old land. But these are small matters. This world is, of course, merely a brief schooling. We will be gathered together again in better realms — of that we are certain. And whether I live in America or Trondheim makes little difference. From either place we can write each other; this means everything. If I should become rich or, rather, somewhat well off — with my boys a bit older — then it would not be so serious a matter to take a trip across the back of my ancient

[14] No documentary evidence has been found to account for Captain Gasmann's activities between 1844, when he visited his brother in Wisconsin, and his eventual move there. This letter indicates that although he was in Norway in January, 1847, winding up his affairs before his final departure, he had taken his family to Wisconsin and bought land there during a recent trip, probably late in 1846.

[15] *Ankerknapper* (anchor buttons) on a marine officer's uniform bear the picture of an anchor. *Smørstikker* (butter piercer) is used figuratively for a sword.

friend (the Atlantic Ocean) to the old places. The Yankees
are not stingy about giving an old sailor a free passage.

I cannot say that I leave my fatherland purely out of desire for a change or because I regard America as distinctly
superior to Norway. Preferably I would continue to live
amidst the ancient mountains. But when, after thirty-six years
of hard toil on the sea, I have nothing except sorrow and
empty pockets; when I see the calling I have followed — a
calling I always regarded as worthy of a man — when I see
this calling derided; when as an old, worn-out man I see no
chance for a livelihood, and when all opportunities for a sea-
man in our land are blocked — then reason must take precedence over emotion.

I do not expect to harvest gold in America, any more than
elsewhere. But I hope and expect that with God's help I will
be able to earn a secure though simple livelihood. And I believe for certain that my children will be better off there, because I cannot give them any training which will put them into
comfortable circumstances in Norway. I do not leave Norway
with bitterness toward anyone or toward the state or any social class. But I leave with a heavy heart because it was impossible for me to remain here — circumstances made it thus.
If I should despise anyone it would have to be our miserable
class of hucksters who parade as merchants, and who harm the
country much more than they serve it; those — those dumb
curs.

As soon as I have gotten things arranged a bit at Round
Lake you shall hear from me. I promised my good friends Ch.
Blom and City Marshal Cappelen that I will write them often,
and this shall be done. And you also will receive letters. I do
not suppose the soil in America will devour my yen to write,
as seems to have happened with many who went across. But
I believe that few who emigrated from Norway had either
much desire or ability to express themselves. If you are willing to write to me at times I will, in my first letter, give you

my address and hints about the cheapest way of carrying on a correspondence.

Now may God keep you, my dear relatives. You have not entirely neglected an old salt and I am certain that from time to time you will hold me in fond remembrance. Lotte and I will always think of you and your home at Otterholdt with kind and tender thoughts.

Farewell. Soon we will be on the vast ocean. May God soon let us joyfully see our new homeland!

Lotte asks me to greet you most cordially. She has so little time and is so busy writing to her sister.

4. THE CULTIVATED AREA EXPANDS EVERY YEAR
Johan Gasmann wrote his sister and brother-in-law from Wisconsin, December 15, 1855.

It is now very long since we last wrote. I must therefore send you these lines so you can see that we are still alive; and I hope that you have not quite forgotten us. I assume that you received my eight-page letter of about a year ago.

Now then, what do I actually have to write about? Not very much. Even though we live in this giant America where mighty things happen every day, life in our neighborhood flows along as smoothly as if we were still in the valleys of old Norway.

First I must say something about ourselves and those nearest to us. My Lotte and I now live very quietly, and — thank God — we are in fairly good health. Carl and Henriette are presently the only ones we have at home, and so the whole household is accounted for. We work and putter around one day after another; thus time passes rapidly by. There is enough for us to do, I can assure you, since we have no hired help. It comes too high. But when one gets used to it, things go pretty well, especially because of the convenient way in which the Americans arrange everything. Harvesttime is the most pressing because then everybody has more than enough to do. At that time you cannot get a man for less than $1.50

93

or $2.00 per day. Last fall was especially difficult because the crop was unusually heavy. There were not enough people to do the harvesting. But since we are farming on a small scale we got along well and could also help others. There is little use in farming on a large scale here because as yet help is too expensive.

Niels and Constance are doing well. They have four fine boys who are developing rapidly. He has a good farm and is making steady progress. The same is true of Maren and Gotfried. He is the best farmer hereabouts and will soon be a well-to-do man. They have one son — a real giant of a child. Caroline and Sørensen live in Indiana . . . Mishiwauki [*Mishawaka*]. They are doing well. . . . [It is a] region I have as yet not visited . . . even though one can go by [train]. . . . Probably it can be done next summer when the passenger trains will run to Oconomowoc. From there we can get to Milwaukee in two hours, and then to Chicago in twelve hours, and finally to Mishiwauki in five hours. Anne is at present with Sørensen and Caroline. I do not remember whether I mentioned earlier that she is engaged to a student named [William] Stoy. He will become a minister in two years and is a very fine man. I must laugh, and so will you also: my family is becoming very ecclesiastical. In three or four years Johan too will become a pastor. As you undoubtedly recall, I was not very clerically minded. But this is all very well. There is room enough here for ministers and enough for them to do, because the country is growing rapidly. It is commendable the way the American nation with all its vigor concerns itself about religion and education as the population increases. A person would hardly believe that Wisconsin is such a new state when one sees the many churches springing up everywhere and the well-equipped schools now found in every township, besides the more advanced schools.

But I will have to tell about our own affairs and not involve myself in statistical observations. We make a little progress as time goes by. The cultivated area expands every year. At present I have 25 acres (or somewhat more than 100 *maal*) under the plow. So we already realize that we can pull through, free of the daily worries; and now we can improve this thing and that which in the early days we had to get along with as best we could. I have fixed the house up nice and neat; have secured better furniture, etc.; have added a new barn for ten cattle, and this winter I will build a new storehouse — in short, the place is beginning to look quite civilized.

Believe me, there is enough to do when everything has to start from scratch. I would scarcely have believed that so much could be accomplished by me practically singlehanded, or by two men, namely, Carl and myself. I have hired some help for woodcutting, but that is all, except a bit of help from the neighbors for housebuilding. A person can do a lot if only he has the will. I cannot deny that I have had many a hard tussle here, and there were times when I wished I had remained where I was. But now I thank God for what I have done. I have a pleasant home and live well and comfortably and see things going forward every year both for us and our children. This is a peaceful country and no one lacks the necessities of life. It is a great blessing to live in a land where there is no real want. Of course, there are poor people here also, but they are few and they are helped liberally. The laws here, in this respect, are excellent.

I must not forget to tell you that I have become an official, namely, supervisor; that means *en formand*. There are three in each township who constitute a so-called board or council. Our function is to oversee roads and bridges, to divide [the community] into districts, to appoint road bosses, to see that the [road] work is being done, to permit or prohibit the sale of liquor, and to see that the poor are taken care of — these are the main duties, besides seeing that order is maintained and reporting all disturbances to higher authorities. I am paid a dollar per day but this is spent in the course of duty. Every year there is a general meeting of all the supervisors in the county. We meet in the courthouse at the county seat and everyone then hands in his account.

In this connection I have been able to acquire some knowledge about our system of government. And I must admit that for a new country affairs are about as well ordered as they need to be. Everything is arranged about as in Norway, but life is freer and founded on equal rights. I have not been able to settle for myself, however, which is the better system of government, a free republic or a constitutional monarchy. I doubt that this democratic system of ruling the country would work well if the population and the struggle for bread were as great here as in many European areas. Were this country inhabited solely by Americans, things would possibly work better, because they are on a higher rung of civilization than the masses of people in Europe. The difference becomes very obvious here — coarser people can hardly be imagined than those who come from Ireland and some of those from Germany. The Norwegians also are uneducated, but in general are peaceful and they have some moral concepts. On the whole there is no racial group which the Americans rate higher than the Norwegians. The Americans always say, "The Norwegians make very valuable citizens." On the other hand, the ill will against the Irish is rising — and against Catholics in general. Many bloody scenes have, unfortunately, been staged in the large cities, and people are somewhat anxiously wondering what the end will be.

The misfortune is that the foreigners, of course, are uneducated people, and since practically all official positions — except those connected with defense, toll collections, and the post office — are elective, the candidates running for office know very well how to win the votes of the immigrants, whom they can fool with promises, fine speeches, and presumably whisky. Very likely the next Congress will correct this matter by extending the period required by foreigners to gain full citizenship. This question and Negro slavery will probably create stormy scenes when Congress meets again. A tremendous hatred of the Southern slave owners has developed, and what the outcome will be is not easy to foretell — possibly a division of the nation. The Northern or Free states have a population of about fourteen million; the Southern states only about six million. The general opinion is that the North should, and shall, rule; slavery must be abolished, since it is a national sin. It seems reasonable that this tremendous land must, sooner or later, be divided into several independent countries — possibly three: the South, the North, and the new states on the Pacific — and Canada. All of these regions have resources enough to become powerful nations in time.

Today is Sunday. It has snowed since yesterday and a foot of snow covers the earth. We have a real Norwegian winter. Dear God, I cannot forget old Norway. We carry many sad memories with us from the old homeland, but still there is something which draws us toward it.

And how are you getting along, dear folks, at the new Horten?[16] I imagine that it must be a very lively place. At any rate I believe I would like it there. Where are Dicken and Mathias? Has Dicken been in the Baltic this year and seen the big fleet which is keeping an eye on the Russians?[17] What is the opinion back home about the war? Can Sweden avoid being dragged in? There will be tough fighting before Russia gives up. But England and France must conquer, otherwise the war will not end soon — and it would be a blessing if the overgrown Russian bear could lose some of its skin before it gobbles up everything around it.

Dear Christiane, please write to us very soon and tell us about everything back home: how you are getting along — about your children, and about conditions generally. If you see Berge . . . Søren . . . you must greet him from us. He is, of course, busy building steamboats or rather machines for . . . . I should be happy if Dicken could come over sometime.

[16] Horten is a town on the Oslofjord.
[17] During the Crimean War an Anglo-French fleet bottled up the Russian Baltic fleet, and bombarded Russian fortifications along the Finnish coast in 1854 and 1855.

I suppose he is the only one we might expect to see out here in the wild West. But no doubt his time is well occupied and I do not suppose he is much interested in visiting us poor farmers. Johan speaks of taking a trip home when he is through with his studies. Believe me, Johan has become quite a man. He is taller than I; and without bragging, I can say that he is undeniably one of the finest-looking young gentlemen at the college. He is very well liked by his teachers and fellow students. He and Stoy, Anne's fiancé, pay us a visit about every third week. The latter is a kind fellow and has a very good head on him. I like him very much and I believe that in him Anne is getting an excellent husband. His father, an officer, fell in the war against Mexico. His mother lives in Indiana. I have seen her picture, that's all.

You asked me, dear sister, to send you a picture of my place. I will do that next summer. But will you be kind enough to send me a view of Horten so I can see where you are living? I have a picture of Porsgrund. How dearly I would love to have some pictorial sketches from Norway! You can send the picture to Consul Habicht in New York with an emigrant ship or by whatever means available. But do not go to much trouble, because the places I loved are clearly imprinted in my memory — among these Otterholdt is not the least memorable. No, these places will not be forgotten. I ought to be happy here because I would scarcely have attained my present place and contentment back home. The sea would, of course, have remained my lot in life as long as my strength had endured, and after that — the fate of so many sailors — poverty and sorrow. But there is always a longing which nothing can erase. I do not really know what I am longing for. The people? No. The ones I associate with here are just as good as the ones back home. On the whole they are probably better, if there is any difference, because back home there was quite a bit of silly pride. I had few friends of any real worth. What is it then that I long for? The old mountains and fjords and lakes? A strange loneliness comes over me when I think of that land which I shall, most likely, never see again.

I would never have left Norway if shameful treatment had not driven me away. But this also must be the ruling of fate. We do not understand the ways of God. My children will be happier here than in Norway, because there the prospects were not bright for the poor. As for my Lotte and myself, I hope that we can live the rest of our lives without any great changes. This is best when one gets old. If the opportunity comes, however, we might move once more in order to secure more land, so that Carl can be a respectable farmer when he takes over.

I wish you and your good Mr. Rye a happy Christmas. Tell him not to go out and fight the Russians. It's not worth the trouble. It would be better for you to come and buy a good farm in Wisconsin and slaughter pigs rather than those poor, stupid Russians. That cousin of yours, Nicolas, must be a real cur. If we had him here we would tar and feather him.

If I ever become rich I will take a trip home and bring along all sorts of machines. We have transportable threshing machines which can thresh five or six hundred bushels a day at four cents a bushel; a machine which cleans the grain instead of winnowing by hand; machines which mow and machines which sow — everything goes with speed. . . . Farmers here sell grain for several thousand dollars a year. . . . You ought to see the roads leading to town . . . in the fall — wagon after wagon with grain and loads with [cattle and] hogs. A person must ask: "Is this a new country?" . . . People do not allow money to rest here — railroads, canals, towns, and grand buildings spring up as by magic. Elegant diligences with four horses run along, as in England. Hotels as large and beautiful as in France [are now] found everywhere. Even the farmers here have healthful [dwellings] . . . instead of primitive log houses. . . . The land now is adorned with beautiful, yes elegant [houses] . . . built in the most tasteful style — this is America. But do not let anyone believe that ignorance

99

and laziness will get ahead any better here than in Norway. By no means! But we have material resources. If intelligence and energy [are put to work] things go forward.

5. HERE NOTHING IS IMPOSSIBLE
Johan Gasmann wrote his brother-in-law from Wisconsin, November, 1860.

A long time has passed since I wrote to you. I will not make any excuses — what is the use? The main reason is that I have been unable to send you any money. The thought that I could not meet this obligation has pained me very much. But impossible is impossible. Now, however, fate has given me an opportunity to fulfill in part my wish to pay you. My wife has received a little inheritance from a relative in Christiania. I have instructed Nils Vauvett in Porsgrund — who is our commissioner in this matter — to send you 50 specie dollars as soon as the money has been collected. If you will, upon receipt, write and let me know how much I owe you, I shall do my best to pay the remainder. I am happy now that the debts to my friends back home are practically cleared. They will not conclude that we forgot all obligations and duties merely because we were forced to seek a new homeland.

It grieves me greatly to learn about the present state of your health, dear Rye — you who used to be so strong and active. But we must bow to the will of God; and this I know you do, as a Christian. How often do I not think of the days I spent in peace and friendly associations at Otterholdt! All has vanished like a dream. How many gloomy hours have I not experienced since then! Still, God has been good. We have much to be thankful for. Even in this strange land he has helped us — yes, given us much more than we deserve. So far we have not lacked anything that we needed. And I have seen our daughters well cared for, that is, well married to able men; and our two sons have grown up to become useful and respected citizens. What else is there to wish for? Some more personal wealth might, of course, be desirable. What we have is not much — a little farm which gives us our daily bread; that's all. But even this is not so bad for an old salt who came here with two empty hands at the age of fifty. Now I am in my sixty-fifth year and still quite spry, so I must thank the good Lord for his fatherly concern.

It pleases me greatly that your children also have gotten along so well, Mathias already a division chief in the government and Dick a lieutenant. I would like to see Dicken — how he appears on the deck of a man-of-war. Tell him that he must take care not to become haughty. But as this is not a family trait I hope there is no danger. Your two girls are also so able that their fame has even reached us on this side of the Atlantic.

I, my wife, and children are getting along well, and their children also; that is to say, our grandchildren, of which we now have fourteen, all of them American born, who in time may become senators, yes, even presidents, because here nothing is impossible. We have just chosen a man to be president, Lincoln, who at one time was a laborer.

There is an infernal rumpus here during elections, but as soon as the matter is decided, everything becomes quiet again. We had the satisfaction this time of seeing the Democrats driven off the field; and it was high time. But according to my humble political opinions I fear that this country will face many turbulent scenes in the future. I do not have as great confidence in the merits of the republican system now that I observe it close at hand — it appears more brilliant at a distance. But humanity must struggle on in this world. We do not grasp the whole scheme of things.

It would please me greatly to receive some lines from you people now and then — from your girls or from your sons. But, of course, they have more important obligations than to tell us old emigrants about our beloved Norway. Despite the fact that I have nothing to complain about in this country I often find myself longing for the old shores and the old mountains — they are not easily forgotten.

C. A. Clausen

6. I LONG FOR THE NORWEGIAN COAST

Johan Gasmann wrote from Amherst, Wisconsin, August 7, 1864, to his niece, Elisa Rye.

I should long since have answered your friendly letter; but you must excuse my negligence. There is so much going on at present that makes me weary of the whole world. We will have to remain here, however, until our time is up. It delights us to hear that you and your sister are very able girls and in good circumstances. It is great — yes the greatest of good fortunes in this world — to be able to depend on one's self. And even though the teaching profession undoubtedly can often be depressing, it is still an honorable occupation which brings you in touch with many respectable families. May God grant you success and happiness! Mathias is now a prominent man, and I saw in *Morgenbladet* that Dicken has been appointed first lieutenant. In time he may become an admiral. If he were here now he would advance rapidly, because there is a great need of officers.

But probably he is better off where he is. God alone knows what will happen here. I get more satisfaction from seeing that our ancient Norway is making progress along all lines than I get out of all America's grandeur. Fate decreed that I had to leave; but it was not from any great desire that I did so. And even though I must admit that God has done well by us in this new land, the eternal longing for old friends and for my dear old Norway is so great that here I neither am nor ever will be really contented.

I will now tell you about our family, and since this is the first time I write to you, I must go into some detail. My old Lotte and I are still alive and in fairly good health. We live on our farm, which, however, I have handed over to my son Carl, who is now primarily responsible for the management — because I am getting tired. We have a fairly good farm, especially if all of it can be put to proper use. But this is a slow process because wages are high and the yield low, so it does not pay to do things on a large scale. We have a good house and a fine garden. The region where we live is very attractive, with hills and valleys and beautiful forests of oak, maple, ash, fir, and birch trees. We also have many beautiful little lakes and streams. On the whole it resembles the less mountainous areas in Norway, but the climate is not so pleasant. The winters are terribly cold and the summers burning hot. It can be said that the climate here resembles the character of the people: it runs to extremes.

Our daughter Maren, who is married to Gotfried Gasmann, lives right next to us on their farm and they are doing fine. They have five children. Niels and Constance live a quarter of a [*Norwegian?*] mile from us in a new little town (Amherst) where he has a store and is doing right well. Caroline, as you undoubtedly know, is married to a Dane, Sørensen, who is pastor in the town of Waupaca, twelve English miles from here. They are getting along extremely well. He is an especially fine man and well liked by everybody. They have seven children. The oldest son is in college already and is an able boy.

As you probably know, Johan is a pastor in the English Episcopal church. I was fortunate enough to get him enrolled in the theological college here, where he studied for six years and was immediately ordained.[18] He has been a pastor in California some four or five years and he has gotten along well; but he wants to return to the eastern states as soon as possible, because California is here looked upon about as Finnmark was by the pastors back home. He is married to a girl named Clarkson, a pastor's daughter from Chicago, where he [*Johan*] was assistant pastor for awhile. The salary, however, is larger in California than here — he is paid $2,000 per year — but the cost of living is high there.

Anne is married to a pastor, [William] Stoy. They also are in California. They have three children. Carl was married to

[18] Nashotah House, an Episcopal seminary near Milwaukee, was founded in 1842 and is still active. John Godfrey Gasmann and William Henry Stoy graduated in 1858; Nashotah House, *Alumni Directory*, 19 ([Nashotah, Wisconsin,] 1966). The directory was furnished through the courtesy of Dean Donald J. Parsons of the seminary.

a Miss Blikfeldt from Molde. He lives with us and is a farmer. So there, you have the whole list. But, no — Henriette, our youngest. She is still unmarried and lives with us or her sisters when she is not teaching school. She is a "schoolma'am," a profession much sought by young ladies here. She spent some time at a ladies' seminary, and she is a very good teacher in English, arithmetic, etc. The pay runs from $16 to $20 per month, but school lasts only some four or six months a year. This, however, pays for her clothes, etc.

Thus you see that we are getting along tolerably well, and if I were sensible I would be quite contented. But I do not like the way things are run here. American republicanism looks well on paper, but in practice it is a helter-skelter affair which allows too much leeway for scoundrels. This becomes particularly plain now during wartime. Our president is undoubtedly a good and upright man, but all his best efforts are frustrated by endless skulduggery. And the constitution, which was supposed to protect and support the state, is often so interpreted as to have the very opposite effect. Royal power in the hands of a poor king is bad enough, but even worse is our anarchical rabble regime. Money is the real god; and what pleasure is there then to live in [such] a country, even though it be richly endowed by nature?

The miserable war still goes on, and God alone knows when and how it will end. If we are fortunate enough to escape a revolution in our own Northern states it will be well. There is much dissension here. It would probably be best if Abraham Lincoln himself assumed command. The army is very loyal to him. But he is not a Napoleon; no, he is an excellent man. It is possible that he will win re-election this fall, and then I believe everything may still turn out well. But if the Democratic party should win — then it would be well if every decent man could leave the country. This is the state of affairs.

To be sure, after the most terrible battles our armies have moved forward, but as yet nothing has been decided. And now 500,000 more men are to be called up, partly to relieve our weary and depleted regiments and partly to enlarge the forces. The people are still willing to sacrifice, but scoundrels are working in the darkness. Oh, if only the cause of humanity would win at last — and this war is the cause of humanity. The struggle would have ended long ago if only that shop-keeper, England, had not aided the South. But England will undoubtedly soon have to suffer for this assistance. It is England that has committed murder and now sees with unconcern the murder of Denmark.[19] God's judgment must strike the rotten aristocracy in England. And that comedy figure, Napoleon: How long will the proud French people tolerate this tyrant who cringes and fawns before the Russians, Austrians, and Prussians? Why this servility? Presumably so that he can hang on to the crown awhile longer. His new emperor in Mexico will soon find that country too hot. And when this war is over (may it be soon) the hegemony of France in Mexico will be ended.

Sweden and Norway should have aided Denmark. We, over here, certainly expected that they would. But they thought they were too weak. If Denmark falls, however, then Sweden and Norway also will fall and, finally also, the perfidious England. No one can imagine the hate which has developed here against John Bull since the war began, while Russia and America have been drawn closer together. The Scandinavians must fight for their freedom! The people are courageous; we can see that here. The Norwegians are respected for their bravery and endurance. But, but—the "higher ups" lack courage. Discretion is a virtue, but there can be too much of it.

Brother Hans's two sons, August and Fin, have served in the army during the war. August rose to be captain but was wounded and has been discharged. Fin started as a sergeant but is now first lieutenant and is still alive. He is presently with the Army of the West near Atlanta, Georgia. A decisive battle is expected there any day. May God be with our men!

[19] Denmark was then involved in war with Austria and Prussia.

If the South loses there and Richmond is taken by General Grant's army, then the rebellion will be over and we will have an army of half a million hardened warriors, ready to march on Mexico; but a tenth of this force will be sufficient.

Everything is quiet hereabouts. Groceries and dry goods are expensive, so we must do without many ordinary things. On the whole, however, life in the Northern states runs its normal course. Our money has fallen in value; but this is really no danger for a land with such resources. If there only were more unity this country would be invincible. America will probably become a happy land if freedom wins and slavery is eradicated. Many changes must be made, however, in the system of administration. The Americans are a vigorous and able people, but a stronger government is needed to rule them.

This has been a poor year in Wisconsin because of the severe drought. For a long time now we have had terribly hot weather, so people have suffered much during harvesttime. We will not get one third of a normal crop. There will be more than enough for the people [here], but there will be little left to sell. Wheat already brings eight dollars per *tønde*; normally it sells for three dollars. Fortunately, we do not need to buy any, but we do not live by bread alone.

This summer I have often longed for the Norwegian coast with its fresh sea breezes. Here, inland, the heat has been almost unbearable. If people can get along somewhat decently back home it is best for them to remain there. Even though they can eat a bit better here, there are many things to keep people more contented back home. The climate has great influence on one's state of mind; and then there is that instability and insecurity connected with all our institutions. Many Norwegians are doing well here, but still I do not see any more happiness here than over there — in fact less.

If a goodly piece of gold should fall at my feet, then, as truly as my name is Johan, I would go back and live and die "where the North Sea foams against stony strands"; and I believe many of my countrymen would say the same. The Americans

106

have a word, "humbug." Its exact meaning would be something like *fjas* or *løgn*. This term can indeed be applied to many things here. But everything is new, and I suppose things must bubble and effervesce, as the case has been with other peoples before they settled down in an orderly community. And when we look at the present behavior of the old nations — exactly those who claim to be at the apex of world civilization — we can hardly expect more from this people which is a lobscouse of all the races.[20]

Now you and Freden must accept this rigmarole for the present. I will do better next time.

We greet you, dear girls, most cordially. Please write to us when you have the time and inclination. It does give a refreshing release to thoughts and ideas. Caroline, Constance, and Lotte will, no doubt, write to you very soon. I had hopes that Cousin Sørensen would not begrudge me a few lines, but I suppose he is so busy with his smiths that he has no time to spare.

May God be with you and guide you as in the past.

"Mutter" sends her special greetings. She has warm memories of the pleasant days at Otterholdt.

[20] Lobscouse is a nautical term for a stew of meat and vegetables.

by BEULAH FOLKEDAHL

5   *Knud Knudsen and His America Book*[1]

W E HAVE everything we had longed for, and are convinced that we will find what we are looking for,"
wrote Knud Knudsen, concluding the description of his journey from Drammen, Norway, to Buffalo, New York, in 1839.
Thus he expressed his faith in America.

Knudsen was born September 29, 1810, presumably in
Numedal, and emigrated to America with the group conducted
by Ansten Nattestad. When the party reached Chicago, some
remained there and others continued with Nattestad to Jefferson Prairie, Rock County, Wisconsin, about ninety miles
northwest of Chicago, where Ansten's brother Ole had settled
two years earlier. Ansten Nattestad seemed reluctant to encourage more Norwegians to settle there, much of the land
having already been taken, so Knudsen and Clement Stabæk
traveled on foot to Rock Run, Stephenson County, Illinois,
about thirty miles southwest of Jefferson Prairie. After surveying the area, they returned to Chicago for their families
and goods and, with some of the others who had remained
there, went to Rock Run to establish their homes.[2]

[1] Knudsen's original account, *Beretning om en reise fra Drammen i Norge til
New-York i Nord-America*, appeared in Drammen, Norway, in 1840. A facsimile
reissue was published by O. M. Norlie (Decorah, Iowa, 1926). A copy of the latter is in the archives of the Norwegian-American Historical Association at St.
Olaf College, Northfield.

[2] Theodore C. Blegen, *Norwegian Migration to America, 1825–1860*, 115

108

Within a short time Knudsen migrated north again, this time to Wiota, then in Iowa County, Wisconsin. The exact date of this move is not known but he seems to have been well established there by 1843. His conviction that "we will find what we are looking for" apparently was justified. Probably the lead mines in Iowa County attracted him to that region. Hamilton Diggings or Settlement (named for William S. Hamilton, son of Alexander Hamilton and founder of the mines) offered him an opportunity to work as a smith, making various types of articles, not only for farms and households, but also for the mine. And so he set up shop in the settlement, became owner of a 160-acre homestead, and purchased land in the village of Wiota.[3]

The Norwegian immigrant leader, Johan R. Reiersen, wrote about Knudsen on December 12, 1843, in a letter to Hans Gasmann, who had recently settled near Pine Lake, Waukesha County, Wisconsin: "Several of the Norwegians here in Wisconsin have by their outstanding ability and enterprise during their few years' residence already attained the acknowledged respect of Americans. Among them I believe I should mention Knudsen, a smith from Drammen, who has a large farm in Hamilton Settlement, thirty miles southeast of Mineral Point, and plies his trade besides, employing several men."[4]

Knudsen expressed his continued faith in America in a letter written for publication in the Norwegian press, dated at Wiota December 20, 1843: "I have recently become acquainted with one Mr. Reiersen from Kristiansand, Norway, who alleges he has come to look over the country and the con-

(Northfield, 1931); Ministerial Records, Wiota Lutheran Church, Wiota, Wisconsin, NAHA Archives; Ansten Nattestad to Peter Valeur, November 6, 1839, in Theodore C. Blegen, ed., *Land of Their Choice: The Immigrants Write Home*, 65 (Minneapolis, 1955); S. G. M[ogan], "Clemet Tostensen Stabeck og Rock Runsettlementet," in *Numedalslagets Aarbok*, no. 11, p. 49–53 (1925).

[3] Johan R. Reiersen to Hans Gasmann, December 12, 1843, quoted in Reiersen, *Veiviser for norske emigranter til de Forenede Nord-Amerikanske Stater og Texas*, xi (Christiania, 1844). In 1846 Iowa County was partitioned into Iowa and Lafayette counties, and Wiota became part of the latter.

[4] Reiersen to Gasmann, December 12, 1843, quoted in Reiersen, *Veiviser for norske emigranter*, xi.

ditions here in behalf of several Norwegian families who are thinking of emigrating. The aforesaid Reiersen showed me a letter dated Galena, December 12, addressed to Mr. Gasmann, in which he gave his opinion of the conditions which he had thus far observed. I found the letter in question to contain such unvarnished truth that, after my four years in America, I can with a clear conscience recommend its publication in the Norwegian press as advice for those of my countrymen who might decide to emigrate to this country." [5]

Knudsen lived in Wiota for a number of years, but then the lust for gold impelled him, like so many others, to California, first in 1849 and again in 1852, when he led an expedition which, besides his own family, included a large group of other Norwegians. For the 1852 expedition, Knudsen and his sons, Hendrik, Christen, and Søren, had money enough to equip themselves with two wagons, eight yoke of oxen, and four cows, and to purchase more livestock during the journey. From the gold fields the Knudsen family moved north to Oregon, where their son John was born about 1856. [6]

Apparently the western adventure was successful, for by 1860 Knudsen was in Barre, La Crosse County, Wisconsin, on a 290-acre farm, 160 acres of which he had purchased in 1851. The farm had a cash valuation of $3,000, and his stock and machinery, of $280; he had on hand 600 bushels of grain as well as a goodly stock of hay and potatoes. During the 1860's he acquired, probably for speculation, several hundred additional acres in La Crosse County, and later in that decade he moved to La Crosse with his wife and son John to a house he bought in 1867. Most of Lot 9, Block 7, in downtown La Crosse, known as Knudsen's Block, was his property. Meanwhile he was disposing of land in Lafayette County, including

[5] Quoted in Reiersen, *Veiviser for norske emigranter*, xxviii.

[6] Tosten Kittlesen Stabæk, "Beretning om en reise til California i 1852," in *Numedalslagets Aarbok*, no. 14, p. 62–85 (1928); *United States Census*, 1870, *Population*, 215. Stabæk's account was translated by Einar I. Haugen in Norwegian-American Historical Association, *Studies and Records*, 4:99–124 (1929). Knudsen came to be called "California Knud" and "Cal Knud"; C. O. Solberg to O. M. Norlie, July 26, 1944, Knud Knudsen Papers, NAHA Archives. C. O. Solberg was a grandson of Ole Nattestad.

the Knudsen homestead, which he sold in 1867 to his daughter Sørena for one dollar.[7] Sørena, who was born aboard ship during the emigrant journey in 1839, had married Isaac Miller, a member of the 1852 California expedition. Members of the Knudsen family occupied the farm until 1920.[8]

Knudsen participated fully in community life. In 1847 he undertook to gather subscriptions for *Nordlyset*, the first exclusively Norwegian-language newspaper in America, which began publication in Norway, Wisconsin, that same year. Naturally, his name appeared on the subscription list.[9]

He was the leader in organizing a Lutheran congregation in Hamilton Settlement, and it was in his house on February 13, 1844, that Pastor C. L. Clausen conducted the first Norwegian Lutheran service in the area.[10] In the same month Knudsen wrote a letter on behalf of the Norwegian settlements at Hamilton Diggings, Rock Run, Jefferson Prairie, and Rock Prairie (Rock County, Wisconsin) to the bishop in Christiania, Norway, asking for a pastor. The communities offered an annual salary of $300, plus ministerial fees and use of a parsonage and of eighty acres of land. The bishop referred the congregations to Pastor J. W. C. Dietrichson, who had emigrated in 1844, but the latter declined the position except on an occasional basis, because of his previous decision to serve the Koshkonong congregation. Then C. L. Clausen, who had already accepted a call from Rock Run for a resident pastor, agreed to serve the Hamilton Settlement also. The letter of call to Claus-

[7] Information about Knudsen's property holdings came from the following sources in Wisconsin: register of deeds of La Crosse County, La Crosse; register of deeds of Lafayette County, Darlington, courtesy of Mr. O. C. Monson; Charles R. Whaley, tax assessor, La Crosse; assessment rolls for Iowa County, State Historical Society at Madison; Mrs. Gilman Hansen to the writer, July 15, 1965, quoting the abstract of deed of the Knudsen homestead. Mr. and Mrs. Hansen are the present owners of the property.

[8] Ann Van Meter of Browntown, Wisconsin, to the writer, July 15, 1965. Mrs. Van Meter's husband was a great-grandson of Knudsen.

[9] Clarence A. Clausen and Andreas Elviken, eds., *A Chronicle of Old Muskego: The Diary of Søren Bache, 1839–1847*, 210 (Northfield, 1951); "*Nordlyset* and *Maanedstidende* Records Book," 12, in NAHA Archives.

[10] At this service Knudsen's son George, who was born August 6, 1843, was baptized, and Knudsen and his wife, Johanne Hendrichsdatter, were communicants; Ministerial Records, Wiota Lutheran Church.

en was signed by the members of the congregations November 28, 1845, but Knudsen's name was not on it. Knudsen continued, however, to participate in church affairs and was mentioned on a local monument erected in 1937 in memory of the charter members of the Wiota Lutheran Church.[11]

Knudsen was said to have been an ardent Democrat when he was soliciting subscriptions for *Nordlyset*. His zeal for politics continued during the 1868 presidential campaign, when Ulysses S. Grant and Horatio Seymour were the chief opposing candidates. Knudsen became the editor, for a few months, of a new Norwegian newspaper, *Amerika*, established in June, 1868, and published from his print shop in the Knudsen Block in La Crosse. *Amerika* declared that the main issue of the campaign was "whether Lincoln's prudent statesmanlike plan or the rash plan of the radical Congress should be followed in an effort to effect a lasting relationship between the North and the South. *Amerika* has in several of its leading articles shown Scandinavians that Lincoln's plan is the right one." [12]

Marcus Mills (Brick) Pomeroy, Jeffersonian Democrat and propagandist, was editor and publisher of the *La Crosse Democrat*. He undoubtedly chose Knudsen as his agent in this presidential campaign. The selection of Knudsen to publish a campaign sheet for circulation among the Norwegians is an indication of his standing in the La Crosse County community.[13]

[11] "Kirke bog for de norsk lutherske menigheder paa Jefferson Prairie," 166, 168, 176, 188, 207–209, and Ministerial Records, Wiota Lutheran Church — both in NAHA Archives; J. W. C. Dietrichson, *Reise blandt de norske emigranter i de Forenede Nordamerikanske Fristater*, 80–83 (Stavanger, Norway, 1846). Other sons born to Knudsen were baptized in 1846 and 1849. He signed the by-laws of the congregation in 1851, and contributed toward the building of the church and the parsonage. Wiota Lutheran Church Archives, Wiota parsonage; *Wiota Lutheran Church 1844–1937*, 7, 25–27, 37 (Darlington, Wisconsin, n.d.); *United States Census*, 1870, *Population*, 215.

[12] Clausen and Elviken, eds., *A Chronicle of Old Muskego*, 210; *Amerika* (La Crosse, Wisconsin), September 10, October 22, 1868; Arlow W. Andersen, *The Immigrant Takes His Stand: The Norwegian-American Press and Public Affairs, 1847–1872*, 13, 115, 141 (Northfield, 1953). A partial microfilm file of *Amerika* is in the library of Luther College, Decorah, Iowa. The quotation is from the issue of October 1, 1868. In the October 22 issue, Johan Schroeder, who was pro-Lincoln, announced himself as the new owner and editor.

[13] *Skandinaven* (Chicago), June 24, 1868; *Fœdrelandet og Emigranten* (La

From the meager evidence garnered above, Knud Knudsen apparently attained success in America and was able to find what he was "looking for." He died October 10, 1889, and lies buried in Miller Cemetery, Wiota.[14]

REPORT OF A JOURNEY FROM DRAMMEN IN NORWAY TO NEW YORK IN NORTH AMERICA
SMITH KNUD KNUDSEN [15]

Because I believe that many of my friends both in Drammen and in the surrounding area would like to hear how we fared on our long voyage, and especially about our experiences, I have in all honesty and to the best of my ability written the following report.

On Wednesday, June 12, 1839, at four-thirty in the morning, we weighed anchor preparatory to beginning our journey to America aboard the ship "Emilie" with Ths. Anchersen of Drammen, the ship's owner, as captain. Since the wind was contrary and of low velocity, the vessel stopped at the moorings right next to the Tangen Shipping Company. From there the captain went back to secure a steamboat to tow us down the fjord. The boat arrived at ten o'clock. As we passed out through Drammensfjord, [Peter] Valeur, the [ministerial] candidate who accompanied us to Göteborg, gave a moving address, admirably adapted to the circumstances of our journey, in which, with obvious spiritual earnestness, he encouraged us all to live moral lives and always have God in our thoughts. By one-thirty we were at Rødtangen, three [Norwegian] miles from Drammen.[16]

Crosse), June 24, 1868; *La Crosse Daily Democrat*, May 28, 1868; *Dictionary of American Biography*, 15:53.

[14] Mrs. M. O. Monson of Wiota to the writer, June 22, 1965.

[15] The writer is greatly indebted to Professor Clarence A. Clausen of St. Olaf College for assistance in editing and translating, especially with reference to maritime terminology. The translation of the verses is his.

[16] The emigrants had petitioned the church of Norway to ordain Peter Valeur for pastoral service among them in America. In November Ansten Nattestad, one of the group, wrote from Jefferson Prairie, Wisconsin, that his community could not support a pastor; Clausen and Elviken, eds., *A Chronicle of Old Muskego*, 191n; Blegen, ed., *Land of Their Choice*, 65. A Norwegian mile equals seven English miles.

After we took leave of an acquaintance from Sandsvær and the captain's brother, who had accompanied us thus far, lively hurrahs rose from both vessels as a last farewell from the fatherland, friends, and acquaintances. After that we had variable wind and weather through the Christianiafjord.

At ten-thirty that evening, at the Fuglehuks Lighthouse, we dropped the pilot, who was from Svelvik. In every respect the ship was well equipped to continue the journey, and at eleven-thirty we arrived at Færder [Island]. There we got a brisk breeze from the north-northeast, and beautiful weather.

On the thirteenth, at two-thirty in the afternoon, Marstrand [Sweden] came into view. At four-thirty we took a pilot aboard from Wingöe and at six-thirty we passed that point. All sails which could be hoisted were set, in order to reach Göteborg that evening. At nine we passed Ny-Elfsborg Fortress, where we were inspected by an officer who took our passports, which were returned just before our departure. At eleven o'clock we anchored at the dock at the Hotel Klippan, where for the next few days we loaded iron ballast.

Experience revealed to us that it was impossible to exchange money at the official market quotations because there were Jews there who supported themselves by conducting trade in foreign moneys. Their zeal for profit caused them to raise the prices exorbitantly — as of any other merchandise — when many people arrived who needed foreign currency. This situation they were clever enough to detect quietly; when they met people on the street whom they took to be foreigners they engaged them in conversation and inquired where they came from, where they were going, and if they had exchanged their money. If they had not, they promised to exchange at a much lower rate than anyone else. With their remarkable gift of persuasion they were able to dupe many an uninformed person who believed their smooth words, that it was precisely with them that money could be exchanged and that they were the only ones who could furnish the needed currency — the exact kind that was most valid in America. If the people then replied that they would like to inquire elsewhere, the answer was, "I am offering you such a good bargain that I cannot repeat the offer another time; take it or leave it; I am not making anything on it," and so on.

If it happened that they already had changed their money, the Jewish brokers immediately asked what rate they had received. Even if the rate were ever so moderate, the Jews claimed that their offer would have been even better. If the foreigners impressed them fevorably, they were simply told that they had made a bad mistake, but if he [*the broker*] sized up the strangers as lacking in understanding, he would declare, "You blockheads! You have surely done it! You have lost a great deal of money. Why didn't you come to me? I would not only have done better by you, but I would have furnished you with money that is worth more in America."

Because of this situation I would advise everybody from Drammen and that vicinity wishing to emigrate to America to exchange his money with one of the brokers in Drammen well in advance (even five weeks before embarkation), so the money can be ordered and secured by mail from abroad if there is no other way of obtaining it. In this respect these [Drammen] brokers are the most reliable men one can meet, because they are officials commissioned to advise the inexperienced. When we left, Bang, the Drammen broker, displayed such praiseworthy solicitude for us, as to both the contract and other matters we did not understand, that I heartily recommend him to others who may desire to emigrate to America. I am sure he will be just as helpful to others of his countrymen as he was to us.

As the wind was contrary, we lay in Göteborg until four o'clock in the morning of the twenty-second, when we weighed anchor, and, with a light breeze from the east, sailed past Klippan in company with several Norwegian ships. At five-thirty we passed Elfsborg, where we had inspection and then continued on our way. At nine we dropped the pilot near Win-

115

göe, after which the ship headed out to sea [*the Skaggerak*]. The winds were variable but always westerly.

On the twenty-fourth, at eight in the evening, we arrived at the Oxøe Lighthouse outside Kristiansand [Norway]. We tacked our way westward, bucking the contrary wind. On the twenty-fifth, because of the stiff breeze, some of the passengers were very seasick. At eleven o'clock that morning we arrived at Udøefjord, from which harbor we were accompanied by a pilot. We zigzagged back and forth without advancing very far, but as the passengers wished to go ashore and the wind was contrary, the captain decided to seek harbor so they might be refreshed. This port is about one [Norwegian] mile east of Mandal, and at four o'clock in the afternoon we anchored there.

On the twenty-ninth there was wind from the east. We weighed anchor at six-thirty in the morning and set sail after we had taken on a little water and all the passengers had returned to the ship. At nine o'clock we dropped the pilot at Lindesnæs and set all the sails that could be hoisted. At twelve noon we arrived at Lister [*Lista*]. On June 30 in the forenoon we set our course toward the English Channel, since the wind was unfavorable for our going north of Scotland. At nine o'clock on Tuesday, July 2, we took our bearings from Gallopers Lightship and at ten-thirty we passed it. This ship lies out in the ocean to serve as a lighthouse for seafarers. At four o'clock in the morning we sighted South Foreland and at seven we passed Dover and Calais. As we sailed close to the English coast, we had a chance to see many towns along the shore. We also observed numerous ships engaged in the coastwise trade and we passed lighthouses, of which there are many along the English coast. Among these I want to mention only the Eddystone Lighthouse, which lies five miles out in the ocean on a small cliff. When the water is high, it rises 'way above the cliff. During the night of the ninth we sighted Falmouth Lighthouse. During the evening of the tenth we had a pilot cutter from Falmouth alongside the ship and at ten we passed Lizard

Point. Because we had contrary wind and weather the whole channel through, we worked our way forward by tacking. That went excellently, as the ship sailed very well. We passed all the other ships in our group.[17]

We then headed toward Ireland. There we wove back and forth for two days before we got past the island and out into the Atlantic Ocean. The winds were variable with alternating rain and sunshine, and storms besides.

My wife, who was pregnant, was delivered of a daughter out on the mid-Atlantic on a quiet, beautiful day. The birth pangs lasted scarcely an hour and a half, the easiest confinement she had ever experienced, she declared. On this occasion the captain was very obliging, both in having food prepared especially for her from his provisions and by practically always supplying her with the same kind of food that he had himself.

Moreover, he showed a sympathetic and friendly attitude toward everybody. Every evening a prayer was said and then we all sang a hymn. This gave us comfort and inspiration during our journey. Nothing is better than thanking Providence, and we lifted up our prayers to him. While we were thus surrounded by the three elements — fire, air, and water — we were all happy, not fearing any danger but thinking only about reaching our destination in that faraway continent.

On August second we grounded on the Newfoundland Banks, the largest and richest fisheries in the world. Here are stationed Frenchmen, Spaniards, Englishmen, Icelanders, and Americans — all engaged in fishing. On the third of August we tried our gear and caught about 70 *bismerpund* [of fish].[18] My brother, Jest Knud, caught two halibut, and one of the crew also pulled out one, the three together weighing 15 *bismerpund*. That was both relaxing and enjoyable.

We often saw large whales, both close to the ship and far-

[17] The Eddystone Rocks are a reef in the English Channel south of Plymouth. On a peninsula to the west are Falmouth and then Lizard Point, the latter the southernmost spot in England and the last to be passed in a direct westward journey.
[18] A *bismerpund* equals about twelve pounds.

ther out. They spurted water through the blowholes or nostrils on top of their heads as high as we could see, the water sometimes appearing in the far distance like a great pillar of vapor or smoke rising from a chimney or steamship. More frequently we saw the so-called springer[?] whales that followed the ship. One morning early, when the air was still, we enjoyed a strange spectacle of the grampuses[?] or dolphins. I believe there were thousands of them; they played with one another on the surface of the quiet water at sunrise. At times they hurtled their whole bodies out of the water, or made such other strange leaps that we were filled with wonder. We also saw many other types of fish, such as sharks, mackerel, and so on.

On August twenty-third we sighted Long Island, with its several lighthouses along the coast. On the twenty-fourth a pilot came aboard. Their boats are so beautiful that they appear to have been cast or molded. This made me immediately aware of the artistic sense and greatness of the Americans. This large cutter was manned by several pilots. Only one boarded our ship and the boat sailed on to direct other vessels.

Late in the evening of the twenty-sixth we arrived in New York, where we first sighted two large lighthouses. Later, there were so many lights along both sides of the channel that the ship was all lit up. During the night we reached the quarantine station, where we anchored, about half a Norwegian mile from the city proper. There we stayed almost two days, washed our clothes, and cleaned up in every respect; otherwise we could not land. On the twenty-ninth we went around in New York and saw sights such as we had never expected. Everything astonished us. Here was a numberless fleet of steamboats and ships; here were buildings constructed of hewn marble and elaborately built, most of them seven or eight stories high. In my opinion, it would take days and years to give an adequate account of this city, for in the short time we were there it seemed incomprehensible to me and the others.

I talked with three Norwegians there. One of them was

called Captain Tybring, a brother of Mrs. Horn and Mrs. Blich in Drammen; the second was John Brons, son of a man in Tangen; and the third was a skipper from Kragerø. My wife's two sisters could have obtained jobs there, for the three Norwegians wanted very much to employ them. They could have earned $60 a year, but since wages are higher rather than lower in Illinois, they preferred to accompany us. We applied to a company in New York, where we obtained tickets clear to Illinois at $14 per person; two children under twelve years went for one adult fare; and children under two needed no tickets. We were allowed to take along a hundred pounds of baggage free, but anything in excess of that cost us $1.75 per hundred pounds. That was the arrangement on the Hudson River; farther on we were allowed only fifty pounds per person.

I sincerely urge everyone who wants to go to America to communicate early with the skipper he wishes to travel with. Anyone more skilled in his trade than Captain Anchersen or his mate Overwein can scarcely be found. Despite the fact that neither of them had ever been in America before, we arrived precisely at the place where we were to dock, quite an accomplishment on such a long journey and with such variable winds. They were courteous and attentive toward the passengers in every respect. The captain always provided medicine for us passengers without cost when we were ailing. I would also counsel everyone who undertakes such a journey to supply himself with the kind of provisions that Rynning suggests.[19] We paid too little attention to this and regretted it often later. Since seasickness leads to nausea and exhaustion, it is well to have on hand a variety of provisions for changes in diet. Therefore Rynning's advice should be carefully heeded. I know from experience that this is true. Lübeck sausage and smoked sausage are very good.

[19] See Theodore C. Blegen, ed., *Ole Rynning's True Account of America* (Norwegian-American Historical Association, *Travel and Description Series*, vol. 1 — Minneapolis, 1926). Rynning's book originally appeared in Christiania in 1838.

On the twenty-ninth, at six o'clock in the evening, we were ready to depart on a steamboat which towed seven large boats that were just as long as the ship on which we had crossed the ocean, but not so wide. We started up the [Hudson] river at night. In the morning we enjoyed a pleasing scene as we beheld the beautiful countryside on both sides. We saw luxuriant trees and delightful meadows with heavy vegetation that was foreign to us. Often when the boat stopped we went ashore to pick apples, which were growing wild. In the pastures, where livestock was grazing, grew large, luxuriant fruit trees.

Along the banks of this river lie many towns, some large, some small. There are numerous steamboats, some carrying passengers, some towing other boats. These steamboats are very skillfully designed. We met one that had two wheels on each side and moved very rapidly downstream. At the same time another came up the river that had quadruple-powered machinery and also moved speedily. Otherwise, there were so many I could not keep count of them.

I feel sincerely that I should mention some of the kindnesses which our noble and kindhearted Captain Anchersen showed us. In Göteborg he gave all the passengers a fresh-meat dinner; in Udøefjord he served us fish; twice in the English Channel and again at the Newfoundland Banks he provided us with halibut, which cost him a lot. Going into Albany ahead of us, he ordered an excellent meal for us passengers at a large hotel. I am sure it cost him between 30 and 40 dollars. The Americans were greatly surprised at this generosity, for they had never before known such concern on the part of captains for their passengers. On the contrary, there was often complaint about their [*the captains'*] unreasonable demands, and their rudeness was even publicized in the New York press.

I can't help mentioning that while we were ashore in a little town on the river, John Pedersen from Eger jumped down from a pile of boards on the wharf and broke a leg. Since, in the rush, cloth for bandages required by the doctor could not be had at any price, the captain hurriedly removed one of his shirts — he generally wore two — and immediately tore it up for bandages, saying: "Look at him as in a mirror.[20] God has brought you and me safely across the ocean; now misfortune had to overtake us. For God's sake do not forget to help him in every way possible." This aroused great admiration among the Americans.

I sincerely hope that many of my countrymen can come over with this great-hearted man. Since both he and his mate are brave, excellent seamen, and since the ship, furthermore, is a remarkable sailer, he is a most dependable man whom I can wholeheartedly recommend to you.[21]

While I was traveling from Albany to the town of Schenectady in a railroad car, I felt the urge to describe this mechanical wonder in the following words:

> Oh Norway's son! You rest content
> With the little you know and comprehend.
> But I go forth to far-off lands
> And see the beauties of the arts.
> Here numerous wonders I behold
> Which liberate man from sweat and toil.
> Wherever improvements can be made,
> This land will surely take the lead.
>
> No sooner had the clock struck eight
> Than the iron horse began to roll.
> The speed with which we raced along
> Was indescribable and strange!
> All fourteen heavy railway cars,
> Which totaled many hundred tons,
> Were pulled along by one machine:
> Our marvelous steam conveyance.

[20] The original phrase, "Speil eder nu ham," is meaningless as it stands, and must be incomplete. The captain probably wanted to emphasize that misfortune might strike the other passengers next and that it would be wise for them to help one another.

[21] Here these lines are interpolated: "Albany, September 1, 1839. Knud Knudsen. Ansteen Natstad. Clemet Stabæk. T. Hougkjem. L. Røstoe. Gullik Gravdal." The second part of the account follows.

121

We rolled up hill,
We rolled down dale;
We passed through channels in the earth
And over bridges spanning valleys wide.
Strange indeed the railways are
Which carry us forward with such ease.
Entranced I sat and gazed about
But time, alas, was all too brief!

On the first of September, 1839, we said farewell for the last time to Captain Anchersen, who had accompanied us by train to Schenectady, a distance of about sixteen English miles. There we began the so-called Erie Canal trip. This canal is 363 English miles long and has eighty-five locks or sluices measuring between eight and ten feet in height. It starts at Albany and ends at Buffalo. Along the canal are located sixty-four towns or cities, some of which are two or three times as large as Christiania, Norway's capital, and each has seven, eight, or nine churches. Besides these, there are many smaller towns with one or two churches. Also, there are stores at every lock. We marveled often at how this canal was laid through the hills and across dales; but when we arrived at Lockport, there were even greater things to see. This city is situated thirty [English] miles below Buffalo.[22] There we floated up a high hill through five successive locks, ten to fourteen feet tall. The job done there was amazing. The canal was dug through a mountain ridge which I estimated to be nearly half a Norwegian mile in extent. The whole canal, when completed, cost nine million dollars.

Now they are going to spend fifteen million dollars extra on this same canal, some for digging new channels where the old one curves, and some in making it twice as wide and several feet deeper. This project employs several thousand people, besides machines and horses. I estimated that about a third of the work was already finished. When it is completed, steam-

[22] Lockport, one of the last points on the westward journey along the canal, is actually northeast of Buffalo.

boats will be used instead of horse-drawn boats. There are over four thousand canalboats continually making stops at the docks. These boats are provided with beautiful rooms and a cargo space in the center for chests and other freight. They are drawn by two or three horses. Along the canal is a railway, where those who want to go faster and who do not have much baggage may travel by train. It is sad to see how the land along the canal lies untilled and how little work the farmer does for his own well-being. But since much of the land in the state of New York is covered with extensive forests, people generally pass it by and go farther west to Illinois and Missouri. There lie large, level, almost treeless plains which do not need to be cleared, and yet there are woods enough for essential needs.

After being on the canal for six days, we arrived at Buffalo late one evening. In the morning I was out early to tour the city. I soon spied a great many vessels at the docks, among which were large full-rigged ships. But I was still more astonished when I saw sixteen steamboats, all fired with wood instead of coal. I had found the same phenomenon in New York also. When I expressed my surprise to a man in the city at seeing so many steamships this far in the interior and on inland waters, he said there were not so many here now; most of them were cruising in other places. In all the cities there are many different kinds of factories, operated by either steam or water power. But since the land is so level, there are few waterfalls and consequently nearly all machinery is run by steam. It is difficult for anyone who has not seen this country's riches to appreciate them, and if I listed some of them, probably people in Norway would accuse me of lying. Therefore, I have decided to keep quiet and not say anything. Should any of them happen to see these things for themselves, they would undoubtedly realize the truth.

When we arrived in Rochester, we talked to a Norwegian from Stavanger who lives there. He told us that Ole Aasland of Numedal, who came over last summer, lives thirty English miles north of Rochester.[23] Since the boat continued on its way, however, none of us could get in touch with him.

The tanner, Christian Knudsen from Drammen, also lives in Rochester. I learned about this half an hour before we left the city, and hurriedly went to see him but found only his wife at home, and she was much surprised to see me. She said they were well satisfied but also told me that they would like to go farther west, to Indiana, which many others are doing, as the land there is more fertile.

On September 8, 1839, at eleven o'clock, we were ready to take off on a large steamship loaded with hundreds of persons of different nationalities, traveling on this vast body of water beginning at Buffalo, called Lake Erie. The boat was equipped with tremendously large machinery and sped along rapidly. There were also three engineers on board. The ship touched at all ports along the coast to take on passengers and wood and to let other passengers disembark. The waves were so rough that the water gushed across the second deck, which was very high. Even the first deck was far above the water. There are always Negroes on board these steamboats, to serve as cooks and attendants. Since I could speak the language somewhat, I engaged them in conversation and found them to be especially good-natured and polite toward strangers. I believe they surpass all other people in kindness.

I would not advise anyone to take along Norwegian and Danish money, as it is not exchangeable here, at least not without a great loss. On the other hand, English, Spanish, and French money are accepted at the regular rate. The Dutch 10-guilder piece is worth $4.00 here; the sovereign, $4.84; the franc, 94 cents; the Spanish piaster is equal in value to the American dollar, which is worth 100 cents or 100 [Scandinavian] shillings; likewise, the Spanish doubloons are among the best (doubloons are figured in piasters). Often you cannot get a quarter of a dollar for a Dutch guilder, but sometimes you get

[23] Ole Aasland took a group of poor emigrants to Kendall Township, Orleans County, New York, in 1838, on condition that they repay him in labor. See Blegen, *Norwegian Migration, 1825–1860*, 108, 109n.

a little more. It happens frequently that these have been clipped; one must always beware of these coins. The Americans often toss such coins on the scales and then one has to be satisfied with their silver value or else take them back.

On Lake Erie I was moved to write two verses, inspired by my wonderment over America's varied accomplishments. (They are set to the tune of *Blandt Norges fjelde er jeg født*.)

> O noble freedom, you are great,
> You crown the lands both far and near.
> You scatter over lands and seas
> The gifts of art to all mankind.
> The steamers ply the watery ways
> And railways serve the land meanwhile.
> The giant, steam, with mighty arms
> Turns the wheels on sea and shore.
> At times we rode the billows high
> Or floated o'er the glassy sea.
> Mighty streams in valleys deep
> Furrowed the bosom of the earth.
> Canals are dug where'er demanded,
> To serve the heart land of the nation
> And bring the overflowing yields
> To cities where the thousands dwell.

From New York to Detroit we traveled 825 miles and moved our chests only twice. We have everything we had longed for, and are convinced that we will find what we are looking for.[24]

[24] At the conclusion of the narrative these words follow: "Detroit, Michigan, September 10, 1899, Knud Knudsen. Gullik Holt. Jens Bagge. S. Berghei. Clemet Stabæk. Ansteen Natstad. Lars Rostoe from Land. Kittil Nyhuus. Gullik Blagstad. Hellik Glaim. Hans Langruud. Niri Fulsaas."

by NINA DRAXTEN

6   *Kristofer Janson's Beginning Ministry*

L ATE in the fall of 1880, some five months after Kristofer Janson had returned to Norway from his lecture tour in America, he and his wife, Drude, went to Italy on a vacation. The trip was the fulfillment of a promise he had made the year before, should the American venture be profitable — as indeed it was. Their seven children were left in the care of a farm woman who had long been attached to the family. Some of their relatives, particularly Dina Krog, Drude's sister, disapproved of this arrangement. She felt the Jansons were somewhat negligent parents not to leave an "educated" person in charge.[1]

In Rome, the Jansons' final destination, they found lodgings on Via Purificatione. Two Norwegian artists, Eilif Petersen and Kristian Ross, and their families joined them as neighbors. All became part of the sophisticated Scandinavian colony then in Rome, of which Ibsen was clearly the Olympian figure, but which also included such persons as Magdalena Thorsen and Camilla Collett — the latter, according to Janson, an ardent feminist virtually to the point of fanaticism.[2]

---

[1] Kristofer Janson, *Hvad jeg har oplevet*, 190 (Christiania, 1913); Dina Krog to Karoline Bjørnson, an undated letter, Bjørnson Papers, University Library, Oslo. Rasmus B. Anderson said that Janson "returned to Norway with fully $3,000 net proceeds"; *Life Story of Rasmus B. Anderson*, 299 (Madison, 1915).

[2] Janson, *Hvad jeg har oplevet*, 192, 196.

Attractive, still young, the Jansons seem to have been an engaging couple, alike in their zest for the new but otherwise highly individual in tastes — Drude, paradoxically, being somewhat the more radical and certainly the more practical of the two. Family legend has it that Drude was much admired in Rome, and this is not hard to believe, for so urbane a man as the Danish scholar and critic, Georg Brandes, who had met her a few months before in Christiania, told how attracted he had been to her, finding her highly original and very charming.[3]

For the Christmas festivities held by the Scandinavian group in Rome, Kristofer wrote a poem which won praise from Ibsen. Janson, in his autobiography, has told of taking long walks around Rome, of reading his short play, *Et kvindesjæbne* (A Woman's Fate) before an admiring audience. He was then working on his novel, *Vore besteforældre* (Our Grandparents), which gives an old man's account of events in Norwegian history from 1790 to 1815. On one occasion the Jansons borrowed costumes of the period of the story from Kristian Ross and invited their friends to a party. Drude's dress is not described, but Janson wore knee breeches, shoes with silver buckles, and a three-cornered hat, and, thus attired, read from his manuscript. During this period Ross painted Drude's portrait, a large canvas showing the three-quarter-length figure of a poised young matron whose slender form and unlined face belied the fact that she had borne seven children in some nine years. When the newspaper *Dagbladet* arrived from Christiania carrying Bjørnson's accounts of his stay in America, Janson discussed them with Ibsen, who had caustic things to say about Bjørnson, then his foremost rival as a Norwegian litterateur. At some time during this Italian holiday — the date cannot be pinpointed — Janson himself received a letter from Bjørnson, saying that a plan was afloat

[3] Mrs. Dina Behr Kolderup to the writer, March 6, 1959; Brandes, *Levned*, 2:360 (Copenhagen, 1907).

to bring Janson to America as a minister, and this prospect, as he revealed later, filled him with great excitement.[4]

Abruptly the Jansons' luck turned. Drude became ill, and, before she had recovered, word came from Norway that their son Sigmund was not expected to live. Kristofer rushed homeward, arriving in Lillehammer the day after the child had died. From such details as we have of the event, it was a lonely time for him. The older children, shocked by their first experience with bereavement, longed for their mother, and a younger one, Arne, was unable to realize what had happened. Janson had to face, besides his grief, the recriminations of Dina Krog, who made it clear that she hoped the event had taught the parents a lesson. The late Dr. Eiliv Janson has reported that Janson conducted the child's funeral himself.[5]

Early in May, 1881, Drude returned home. By that time Janson had received a proposal from Professor Rasmus B. Anderson of the University of Wisconsin that he return to America to organize a liberal religious movement among the Scandinavians. Janson was at first inclined to refuse, dreading the prospect of another long separation from his family, and Drude advised him at least to sleep on the matter.[6]

Anderson's letter has not survived, but in his autobiography he gave this account: He wrote Janson immediately after meeting two prominent Unitarian clergymen, Jenkin Lloyd Jones and Henry Martyn Simmons, in Madison. He had promised Bjørnson that he would do something to establish Janson in America, but had no idea how to proceed. This chance encounter with the ministers, whom he knew well, gave him an opening. If the Unitarians were interested in missionary

[4] Janson to Rasmus B. Anderson, July 18, 1881. Letters from Janson to Anderson here cited are in the Anderson Papers, State Historical Society of Wisconsin, Madison. *Et kvindesjæbne* was published in Bergen, Norway, in 1875, *Vore besteforældre* in Copenhagen in 1882. The portrait of Drude Janson is in the possession of Mrs. Betty Lou Nelson of Seattle, Washington, a great-granddaughter.

[5] As Janson approached his home, Arne, then about seven, ran out to meet his father, his face beaming, and shouted, "Sigmund is dead!" Interview with Mrs. Elinor Janson Hudson, daughter of Arne Janson, July, 1965; Dr. Eiliv Janson to the writer, July 4, 1959.

[6] Janson, *Hvad jeg har oplevet*, 198.

work among the Norwegians in this country, he had the ideal man for them, and he described Janson's career as a writer and speaker, and his theological training at the university in Christiania. Jones and Simmons were at once interested; they were going to Boston for a church conference, where they would present the matter before the American Unitarian Association. Anderson then suggested that Janson be guaranteed an annual salary of $1,000 for the first three years. They agreed, promising to write Anderson from Boston. Encouraged by all this, Anderson at once wrote Janson, saying that if the matter turned out as he expected, he would send a one-word cable, "Come!" Sometime afterward Anderson received confirmation of his proposal, whereupon — to quote the professor — "I cabled the word 'come' to him and he immediately packed his grip and came."[7]

No one can doubt that Anderson was responsible for bringing Janson to America as a minister, but he has gilded his story a bit. Things did not move so fast. If (as Janson said) he received the professor's proposal early in May, he must have mulled the matter over through a great many nights, for he did not reply until the middle of July. Then he did not mention the Unitarians, apparently considering the ministers' show of interest a flimsy prospect on which to risk his future. Much of Janson's letter was given to an analysis of his own situation. He was forty years old and had six children to support. His wife was not robust and needed household help. Janson, knowing full well the privations some Lutheran ministers and their wives had to endure in America, could not tolerate Drude's giving up a comfortable life in Norway for one of hardship in America. Unless he were assured an income of at least $1,500, he would not consider the matter.

Yet, as he ruefully explained, his prospects in Norway did not seem good. He felt isolated, for those who shared his religious views differed from him politically, and vice versa. Nor did he foresee much of a future as a writer. Public interest

[7] Anderson, *Life Story*, 300.

in tales of rural life had waned in favor of the social novel and drama, a field Janson felt had been pre-empted by Ibsen, Bjørnson, and Alexander Kjelland. Furthermore, the *landsmaal* issue had been resolved, for that language was even taught in the schools: Janson was no longer needed as its champion.

But more than anything else he wanted to go into religious work; were he able to get congregations, he would give all his energy to the development of their spiritual life. Anderson had suggested that he establish churches in several localities, dividing his time among them. Janson agreed to this, but vetoed Anderson's recommendation to include Chicago. He was set on living in Minneapolis, and traveling between the two cities would be too wearying. Besides — and here he asked Anderson to respect his confidence — Janson had not much liked the Scandinavians in Chicago, and though he might lecture there from time to time, he did not relish closer contact with them.

Janson then instructed Anderson how to go about organizing congregations. He drew up a proposed program, sending three copies, which he called circulars. Each was to go to an energetic but discreet man in one of three cities: Minneapolis, Fort Dodge, Iowa, and a third that Anderson might pick — possibly Madison. In each town, the man selected was to call a meeting at which Janson's program would be discussed, and those willing to support a congregation based on the principles given were to sign their names and pledge an annual sum, to be continued for at least three years. All of this, Janson cautioned, must be kept out of the newspapers, for if orthodox ministers got wind of it, they might frighten away people who would otherwise support the movement. After the circulars had made their rounds, Anderson was to forward them to Janson with whatever explanation was necessary. Toward the end of the letter Janson asked if it was legal in America for a man who had not been ordained to function as a minister, reminding Anderson that he had not been; nor could he go through the rite in Norway, for ordination there required taking an oath to uphold the Augsburg Confession.[8]

Had Anderson tried to put this plan into operation, he might well have been thrown back on his heels, for it is hard to publicize a man's activities and be quiet about them at the same time. But he faced no such dilemma. By the time he received Janson's letter he seems to have been sufficiently confident of his own plans to disregard the circulars. Instead of a single-word cable, he wrote Janson, and while this letter too is lost, its contents can be surmised from the response it drew. Anderson seems to have made it clear that the time for ambivalence was over. Prospects for support from the American Unitarians were good, but they were not going to commit themselves until they had met Janson. He must come to America in the fall, accepting the risks, or the matter would be dropped. While negotiations were going on, he could be lecturing, with Anderson again acting as his manager. A friend of Anderson's in Madison, John A. Johnson, had offered to keep Janson at his home until he was permanently located, and to donate a sum of money to him, a suggestion that was apparently tantamount to saying he would support Janson for a time if the worst came to the worst.[9]

On September 8 Janson cabled that he would come. In a letter of the same date, Professor Anderson wrote *Skandinaven* in Chicago, announcing that Janson would return to America in the fall for another lecture tour.[10]

In Norway Janson agonized over the sudden turn of events. On September 9, the day after he had sent his cable, he wrote the professor, revealing his anxiety over the future and his humiliation at coming under such circumstances. "Your letter gave me a great shock! All my plans have been ruined. Had you realized what you were doing, taking me away from my

[8] Janson to Anderson, July 18, 1881.

[9] Janson to Anderson, July 18, 1881. Johnson was a pioneer industrialist, founder of the Gisholt Machine Company. A biography of him by Agnes Larson is to be published by the Norwegian-American Historical Association.

[10] *Skandinaven* (Chicago), September 13, 1881. The letter was reprinted in *Folkebladet* (Minneapolis), September 22, 1881.

home, my wife and children, giving me a long voyage across the ocean, forcing me to come — uncalled — to struggle with an uncertain future, you would have thought twice about it. However, now I have cast my lot, and I must try. I have set my life's hope on a future there with you. If I fail, woe is me!" [11]

Janson went on to say that he expected to arrive before the middle of October. He gratefully accepted Johnson's offer of hospitality but not the money, which he would accept only in extremity and then strictly as a loan. He was, nevertheless, concerned about finances; he had to earn enough to support his family in Norway and to lay aside money to bring them over and establish a home. For a lecture he needed a minimum guarantee of twenty-five dollars, and fifty dollars in the larger cities. He hoped to stay out of controversy, adding resignedly that he supposed that was unlikely, at least so far as the Norwegian Synod was concerned. He added in a postscript that Bjørnson disapproved of his decision to go and could not understand why Anderson had done nothing with the circulars. "I would stay in Norway until a congregation was knocking at my door," he quoted Bjørnson as saying. [12]

Anderson apparently felt no qualms. Shortly after his ultimatum went to Janson, he wrote Bjørnson that he was working on the Janson matter and had good prospects for getting him a yearly salary of $2,000. Just what encouragement he had received thus far is not known, but it is clear that the American Unitarians were talking about Janson and were indeed eager to see him. On September 27 Aubertine Woodward, who had translated Janson's *Den bergtekne* (The Spellbound Fiddler) two years before, wrote Anderson from Boston that the Reverend James de Normandie, editor of the *Unitarian Review and Religious Magazine*, wanted to get all particulars from her on Janson, about whose coming he had heard from the wife of a Unitarian clergyman. On October 11, in the postscript of

[11] Janson to Anderson, September 9, 1881. Excerpts from Norwegian sources here quoted have been translated by the present writer.
[12] Janson to Anderson, September 9, 1881.

another letter to Anderson, she wrote: "I have seen Mr. De Normandie. He is delighted about Kristofer Janson, and says he must by all means come to Boston where he will himself introduce him to the Unitarian Board and he has not the slightest doubt of getting a salary appointed for him. He also says that the columns of the Unitarian Review are open whenever we want to use them. . . . Mr. De Normandie is very influential, and passes much time in Boston." [13]

Meanwhile many readers of *Skandinaven*, unaware of any prospective ministry for Janson, read Anderson's announcement of another lecture tour glumly. Bjørnson's tour had taken place the year after Janson's; both men had proved to be apostates from the Lutheran Church and both had been highly critical of Norwegian immigrant life. Even the Reverend Erik L. Petersen, who a year and a half before had applauded Janson's outspoken final lecture, "The So-called 'Pure Teachings,'" now thought that enough was enough. "Let as many cablegrams come as will," he advised readers of *Skandinaven*. "Twice you have been taken in; don't let it happen a third time," he said, citing the proverb that a fool and his gold are soon parted. "Neither Kristofer Janson nor Rasmus B. Anderson is a poor man," he continued, "and you would be foolish if you filled Janson's purse with thousands to use in enjoying himself later in Paris or Rome while you slave in the summer heat and winter cold. If you love God, you won't put out a cent for those who scorn God and His Holy Word, and whose living is made by driving Christianity out of the believer's heart." [14]

Janson apparently arrived in New York rather early in October. His initial activities are not known; possibly he stopped there to visit Hjalmar Hjorth Boyesen, something he had speculated on in his letter to Anderson of September 9. He

[13] Anderson to Bjørnson, August 27, 1881; letters to Bjørnson here cited are in the Bjørnson Papers; microfilm copies of Anderson's letters in this collection are in the State Historical Society of Wisconsin. Aubertine Woodward's letters are in the Anderson Papers. The *Spellbound Fiddler* had appeared in Chicago in 1880.

[14] *Skandinaven*, October 11, 1881.

may, under a directive from Anderson, have gone to Boston to meet directors of the American Unitarian Association. It seems likely, not only because the way had been cleared for such a meeting but also because missionaries were paid by the association from Boston, even though those working in the Middle West were directed by the Western Unitarian Conference. By October 24, 1881, Janson was in Madison, still awaiting definite word from the Unitarians. On that day he wrote a twenty-page letter to Jenkin Lloyd Jones, secretary of the Western Conference. Probably he had not yet met Jones, for he was, in effect, introducing himself. Quite likely the first letter Janson ever wrote in English, it reveals his early difficulties with idiom and syntax, but also indicates that the shift in language did not hamper him from presenting himself in an appealing way:

"You must excuse me, that I dare to trouble you with a so very long letter, as this seems to be; but when you have read it through, you will find reason in it, I hope. To you perhaps have been told, my friend in Madison, Prof. Anderson, had written to me a while ago a letter, asking me to emigrate to America for the purpose of working for a more liberal spirit among my countrymen here, especially concerning their religious views, and make them good American citizens. I felt a desire to do it, because it seems me a necessary and blessed work too — but I had a large family, I was well off in my home, and I did not dare to do it without any assistance. Then Mr. Anderson told me about his meeting with you and your readiness to accept his proposals. I was quite surprised, for such a thing could not happen in any other country than America, I suppose, where public confidence has become an educating power. Relying upon this magnanimous and noble offer, I have left my home and am willing to try the hard task. I hope that you, dear Sir, may be able to get Mr. Andersons proposals realized, and that your confidence in me will not be misplaced. I hope, that the spiritual capital, which my countrymen, when once awakened, will bring to their new fatherland, will reward the generosity of your society toward me and the Scandinavians. I promise you as an honest man to put in all my vigour and energy in this work."

Janson went on to a description of the dissension among the Norwegian Lutherans in America — the five rival synods, and the Norwegian Synod's affiliation with the German Missouri Synod, the schism then threatening it over the predestination issue, and its actions in the past: its defense of slavery, its opposition to the common school, its rigid fundamentalism, and (the allegation Janson had made before) its policy of keeping its parishioners cut off from American society. With some stylistic changes, this discussion was later printed in *Unity*, the publication of the Western Unitarian Conference, and then was widely disseminated when an excerpt from it appeared in the *Independent*, an interdenominational magazine devoted to news of the various Protestant churches.

Janson next assessed his chances of success as a missionary:

"I thought it my duty, dear Sir, to tell you the very truth about the distressing condition of my fatherlands church here in America. You may see that my task will not be easy, and that I may not hope to organize free societies in a hurry. I am sure, that all the Lutheran congregations will agree in my persecution. I have already got a little taste of it by several mean articles in the Norwegian newspapers here. In one of them they recite the words of St. Paul as a salutation to me: 'if any man preacheth unto you any gospel other than that which ye received (from the Norwegian synod?) *let him be anathema.*'

"But I will also find my defenders.

"Besides the members of the mentioned congregations you will find many thousands of Norwegian people outside the church, floating and drifting for all winds, spread over all the country. Among them I will probably find the first stones for my church. But I am not sure, how far I will succeed among them. A large part of them have thrown the christianity over board and do not care for any Christian membership; another part are business men, who are afraid to loose [*sic*] their customers if they declare themselves to be members of a free church. For it is not so among the Norsemen as among the Americains [*sic*], that nobody in affairs asks, whether a man is Methodist or Episcopalian or not — no — they make business with their own fellows and look at the others with a shy look as something strange and horrible.

"Without your assistance I will be compelled to lay my religious work a side and earn my living by lecturing about esthetical, historical, and social subjects. With your assistance I will put my other lectures in the background and employ all my power in a labor for a free church, and shall be able to stay here for a number of years at least. In that case I intend to go back to the old country next May, arrange my affairs there and take my family over with me. The summer months spent at home I will use for collecting a hymn book, which will be necessary, because the largest number of the common hymns in the Norwegian church are so inwoven with old creeds and singular Lutheran dogmas, that these will be of no use to me.

"Finally, I may beg your pardon, dear Sir, that I have engaged your attention for so long time. You may also excuse my bad language, but I am a beginner and must still compose my letters by means of the dictionary. In a year or two I hope I will improve so much in English, that I may be able to preach my sermon in that language. That will be necessary, if I shall think upon conquering the growing up people. If any of this information should have interest for your society, I will leave them entirely at yours disposal."[15]

This prospect of support made it mandatory for Janson to become known to the American public. Apparently Anderson had this in mind. He had recently published a translation of Bjørnson's *Arne*, and arranged to have Janson review it. The article, composed in English by the reviewer himself, ap-

[15] Letters to Jones are in the Jones Papers, Library of Meadville Theological School of Lombard College, Chicago. Italics in the section quoted are Janson's.

peared in the November, 1881, *Dial*, and was entitled, "A Norse Prose Idyl"; the fact that Janson spoke well of the translator's work does not seem strange under the circumstances. As soon as the magazine came out, Janson sent a copy to Jones.

In the last week in October Janson received favorable word from the American Unitarians, and the news that his ordination would take place in Chicago during the following month. On November 1 Janson wrote Jones, asking if Sunday, the thirteenth, would be convenient — not, it appears, because he had a preference for that date but because he was considering giving a free lecture in Chicago while he was there and needed to make preliminary arrangements. Four days later he gave an address, "Vore forfædre" (Our Ancestors) in the assembly hall of the University of Wisconsin. It was of course delivered in Norwegian, but received a lengthy and very favorable review in the *Wisconsin State Journal* (Madison) which, in translation, appeared in *Skandinaven*.[16]

On November 21, 1881, the directors of the American Unitarian Association formally accepted Janson's application into its ministry and voted him $1,000 for the first six months of his work. On Friday evening, November 25, he was ordained in the Third Unitarian Church in Chicago. Besides Jones, three other Unitarian clergymen, Brooke Herford, E. L. Garvin, and George C. Miln, took part in the ceremony. After the ordination, Janson, apologizing for his English, spoke of the event as one of the high lights of his life, likening it to the day he became a university student, the day his first book came out, the date of his marriage, and that of the birth of his first child.[17]

The event had extensive coverage in Unitarian journals. In the *Christian Register*, the official organ of the American Unitarian Association, the article was entitled "A New Prophet in Israel." In *Unity*, Jenkin Lloyd Jones quoted Bjørnson that

[16] *Skandinaven*, November 15, 1881.
[17] *Christian Register* (Boston), November 24, December 1, 1881.

no better protest against the dogmas of the orthodox church could be found than in Kristofer Janson's liberal religion, "sustained by the purest personal character and most charming intellect." Jones, extending the good wishes of the Western Conference to its new missionary, made use of Norse mythology: "May his be Thor's hammer to smite wrong, and Balder's smile to woo the right." [18]

Meanwhile Aubertine Woodward had been waiting until after the ordination to write about Janson. In the *Unitarian Review and Religious Magazine,* under her pseudonym, Auber Forestier, she described the ordination, gave a biographical account of Janson, and spoke of Professor Anderson as the man who had paved the way for Janson by his truthfulness about the Norwegian Synod and his "brave, single-handed fight on the common school question." The work of the two men would harmonize, she declared, concluding her article with a eulogy of Janson.

"And now this man, so rich in endowments, in experience, in honors, a true liberal in religion and politics, his poetic nature and loving heart overflowing with a Christ-like yearning to aid and lift up his people, leaves his home with a self-sacrifice that we can perhaps scarcely estimate, and comes among us on a noble and exalted mission. His genial presence, his deep earnestness, his strong personal influence, cannot fail to help his cause and attract many about him. May his endeavors be crowned with the grandest success!" [19]

On the Sunday following the ordination, Janson gave his free lecture, "The Norwegian Synod," in Chicago. *Skandinaven,* in an objective account, reported that every seat was taken, on both the main floor and in the balcony, and crowds took standing room in the back of the hall. Otherwise, the Norwegian press of the city took a dour view of this as well as the proceedings of the Friday evening before. "He chose a rich theme for one who claims to be the apostle of brotherly love.

[18] *Unity* (Chicago), December 1, 1881.
[19] *Unitarian Review and Religious Magazine* (Boston), January, 1882.

Janson is a hypocrite," *Den Nye Tid* lashed out angrily. *Norden* concluded its remarks with the statement, "We hope Janson's mission will have no future among our countrymen." *Verdens Gang* was more temperate. Janson's significance, as both poet and theologian, had been greatly exaggerated by his admirers, the editor maintained. Nevertheless, his coming meant a struggle which should stimulate the spiritual life of the Norwegians, something they greatly needed. A man had a right to ally himself wherever he chose, the editor continued, even if it meant breaking with the old. In Norway many in the higher classes were certainly not Lutheran, were actually closer to Unitarianism, and it was better for church and society that they be openly so. The editor felt, however, that Janson's Sunday lecture did not leave a good impression, because of its bitterness and the circumstances under which the material had been gathered — the latter a reference to Janson's lecture tour of 1879–80.[20]

In La Crosse, Wisconsin, *Fædrelandet og Emigranten* prefaced its account of the ordination by saying that Unitarians accepted only one God and denied the divinity of Christ and the verbal inspiration of the Bible. In England, the editor continued, they were considered freethinkers. In America they tried to gloss themselves over as Christians, but were really freethinkers, nothing else. The same issue of the paper carried another column-long article entitled "Unitariernes sekt," a history of Unitarianism beginning with Servetus and concluding with the statement that in America there were no more than 17,960 members.[21]

On December 2 Anderson wrote exultantly to Bjørnson:

"I must report the news on Janson. He received the salary from the Unitarian Association that I predicted at the outset. Beginning yesterday (December 1) he has $2,000 as a missionary to the Norwegians in the Northwest. . . . Slightly

[20] *Skandinaven*, November 29, 1881. The other newspapers mentioned were quoted in *Budstikken* (Minneapolis), December 6, 1881.
[21] *Fædrelandet og Emigranten* (La Crosse), December 6, 1881.

over a week ago he was ordained in Chicago, and soon afterward he gave a fine address in the old Turner Hall before a *packed* house. Theme: the Norwegian Synod, and it took! Yesterday he went to Minneapolis. There will be a life-and-death battle, but Janson, with the backing of the Unitarian Association, can laugh at the neck-breaking exertions of the opposition. He will bring life and the Norwegians will develop into independent thinkers. I hope Janson himself will become a more independent man, for he still holds on to a great many dogmas. However, by this he builds a bridge for many others. I shall keep you informed; you can depend on that." [22]

II

At this time Minneapolis was entering a decade of great expansion; its population was to increase fourfold, from 36,887 to 164,738. The great influx of Norwegian immigrants had already begun; their number was to grow with every passing year, increasing from 2,500 in 1880 to 12,624 in 1890.[23] Nor do these figures tell the full story: for one thing, the census of the time did not include the native-born children of immigrants, and for another, there were, every year, newcomers streaming into the city who used it as a stopping place before moving on to find homes elsewhere.

Minneapolis covered some thirty-three square miles, extending seven and a half miles from north to south and slightly over six miles from east to west. To Janson — as he was to write a year later — it was a place of dramatic contrasts; one hardly knew from one moment to the next whether he was in a pioneer settlement or in a city. On the outskirts of town were log cabins separated by wide gaps of unsold lots where, weather permitting, cattle roamed. Toward the center of town were impressive mansions. Pictures show them to be many-gabled structures that probably held twenty or more rooms. With no fewer than three chimneys, some houses rose to three and a

[22] Anderson to Bjørnson, December 2, 1881. Italics are Anderson's.
[23] Carl G. O. Hansen, *My Minneapolis*, 52 (Minneapolis, 1956).

half stories; characteristically they had a profusion of projecting dormer windows and were elaborately hung with balconies and porches. Some were built next to the humble cottages of earlier settlers, who were often able to make a pretty profit as land values went up. Downtown an electric tower had been erected which flooded the area with white light; otherwise the streets were lighted with gas. Only the principal streets were paved; the others, frozen and rutted in winter, were so deep in mire in spring that the mud went over the galoshes of anyone who had to cross. Everywhere were signs of hectic activity: small cottages were moved from one location to another; streets were torn up as water and sewer pipes were laid.[24]

Janson was to characterize Minneapolis as a city "coming into being," saying that contrasts were also to be found in its cultural life. The Academy of Music, then the leading theater, one night might present a minstrel show where spectators were convulsed at the antics of blackface singers; the next evening *Hamlet* was on the boards; and on the third, the offering might be *Jesse James* (which Janson disparaged as a "so-called drama").[25]

As one might expect, immigrant life was humble, although it in no way approached the squalor found in the tenements of New York and Chicago. Even so, most newcomers got along on the narrowest financial margins and accounts of suicide in Norwegian weeklies of the time point the trail of those who could not make it. Immigrant life was to become increasingly hard with the years. The nation as a whole had known a labor shortage in 1870, but this situation was to be reversed in the period 1881–1900, when immigration, technological changes, and other factors were to swell the number of unemployed to a million.[26] In other words, the contrasts Janson observed in his early days in Minneapolis were to be radically sharpened, with

[24] *Tribune Hand Book of Minneapolis* 44, 115 (Minneapolis, 1884); Janson, "Fra Amerika," in *Nyt tidsskrift*, 2:22 (Christiania, 1883).

[25] Janson, in *Nyt tidsskrift*, 2:22.

[26] Charles Howard Hopkins, *The Rise of the Social Gospel in American Protestantism 1865–1915*, 79 (New Haven, 1940).

great wealth in the hands of a very few and at the other end of
the continuum an impoverished laboring class. Within a few
years this disparity was so to arouse Janson that the "oppres-
sion" of the Norwegian Synod became a secondary concern.

Although it may be assumed that there were Norwegians
living in all sections of the city when Janson arrived, places
of their heaviest concentration may be identified. The largest
colony — and the area where Janson first directed his efforts
— lay along both sides of Washington Avenue, roughly
bounded on the north by Eleventh Avenue South, moving toward Cedar Avenue and the Riverside area. Washington Avenue from Eleventh to Fifteenth was lined on both sides with
establishments kept by Scandinavians — grocery, dry goods,
shoe repair, furniture, and hardware shops — and saloons.
Some buildings towered to three stories, but most seem to have
been single-story, gable-fronted stores. To the west of Washington Avenue, on the corner of Second Street and Twelfth
Avenue, was Beard's Block, a three-story building commonly
known as Noah's Ark, which contained some sixty apartments
renting from eight to thirteen dollars a month. In windows
throughout the area were such signs as "Scandinavian Boarding Day or Week" and "Scandinavian Midwife." A few blocks
off Riverside Avenue was Augsburg Seminary, the theological
school of the Norwegian-Danish Conference, the second largest
of the five Norwegian Lutheran synods. This academy had
been in the city since 1872, and the church established by the
Conference — Trinity — also in this area, was the oldest Norwegian congregation in Minneapolis. There were four other
Norwegian churches: Two were Lutheran, Our Savior's and
St. Paul's — of the Norwegian and Hauge synods, respectively
— while the other two were Methodist and Baptist.[27]

A second colony, in north Minneapolis, extended north from
Plymouth Avenue to what is now West Broadway, and from
Second Street North westward toward Emerson. This group,
drawn largely from the Trondheim province in Norway, seems

[27] Hansen, *My Minneapolis*, 23, 51–54.

to have been generally interspersed with other nationalities, for the area as a whole was not dominated by Scandinavians. Years before, these Norwegians had made some efforts to form organizations: In the early seventies a number of families banded together to set up a primary school but abandoned it after a few years. In 1874 the Conference established St. Olaf congregation, but this too had petered out by 1877, and in 1881 the Norwegians in north Minneapolis had no church. (Later, for several years, Janson valiantly held weekly meetings on Plymouth Avenue in an effort to establish a congregation but finally gave up and turned his attention to St. Paul.) In northeast Minneapolis was another colony about which little is known except that it was sufficiently large to maintain a church, Immanuel, established by the Norwegian Synod in 1874.[28]

Such, in brief, was the city and such its concentrations of Norwegians when Janson arrived on December 3, 1881, to try his luck. While all the Norwegians certainly were not pleased at the prospect, the event caused virtually no surprise. Months before, in the spring of 1881, a rumor had circulated that Janson was to organize a liberal congregation in the city. The report reached Norway, where it was laid to rest by Janson himself in *Dagbladet* — a denial which was printed sometime after he had opened his correspondence with Anderson. Although the statement was reprinted in *Budstikken* in Minneapolis (which traced the rumor to the efforts of a Pastor R. Egeland to organize a "free" congregation), many people who had heard the report seem not to have read the denial, for after Janson's ordination, correspondents to the paper frequently spoke of it as something they had been hearing about for a long time.[29]

In announcing Janson's arrival, Luth Jaeger, editor of *Budstikken*, said he was sure the majority of his readers would join in wishing Janson a hearty welcome. Janson had come, not to destroy the synod, but to work for religious toleration and

[28] Hansen, *My Minneapolis*, 23.
[29] Janson's denial was reprinted in *Budstikken*, August 30, 1881.

spiritual freedom. Now prospects were better than ever for the Norwegian people to be emancipated from blind dogmatism, Jaeger said, adding, "All free-minded Norsemen who, like us, long for this, will wish Janson the best of luck." [30]

In many ways Janson was fortunate in his choice of Minneapolis. He had prominent friends there, among them Dr. Karl Bendeke, Andreas Ueland, and Dr. Jacob Schumann. Besides Luth Jaeger, the publishers of *Budstikken*, Gudmund Johnson and John Gjedde, were friendly to him and from the beginning the columns of the paper were open to him. He was welcomed by the minister of Unity Church in St. Paul, the Reverend W. C. Gannett, a man with impressive Unitarian credentials, for he was the son of the famed Boston preacher, Ezra Stiles Gannett, and the namesake of the great William Channing, who had, indeed, christened him. Then Janson was to have the guidance of a Unitarian colleague near at hand — the Reverend Henry Martyn Simmons, who, the month before — in November, 1881 — began what was to be a long ministry in Minneapolis when the already organized Liberal League became the First Unitarian Society. The two men liked each other from their first meeting.[31]

The time when Janson arrived — even though it was wholly adventitious — was also in his favor. The two major Norwegian Lutheran organizations — the Norwegian Evangelical Lutheran Church, popularly known as the Norwegian Synod, and the Conference of the Norwegian-Danish Evangelical Lutheran Church in America, generally referred to as the Conference — paid little attention to him, absorbed as they were in internal problems. In the Norwegian Synod a controversy had erupted (as Janson had mentioned in his letter to Jones) over the issue of predestination, led by a group that came to be known as the anti-Missourians. In the Conference, efforts to raise an endowment fund of $50,000 for Augsburg Seminary

[30] *Budstikken*, December 6, 1881.
[31] Janson to Anderson, December 11, 1881; Simmons to Jones, December 12, 1881, Jones Papers.

had been received coolly by some congregations and was sparking some newspaper debate. It has been said by those who knew Janson, among them his protégé and successor, Dr. Amandus Norman, that Janson was denounced from pulpits; if this was the case, these attacks were not reported in the papers. What Janson had to endure was harassment from laymen — some of it so crude that it aroused public sympathy for him.

Six days after Janson arrived, on Friday, December 9, he lectured about the Norwegian Synod before an audience of 249 people, a fraction of the number who had heard the same address in Chicago; but those in Minneapolis paid twenty-five cents admission. Shortly afterward he was invited to give the speech in St. Paul. Thus far, however, he was only warming up. What he regarded as the opening salvo of his mission was a mass meeting he called for the following Sunday. For this he hired the largest auditorium in Minneapolis, Harrison Hall, on Washington and Nicollet avenues. According to Simmons, who attended as an observer, the crowd was so huge that people thronged the aisles. Janson has told, with sardonic humor, incidents that immediately followed the meeting. At the end of the address he announced that he would remain for a time in a small adjoining room, available to anyone who wished to talk with him. First to take advantage of this offer was an old woman carrying a copy of the Lutheran catechism. Brandishing the book, she demanded whether he was going to uphold its teachings. On hearing that he would not, she warned him that she would call down a curse on his work. Another person was an elderly man, his eyes glistening with tears, who clasped Janson's hand warmly. But then — as Janson has described it — the man suddenly came to his senses, and, realizing that the devil had been tempting him, hurried away.[32]

These instances, however, were mere bagatelles, and did not depress Janson in the slightest. That night he wrote Professor

[32] Simmons to Jones, December 12, 1881; Janson, *Hvad jeg har oplevet*, 205; Janson, "The Scandinavians in America," in *Christian Register*, June 22, 1882.

Anderson — in English — his salutation revealing his exultant mood:

"My dear, sweet, young, old boy Rasmus!

"I have just delivered my program — a splendid meeting, the large hall crowded. I think 1500 persons were there! When I protested the tyranny of the ministers and abolished the eternal hell there was perfect joy and applause: only two whistles were heard, but I do not know if they whistled in *American* or on [*sic*] *Norwegian*. I suppose the latter. It seems as if my program has made a deep impression. My friends told me that many people, walking out, declared they would join my congregation. Next Sunday I will commence my regular services, in the beginning at the same hall 3 o'clock in the afternoon. My first theme will be: 'God is Love!' After my lecture several persons walked in to me — and clasped my hands with sparkling eyes; the largest number of them *Swedes*. In Sweden, you see, those thoughts are not quite unknown, there has Nils Ignell and V. Rydberg worked and I think I here in Amerika will gather the fruits of their work in Sweden."

He mentioned two prominent persons as likely members of his church: Miss Nanny Mattson, Luth Jaeger's fiancée and the daughter of Colonel Hans Mattson, and Alfred Söderstrom, editor of *Svenska Folkets Tidning* (Minneapolis). He had other reasons for being encouraged. Even before his mass meeting he had been approached by N. T. Sjøberg and a group of the latter's friends about forming a congregation. These men, Janson explained to Anderson, had withdrawn or been expelled from Lutheran churches because they had joined fraternal organizations with life-insurance programs. They showed Janson the constitution they had drawn up. He was momentarily dismayed: "It was just the same as every Lutheran church — the name ought to be a Norwegian *Lutheran* congregation and they would oblige the minister on symbolium, Nicanum, Athanasianum." Janson told them he could not accept it and, after explaining his reasons, asked if he had frightened them away. They answered that he had not, and after that they had sold tickets for him and performed other services. He also received a letter from a group in rural Brown County, and in return sent them what he called a "friendly and prudent letter," saying he would soon deliver a lecture in nearby Madelia, and when he was in the area he would preach for them and hold a conference to discuss their offer. He had been busy with other things too: working out a constitution which he planned to present to Sjøberg and the group in Minneapolis and later take with him to Brown County, preparing the announcement of his program for publication in *Budstikken* and *Skandinaven*, compiling a small hymn collection to be used at his services, and sending out a list of the titles of lectures he was prepared to give, for advertisements to be run in *Budstikken*, *Skandinaven*, and *Fædrelandet og Emigranten*. "I answer letters, make acquaintancs, write sermons — so you will see I have my hands full," he wrote Anderson, adding cheerfully, "But I have good hopes of success, old fellow, and I see it will only depend on my personal influence, so I have to be as amiable and vigorous as possible. I have suffered from backache these last days, and that is not very pleasant, but I must be thankful that my head is clear and that I can work." [33]

The following day he sent off a lengthy report to Jenkin Lloyd Jones, of much the same content as the one to Anderson. This letter, although more restrained in tone, was also buoyantly optimistic. Balder's smile, he remarked, referring to the secretary's comment in *Unity*, was likely to be more useful than Thor's thunderbolts. Still feeling the need to interpret the Norwegians to Jones, he added a few comments on a letter from the people in Brown County:

"The man [*Johannes Mo*] who writes it, writes in the name of a lot of Norwegian peasants [*farmers*] who have separated

[33] Janson to Anderson, December 11, 1881. Italics in the letter are Janson's. The Lutheran Church (and other orthodox Christian religions) accepted both the Nicene and the Athanasian symbols or creeds. Janson is here explaining that he was presented with a constitution suitable for a Lutheran church, not a liberal congregation.

themselves from the Synod because they were always quarreling there. They ask me to come and be their minister, and they send me their constitution—the same as the former 'Nicanus Athanasium, the confession of Augsburg, etc.['] They do not know any other thing, poor fellows, and they will try to do it as well as possible. I returned a very friendly letter, thanked them for their confidence in me but told them I preferred to be a Christian for [*rather than*] a Lutheran." Janson had asked them if it was not time for the different Christian churches to unite rather than separate.[34]

"Kristofer Janson's Program," which was published in *Budstikken* on Wednesday, December 13, informed those who had not attended his mass meeting how Janson interpreted his role as a clergyman. It had long been his wish, he said, to engage in religious work, but his convictions were such that he could not serve within the state church in Norway. As for otherwise serving the liberal cause there, Norway was already well supplied with active leaders; his efforts could be put to better use among the Norwegians in America. Since most of them came from the working class and had little education, it was hard for them to develop a leader from their own ranks. Janson wanted to become their spokesman, helping them in their adjustment to American life. Lutheran pastors, he said, were tyrants rather than helpers. They had changed the Bible into a procurator's lawbook and embalmed Christianity into a mummy with their literally interpreted scriptural passages. This tyranny, Janson declared, he would oppose with full vigor.

Outside of that he wanted no controversy. He had no intention of going into congregations seeking converts, for he respected all faiths; he was instead making an appeal to Scandinavians who could not accept the dogmas of the orthodox church but were unwilling to renounce Christianity. The liberal church he planned to organize would be founded on "love to God the Father, and to our Saviour, Jesus Christ." Listing

[34] Janson to Jones, December 12, 1881.

his major principles, Janson said he followed St. Paul in regarding Jesus as "the one mediator between God and man." He did not accept the divinity of Jesus, saying the crucifixion of a god amounted to an absurdity. Nor did he consider the Bible to be verbally inspired: the Old Testament he regarded as the history of the Jewish people and the New Testament as the earliest account of the lives of Jesus and the apostles, but both were the work of men who bore the prejudices of their own milieu. He did not accept the doctrine of the Trinity; he did not believe in an everlasting hell — although he was convinced that all wrongdoing was punished by mental and physical suffering, in accordance with natural law.

For his church services, Janson would use some of the practices of the church in Norway. Unless parents wanted it otherwise, he would baptize in the name of the Father, Son, and Holy Ghost. In celebrating the Lord's Supper, he would follow some of the conventional usages of the church at home.

Some parts of this statement seemed paradoxical; and Janson was shortly to be called to account. Yet, in terms of his rationale, it was entirely consistent. There was one God; Jesus was indeed the son of God, but not because of any mystical circumstances attendant on his birth, rather in the sense that all human beings are the children of God. Nor was he the Saviour for having served as a sacrificial lamb who redeemed mankind, but because he had, by his teaching and example, shown the way to God. Christians were to be identified by their way of life, not by a mere profession of faith. To Janson, what one believed was an intimate, personal matter, governed by inner conviction. An earnest Christian, looking to Jesus for guidance, never presumed that his particular belief of the moment constituted a monopoly on truth; instead he strove for new insights so that his religion, never a static body of doctrine, was always growing and developing.

Since belief was a matter of the individual conscience, no one who joined Janson's movement was under any compulsion to agree with him on what he had outlined as the major tenets of his faith. He was to meet shortly with those who could not, and this fact he accepted with equanimity. He also recognized that people were emotionally attached to many Norwegian church customs, associated as they were with memories of home. He saw no reason for dispensing with these when they could be reinterpreted by deleting the mystical elements. Thus Janson accepted the use of baptism, the Eucharist, confirmation, and other established practices.

All in all — as an outsider might view it — the orthodoxy Janson rejected and the "free" Christianity he espoused differed most fundamentally in that the latter lacked the punitive features of the former (a Jehovah punishing the sins of the fathers upon their children unto the third and fourth generation, a hell awaiting those who would not accept prescribed articles of faith) and in the breadth it gave religion; according to Janson's definition, one could find Christians in all places and ages — even among the ancients who had lived before the time of Christ — and Janson frequently did find them. Yet even his denial of the divinity of Christ becomes academic, for one is hard put to find greater reverence for Jesus than that in Janson's sermons and poems. In the course of time some Lutherans came to concede as much; for instance, Pastor Lars Heiberg, who, after the publication of Janson's *Jesus sangene* (Songs of Jesus) sent the author a warm letter of appreciation.[35]

In the week following the appearance of Janson's program in *Budstikken*, it was reviewed in *Folkebladet*, a weekly also published in Minneapolis. The paper was owned and edited by Sven Oftedal and Georg Sverdrup, professors at Augsburg Seminary, the theological school of the Conference, which had its headquarters in Minneapolis. Although the professors used *Folkebladet* to expound their views on issues related to the seminary and the Conference, it was essentially a secular paper, written in a highly readable style. Of the two editors, Oftedal was to emerge as Janson's most implacable critic, and

[35] *Saamanden* (Minneapolis), November, 1893.

until 1887 he was to be nipping at Janson's heels much of the time. The differences between him and Janson — so Oftedal declared — were not to be interpreted as *en lærestrid* (a theological debate), for the professor could not be drawn into any such discussion with a person who denied the divinity of Jesus.

From all accounts, Sven Oftedal was highly gifted — a scholar, an eloquent speaker, and a beautiful singer; during the eighties and nineties he came to play a leading part in the cultural life of the city. He was, however, not one to shrink from controversy and, once involved, he used little restraint in verbally pummeling an opponent. Long before Janson appeared on the scene, Oftedal had become well known for his broadsides. In 1874 — shortly after he arrived in America — he had published a scathing attack on the Norwegian Synod that, even in those days of bitter exchanges, made something of a high-water mark.[36] Later, angered by the prospect of Bjørnson's lecture tour, he belittled the poet as a "clown," an epithet critics then and later found singularly inept.

After Janson's ordination, *Folkebladet* contained allusions to Janson that seemed to be in Oftedal's idiom. Janson was mentioned as "a petite edition of Bjørnson" and as "one of Bjørnson's living proof sheets"; in the latter case, there was an added comment that all such persons might better be removed to Alaska, where the wilderness would appreciate their new form of civilization. Yet, all this was missing from the treatment of Janson in the December 22, 1881, issue of *Folkebladet*. For one thing, a dispatch written by a correspondent in Madison for a paper in Norway, highly complimentary to Janson, was reprinted without comment. Then — without any recourse to name calling — Janson's program was reviewed. As none of the articles were signed, the author cannot be identified with certainty. But the piece suggests a hand other than Oftedal's — that of Georg Sverdrup, an introspective man, somewhat austere in bearing, who today has the reputa-

---

[36] See E. Clifford Nelson and Eugene L. Fevold, *The Lutheran Church among Norwegian-Americans*, 1:224 (Minneapolis, 1960); S. Sondresen, "De norske kirkesamfund i Amerika," in *Norsk-amerikanerne*, 53 (Bergen, 1938).

tion of having been an unusually able dialectician. The review was not an exercise in dialectics, however, but more of a satire in which the writer generously conceded Janson's talents and then thrust the dagger where he was vulnerable.

The writer in *Folkebladet* reported Janson's statement about coming to serve as a leader for the Scandinavian people in America, adding with quiet irony "since they have none other than Lutheran ministers." Citing Janson's five major points as well as his resolve to retain practices from the church of Norway, the reviewer noted that although Janson denied the Trinity, he would baptize in the name of the Father, Son, and Holy Ghost; and while he did not accept the divinity of Christ, he would celebrate the Eucharist using the words, "This is my body" and "This is my blood." Janson would be both pastor and teacher; he would preach and deliver lectures. "Such is the program," said the writer, adding resignedly, "and so it must be, coming from a Unitarian." He assessed these principles as outworn rationalism, something long since discarded by Europeans but propounded in America by the Unitarians. This teaching could only be regarded as freethinking. Serious as the threat was, one could take comfort by recalling events in Norwegian history: It was just such rationalism that had precipitated the great religious awakening led by the lay preacher, Hans Nielsen Hauge.[37] One must remember this precedent while grieving over Janson's defection:

"It is disheartening to see a Norwegian poet become a minister in order to propound such a teaching, one regarded in the Lutheran countries of Europe as stable fodder and a crop of potatoes. It is discouraging to see a man who has fought for freedom now work for the teachings once preached in Norway by men who put Hauge in prison and sought to quell the workings of the spirit by physical force. It is disappointing to see a talented man from the Norwegian church openly declare views which the Christian church has never acknowledged.

[37] Hans Nielsen Hauge (1771–1824), a lay preacher, brought about a religious revival in Norway despite persecution from state authorities.

"There is no reason, however, for Norwegians in America, who have worked to establish free congregations to safeguard the teachings of their childhood, to nourish anxious or bitter thoughts over Pastor Janson and his mission. The same thing has often happened in the history of the church, that heretical and rationalistic views have been preached and people have had to protect themselves by regarding them critically. That is especially true in this country, which has so many sects. Congregations must choose between the new teachings and the proven truth." [38]

Janson seems to have been somewhat puzzled about how to answer. He had no wish to quarrel with the Conference. The Norwegian Synod had been his prime target, and on several occasions, he had praised the Conference, both for its confederation of independent congregations as against the centrally administered synod and for its use of lay preachers.

In his reply, Janson began by thanking the editor of *Folkebladet* for the generally courteous tone of the article, saying, "In these days of bitter strife, that is something one rarely encounters in an opponent, especially here in America." If the writer chose to adopt an attitude of levity and superiority toward his program, Janson must accept that interpretation. The same might be said about the comments on his similarity to the clergymen who had persecuted Hauge, although Janson added parenthetically that he was well versed on these men and on Hauge too, having recently dealt with them in a still unfinished book — a reference to *Vore besteforældre*. He could not acknowledge these ministers as his kindred, nor did he feel, especially at Christmas, any inclination to preach on potatoes. "All such imprecations," he said, "strike me as making use of old, but, unfortunately, not outworn tactics, designed to create mistrust in people's eyes. And I must admit I am surprised that you express yourself thus, for recently in my lecture on the Norwegian Synod I spoke of my admiration of

[38] *Folkebladet*, December 22, 1881.

the Conference's use of lay preachers. Do you call that persecuting Hauge?"

Janson complained that his program had been reported in terms of contradictions, and that such practices as the use of the Eucharist were not part of original Christianity but had been introduced by the early church fathers in the year 381. He conceded, however, that it was natural that he and the Conference should look upon such matters differently; each must choose according to his taste. He thanked the editor for reprinting the favorable dispatch by the correspondent from Madison. And he agreed that future debate between him and the Conference was unnecessary, adding, "I should value it very much if you would accept me as a neighbor with whom you could be on personally friendly terms, and that both our congregations might work side by side without either casting aspersions on the other."

This overture was rebuffed. Janson's letter was printed in the January 5, 1882, issue of *Folkebladet* and followed by editorial comment couched in coldly civil terms:

"*Folkebladet* has printed the above communication from Pastor Janson because it clearly reveals his rationalism as much as anything we could have written. Christianity is not, for us, something one chooses according to his taste, and it cannot be for any Christian. There can be no talk of working side by side with a man or an organization that denies the divinity of Jesus, which Christians have acknowledged through the ages, not just since 381, but from the days of the apostles. If Janson is familiar with the events of Hauge's time, he knows that the ministers who opposed him had a spiritual lack, intricately bound up with their heretical views and their denial of the divinity of Christ. Mankind, therefore, is prepared to fear the fruits that come from the same root in church work." [39]

The exchange took several weeks. In the meantime Janson proceeded with his original plan to hold services every Sun-

[39] *Folkebladet*, January 5, 1882.

day. Thus, one week after his mass meeting, he preached in Harrison Hall in Minneapolis at three in the afternoon before an audience of twelve hundred. In the interval between the two events, he heard from Jenkin Lloyd Jones. We do not have Jones's letter, but Janson's reply indicates that the secretary had some misgivings about Janson's hiring the largest hall in the city to attract great crowds, most of whom attended out of curiosity. He seems to have felt too that any further pillorying of the Norwegian Synod was unproductive, that Janson could be better employed emphasizing the constructive aspects of his mission.

"Thank you for your kind advice," Janson began in his reply of Monday, December 19. "I will try to get so sagacious as possible and behave as a 'business man' in all regards. Though I do not like serpents at all, I will nevertheless be 'as wise as the serpent and harmless as a dove.'" Yet, though he was willing to be counseled, he wanted Jones to know that he had been prudent in his management and by no means neglectful of the real purpose of his mission. As long as people continued to come, he had to have a place large enough to accommodate them. Daytime rental of Harrison Hall was ten dollars, but there had been no difficulty meeting expenses. Rent for the mass meeting had been paid from proceeds of his lecture on the Norwegian Synod; for the two following Sundays, friends had offered to assume the burden; and thereafter he planned to take up a collection to cover costs. He went on to say that at least Norwegians knew he was in the city. "I have been reported, that the Norwegians do not speak about other things now, whether they meet one another on the street, in the shops or in the saloons. The worst thing is I have abolished the eternal hell; they cannot dispense with their pet child. I have been very careful in my utterances, trying not to frighten them away." Then, as if to reassure Jones, he summarized his sermon of the day before:

"Yesterday I spoke of 'God is love.' I took my starting point from the beautiful story of Elias when he stares for the Lord

155

in the sturm [*sic*] and the earthquake and the consuming fire —
but the Lord was not there. And then came a mild breeze, and
the prophet covered his head for the Lord was near him. With
short pencil strokes I painted to them the development of the
Jewish opinions of their Jehova[h], first as a Sun-God, then
as a War-God and the God of their nationality til [*sic*] the idea
reached its highest top in Jesus Christ who taught 'the father
in heaven.' That was one of the reasons, I said, why there is
such a confusion in my countrymen's reading in the Bible and
in their religious opinions, that they do not make any difference between the Jewish God and the Christian God. I showed
them, how that is to disgrace God to tell that he sends famine
and pestilence and war, etc. as special punishments upon us,
how such an opinion is reminiscent from olden times, when
they stared for God in the sturm, in the earthquake, and in
the consuming fire. I showed them, how all suffering here on
earth are brought by the humanity over the humanity, but the
blessings, which sprout from the sufferings are his, our father's, and advised them to trust upon him as the boundless
mercy and charity."

Several staunch synod men had been in the audience, yet
Janson was told that on their way out they had remarked that
they could see nothing harmful in what he had said. "May I
not then have been sagacious, Brother Jones?" he asked, a bit
slyly. He said he expected to hold his next service on Christmas Day, and on the following day preach in Fort Dodge,
Iowa. Enclosing four photographs of himself, he asked that
Jones keep one and distribute the others to the rest of the
clergymen who had taken part in his ordination.[40]

On the same day that Janson wrote this letter, Anderson
sent one off to Bjørnson. Still relishing the fact that he had
been "right all along," he reported that Janson was assured of
a salary of $2,000 a year from the American Unitarian Asso-
ciation. On this point, however, Anderson was overstating the
case. True enough, the salary was to become a reality and the

[40] Janson to Jones, December 19, 1881.

professor's statement may only reflect his confidence in Janson's ultimate success. Janson had no such assurance: he was going through a trial period of six months, for which he was to be paid $1,000, and although, as it turned out, subsequent support was to be forthcoming, the understanding was that the American Unitarian Association would continue this only until Janson's congregations became large enough to bear their own burdens. Yet Anderson was in no mood for qualification. Janson was doing wonderfully, he reported, better than all expectations. He would get congregations in Minneapolis, Madelia, and Fort Dodge. "The struggle with the synod will be a life-and-death one, but he is on top. Attacks on him have already started in a thousand ways, and there is the same irresponsibility and bitterness in the attacks as those on you last year." [41]

A newspaper article that Anderson seems to have found especially "irresponsible" had appeared in *Fædrelandet og Emigranten* on December 6, characterizing the Unitarians as a small sect of about 17,960 people. Anderson, in a letter to *Budstikken* published December 20, 1881, declared the estimate to be patently false. Acknowledging that he had not the exact figures, he said he would judge the number to be nearer 300,000, and, more than that, they included the most gifted and distinguished citizens of the United States. To illustrate, he listed an impressive array of presidents, poets and novelists, historians, clergymen, teachers, and philanthropists, concluding with a suggestion that he found men of distinction and Unitarians to be virtually identical:

"To the Norwegian people in America I have only this to say: Watch out for the talented, worthy, popular, great poet and speaker, Kristofer Janson. If you allow yourselves to be led astray by him, you may find yourselves, on the other side of the grave, with the men and women I have named in this article, and among them you will also find Milton, Locke,

[41] Anderson to Bjørnson, December 19, 1881.

Macaulay, and James Martineau from England. A dangerous society, is it not?" [42]

At Christmas Janson received gifts from the Andersons and Miss Woodward; he was the dinner guest of Dr. and Mrs. Karl Bendeke. At his service on Christmas Day (which in 1881 fell on a Sunday) an incident occurred that incensed his friends. As *Budstikken* described it, three persons attended who obviously did not belong there. One was a Swede, the other two, Norwegians — one of the latter so staunch a synod man that he did not send his children to the public school. During the sermon he and his Swedish friend kept up a lively conversation in spite of repeated remonstrances from Janson. At one point they walked out but returned shortly, continuing to make comments. Finally when another person went out as if to summon the police, the men became frightened and left. Such conduct was inexcusable, Jaeger declared, warning that if such an incident was repeated, he would publish the names of the offenders. [43]

On January 2, 1882, a month after Janson had arrived in the city, he organized the Free Christian Church of Minneapolis. (Four years later, after it had erected its own building, it became known as Nazareth Church.) As congregation records are not available, the exact number of charter members is not known, but in February Janson wrote Anderson that he had thirty-four, some of them men with families. [44] The immediate result was that on the following Sunday, January 8, the time of the services was shifted from afternoon to the conventional morning hour. Attendance dropped from the great numbers he had been drawing at afternoon meetings, but it was still much larger than the actual membership count would indicate, ranging throughout the winter and early spring from two to four hundred people — the fluctuation, according to Janson, depending on the weather. [45]

[42] *Budstikken*, December 20, 1881.
[43] *Budstikken*, December 27, 1881.
[44] Janson to Anderson, February 9, 1882.
[45] Janson, in *Christian Register*, June 22, 1882.

Certainly some who attended Janson's church services, not only in the early days of his ministry but later, too, were there to see the man. This is mentioned not only in memoirs but also in the immigrant fiction of the period; one of the first things a Norwegian newcomer did on arriving in the city was go to hear Janson. Yet the sermons were memorable in themselves — rich in imagery, with illustrations drawn from all places and all times. Sometimes they had evocative titles ("When Will the Day Come?" "How Wonderful to Be a Human Being!") Luth Jaeger found one, "Our Leading Stars," magnificent and published it in *Budstikken*.[46]

Many testified to the comfort they derived from Janson's sermons. Those cited here occurred after the period of Janson's trial ministry, but are typical. In 1935 U. H. Lindelie wrote in *Decorah Posten* about his early life. During a brief stay in Minneapolis before he went to take up a homestead, he heard Janson preach a sermon, "Jacob's Struggle with God," in which he enlarged on the injured Jacob's refusal to give up until he had received the blessing. Almost fifty years after hearing the sermon, Lindelie said it was still fresh in his memory and that many times in his life as a farmer, combating the forces of nature, he had been tempted to quit, but he had remembered the theme of the sermon— not to surrender until he had received the blessing. In 1890 Oscar Gundersen, the self-taught immigrant writer and scholar of Chicago, wrote a perceptive article on Janson. He had only faint praise for him as a writer; he found his theology anachronistic; and in his judgment Janson had no real understanding of the physical sciences nor, for that matter, of history. Yet when Janson rose to speak, all this was forgotten. Instead, one sensed his kindliness and deep sincerity; the listener became morally uplifted and, close to tears, found his thoughts drifting to the Son of Man, who had urged men to love one another.[47]

[46] The sermon is included in Janson's *Lys og frihed*, 70–78 (Minneapolis, 1892).
[47] U. H. Lindelie, "Nogle erindringer og betragtninger," in *Decorah-Posten*, May 31, 1935; Oscar Gundersen, "Kristofer Janson," in *Minneapolis Tidende*, August 17, 1890.

Early in January, 1882, Janson was the victim of a trick which aroused considerable resentment in the Norwegian community. One morning a man invited him to take part in a program given by a young people's literary society. The group, according to the caller, had been organized by the Norwegian Synod pastor, the Reverend Ole P. Vangsness, but it was open to anyone who cared to join. As Janson explained later, he was pleased to hear of the organization; he thought it fine to have a society in which Norwegian young people, regardless of church affiliation, could meet. Ordinarily, on the evening in question, Janson attended a literary group organized by Henry M. Simmons, but he said he would gladly forego that. The caller asked what subject Janson would choose to speak on, saying that programs were to be printed. When Janson said he needed time to make a choice, the two agreed that "Reading by Kristofer Janson" would serve. On leaving, the visitor said he would give this information immediately to Dr. Prydz, chairman of the program committee.

When Janson entered the hall on the evening of the meeting, one of the first persons he met was Pastor Vangsness, who greeted him courteously, but, as Janson later recalled, seemed somewhat surprised to see him. No printed programs were in evidence; instead Dr. Prydz announced each number. As the evening wore on, and one selection followed another, Janson began to feel apprehensive. Finding an opportunity to speak to the chairman, he asked when he could expect to be called upon. Jocosely Dr. Prydz answered him, "Your turn will come next Sunday!" Stung, Janson found his way back to his seat; someone helped him with his coat, and he left the hall. Recounting all this in *Budstikken*, Janson concluded the tale of his humiliation somewhat bitterly, "I hope none of the righteous men and women who remained contracted a disease as a result of having so dangerous a person in their presence for a few hours." [48]

Exactly who was responsible for the trick seems never to

[48] *Budstikken*, January 10, 1882.

have been ascertained. Dr. Prydz later stated that he did not know that Janson had been invited, adding that he considered his refusal to allow him to speak justified "on Christian grounds." The matter enlivened the columns of *Budstikken* for several weeks. One correspondent, signing himself "En Bondegut" (A Farm Lad) found Dr. Prydz's excuse a lame one. It was impossible, he declared, for the committee to be unaware that Janson had been invited. Yet even had that been the case, Dr. Prydz knew that Janson had been in the hall for several hours before he made his inquiry, and then, the writer declared angrily, the doctor's rude retort had been made on "synod grounds" rather than "Christian." Somewhat later, Peter J. Hilden wrote from Montevideo, commending "En Bondegut" for his letter and implying that it was high time for the Norwegian farmers to forget their subservience to the "better classes" and act independently. "Better conditions are in store for Norwegian Americans," he prophesied. "We have Kristofer Janson, who has studied us well. . . . I give you this advice: Don't be afraid to hear Janson or others." To this he added a bristling statement: "I am the son of a *husmand*. Some may think I have no right to express an opinion, but I certainly have."[49]

The greatest impact of the incident was felt by the literary society itself. A strong faction insisted that an apology be sent Janson. When, after several meetings given over to stormy debate, one was not forthcoming, the group withdrew to form a rival society which they called "Fram" (Forward). An active organization from the first, it frequently invited Janson to take part in its programs.[50]

Humiliating as Janson had found the incident, he was soon to have a gratifying experience of a different sort. On January 10, 1882, negotiations came to a head with the already organized congregation in rural Brown County. Janson became the minister of what was thereafter to be known as the Nora Free

[49] *Budstikken*, February 21, April 4, 1882. A *husmand* is a tenant farmer.
[50] Hansen, *My Minneapolis*, 58.

Christian Church. What perhaps makes the history of this congregation unique is that up to the moment when the parishioners met the man who was to be their preacher, their sole intent was to continue as Lutherans.[51]

This group had been part of the Lake Hanska Lutheran Church. In the summer of 1881, months before Janson arrived in this country, they broke away, saying that they could no longer tolerate the bitter dissension that characterized congregational meetings. Presumably several issues were at stake, but one of them centered about who should be permitted burial in the church cemetery. In August the seceding members met in a local schoolhouse and organized an independent congregation. Shortly afterward they drew up a constitution and elected officers, with Johannes Mo as president. From time to time in the months that followed, they invited a Lutheran minister from another synod to preach (the Lake Hanska Church had belonged to the Norwegian Synod), but were always refused. At one time they considered writing the university in Christiania for a theological candidate, but gave that up for financial reasons. In December they read of Janson's ordination. Many of them had heard Janson lecture in near-by Madelia less than two years before, when he gave an address on peasant reform in Norway that so captivated the audience that at the end they gave three rounds of cheers for Kristofer Janson and Bjørnstjerne Bjørnson. In December, 1881, the Brown County group, somewhat uncertain what to make of Janson's Unitarianism, had instructed Mo to write him, sending their constitution.[52] In return, Janson sent them a cordial but guardedly worded letter.

When Janson faced the congregation on that January day, the time for reticence was over. "I told them openly and honorably where I stood, making it clear I was opposed to the

[51] Ole Jorgensen, "Speech at the Laying of the Cornerstone of Nora Church Parsonage, June 24, 1906," in *Nora fri-kristne menighed*, 21 (Hanska, Minnesota, 1906), a twenty-fifth anniversary pamphlet. "Nora" is a symbolic term for Norwegian.

[52] *Budstikken*, April 11, 1882.

kind of preaching to which they had been accustomed." Watching his auditors as he spoke, Janson noticed from time to time that men would nudge and eye one another, nod and smile. When he had finished, some of them declared that on many issues they had long felt much as he did, but had never dared say so openly. They found it easy to relinquish dogmas of the Trinity, the verbal inspiration of the Bible, and the existence of hell, but some found it impossible to give up their faith in the divinity of Christ. These Janson comforted by saying that they not only should but *must* continue to believe it if it seemed to them to be the truth. Before the meeting ended Janson was asked to revise the written constitution; this and other practical matters were completed shortly. In February Janson wrote Anderson that he had forty voting members and twenty-five children under eighteen. The "peasants," however, as he still called those living in farming areas, were poor and could not pay their minister much. Several non-members in the neighborhood pledged support, but even then he could expect no more than $140 to $150 a year.[53]

In the months that followed, the congregation was bitterly assailed, but stood its ground, with Johannes Mo acting as chief spokesman. Much of the opposition apparently came from the immediate neighborhood of the church. Thus, shortly after Nora Church was organized, when *Budstikken* announced that Janson had preached and lectured in Madelia and Waseca and started a congregation in the former, M. Olsen wrote to reprove the editor, denying that such a church had been established. Unitarianism, he said, was a bloody pillow under the sleeping head. Then, wrathfully mixing his metaphors, he added, "I hope this dangerous teaching will not throw dust in the eyes of our countrymen. *Budstikken* would do well not to champion a movement aimed at destroying Christianity." Luth Jaeger, unrepentant, admitted that he had erred about the location of the congregation: "It was one in

[53] Janson, *Hvad jeg har oplevet*, 207; Janson to Anderson, February 9, 1882.

the vicinity of Madelia which had the honor of calling Janson as its minister." [54]

In January, 1882, *Evangelisk Lutherske Kirketidende*, official organ of the Norwegian Synod, reprinted a section of an article by Janson, his account of the shortcomings of the synod that had originally appeared in *Unity*. Accompanying the excerpt was an editorial statement that no comment was necessary, the implication being that the charges were preposterous. Yet, at the same time similar criticism of the synod was being aired in the *Critic*, when Hjalmar Hjorth Boyesen, long a foe of the Norwegian Synod, published an article on Janson. After sketching his career as a writer, a pioneer in the *landsmaal* movement, and a teacher in the Norwegian folk school, Boyesen said that Janson was merely transferring his work to a new field — the Middle West — where the Norwegians needed enlightenment:

"They are sorely in need of the liberalizing influence of just such a man as Mr. Janson, having been too long shut off from intellectual contact with the Nineteenth Century by their 'evangelical' Norse Lutheran Synod. It speaks very poorly in fact for the culture and intellectual status of the Norwegians that they have allowed themselves to be ruled so long by a corporation which would find its proper place in a museum of antiquarian remains. It is the soul-paralyzing tyranny of this body of clergymen that Janson is endeavoring to break, apparently with encouraging success." [55]

Janson was succeeding far beyond his expectations. He had lectured in St. Paul and Lake Park in Minnesota and La Crosse, Wisconsin. Subscription lists for the support of his work were circulating in Eau Claire and La Crosse, besides several in Minneapolis, and he had recently received $112 from Dodge City, Iowa. All of this he mentioned in a letter to Anderson. If his letters to the professor frequently mentioned money, it must be remembered that at the time he was wholly

[54] *Budstikken*, January 31, 1882.
[55] *Evangelisk luthersk kirketidende*, January 13, 1882; *Critic* (New York), January 14, 1882.

self-supporting, having as yet received no payment from the American Unitarian Association. Through Anderson, lists also circulated in Madison.[56]

Grateful though Janson was for the professor's help, he came to realize that at times Anderson's patronage was a mixed blessing. Long before Janson arrived in the United States, Anderson had become involved in a bitter feud with Halle Steensland, a businessman in Madison, over the latter's candidacy for secretary of state in Wisconsin. After a series of acrimonious exchanges in the newspapers, Steensland sued Anderson for libel. Anderson had called upon his friends for support. John A. Johnson in Madison and Bjørnson in Norway both wrote articles, and Janson, after his arrival in America, wrote an account for a newspaper in Norway. Since Steensland was known to be a strong supporter of the Norwegian Synod, Anderson represented himself as the liberal champion engaged in a desperate struggle against orthodox tyranny, publicly appealing to those who sympathized with him to send ten-cent contributions for his defense. While many did so, cooler heads among the liberals (Luth Jaeger, for instance) disapproved of Anderson for having started the feud in the first place. Steensland, for his part, bitterly resented the interference of Bjørnson and Janson; shortly after the latter's ordination, he reproved him sharply in *Norden*, concluding bluntly, "Mind your own business, Reverend Sir, and let those who have not bothered you live in peace."[57]

After the turn of the year, the dispute having become increasingly bitter, Steensland turned more of his attention to Janson. On February 9 Janson wrote plaintively to Anderson:

"And what to say about that story with Halle Steensland! I very seldom felt myself so like a wet rooster as on that occasion. I had myself drawn my formidable sword defending you and now *quil bruit pour une omelette*. That was the little mouse, the mountain brought forth after all woes and throes

[56] Janson to Anderson, February 9, 1882.
[57] *Norden* (Chicago), November 20, 1881.

in the newspapers and the ten cent subscription and the boasting of your lawyers. The result of all is, that he now threatens me with libel suit too! He has written several letters to me and promised that my expressions in the article to 'Verdens Gang' shall cause me trouble." [58]

Fortunately, by the time Janson wrote this letter the matter had already been settled out of court when Anderson made a public apology in *Skandinaven* on February 24, 1882. And Janson, worried though he might have been, had not let the matter interfere with his work. Shortly after the organization of his Minneapolis congregation, he announced that he would give a series of weekly readings from literature. Because of difficulties in finding an evening when Harrison Hall was available, these did not begin until January 23, when Janson read the first part of his *Fante Anne* (Gipsy Anne) before an audience said to be as large as the hall would hold. [59]

These readings were to be a part of Janson's program during all the years he remained in America, and the legend of their excellence still lingers. The late Mrs. Marie Stoep of Minneapolis declared she had never known anything to be so interesting, adding, "We could hardly wait from week to week." Miss Borghild Lee of Seattle reported that her mother, who had been an immigrant in Minneapolis in the eighties, said that on Mondays her work began at four in the morning, but even so she could not forego hearing Janson's reading the evening before. [60]

Sometimes it was the readings alone that drew people to Janson. A farmer living on the northern outskirts of the city, disgusted with the controversies taking place among the Norwegian Lutherans, steadfastly refused to go near Janson, whom he regarded as "another troublemaker." Finally, in the winter of 1888, to entertain a visiting relative, he attended

[58] Janson to Anderson, February 9, 1882. On the Steensland-Anderson dispute, see Lloyd Hustvedt, *Rasmus B. Anderson: Pioneer Scholar*, 171 (Northfield, 1966). A loose translation of the French words would be, "What a noise over one omelet!"

[59] *Budstikken*, February 7, 1882.

[60] Interviews with Mrs. Stoep and Miss Lee, spring and summer, 1960.

one of the readings and his hostility vanished. "Father came home a different man," his son reported. "He said he had never heard anything like it, and after that he couldn't get enough of Kristofer Janson." In 1892 the Reverend Axel Lundeberg, a graduate of the University of Uppsala in Sweden and a Unitarian colleague of Janson's, wrote in the *North*: "As a reciter Janson is masterly. Indeed, it may truthfully be said that in that field he can fully cope with America's most prominent readers, and he surpasses everything which ordinarily is offered here in the West." [61]

The reviews that appeared in *Budstikken* glowed with the same enthusiasm. Through the years Janson offered not only the plays of Ibsen, Bjørnson, and other Norwegian writers, but the works of De Maupassant, Zola, and even Shakespeare. Obviously these could not be read coldly from the text to an untutored audience. From the brief comments Janson has made to Anderson, we glimpse something of his procedure. First he sketched in the background, pointing up the lines of essential conflict, and then throughout the reading he made whatever interpolations were necessary to bring the material within the experience of his audience.

Throughout February Janson's work went on with encouraging success. *Unity*, commenting on the growth of the two new Unitarian churches in Minneapolis, observed that St. Paul had better watch lest Minneapolis eclipse it and become the cathedral city of Unitarian Minnesota. Professor Anderson, beguiled because Janson was not getting more opposition from the orthodox, wrote exultantly to Bjørnson:

"What's so amusing is that the synod is in the midst of a great struggle within its own ranks on the predestination issue, a fight that is driving people out of the synod and will eventually divide them a thousand ways. They are so absorbed in this internal quarrel that they have wholly forgotten Janson, who takes one province after the other from them. In the Con-

[61] Axel Lundeberg, "Kristofer Janson and His Work," in *North* (Minneapolis), May 11, 1892.

ference things are not better. They are fighting over something they call the issue of professors' salaries and go at one another like mad dogs." [62]

Yet, if Janson was escaping attack from official quarters, Nora congregation was feeling the wrath of laymen and clergy alike. Late in March, Johannes Mo wrote to *Budstikken*, recounting the history of the church and pleading that Norwegians in America live and let live. From the time the group had left Lake Hanska Church they had been barraged with slander and abuse on every side, even from pulpits. They had been called mockers of God, a rotten congregation, freethinkers. Attacks had appeared in *Nordvesten* in St. Paul, in *Norden* and *Skandinaven* in Chicago. A letter in the last-named paper, bearing the signature of a neighbor in Brown County, had berated Mo and Ole Serumgaard for being leaders of a congregation served by Janson, who was undermining Christianity. No one, Mo went on, need speak for Janson, who was fully able to defend himself. Instead of destroying, however, he devoted himself to raising the downtrodden and righting what was wrong and false. In his last sermon, Janson, knowing the calumny people had endured, had urged them to be patient, not to repay evil with evil. Mo, for his part, was not ashamed of his function in the congregation, but was proud of the confidence others had placed in him.

The writer of the letter to *Skandinaven* had said that the group left the Lake Hanska Church because of a dispute over the graveyard. Mo, insisting that this was only one issue, explained that Nora Church was going to have its own burial ground, and in it anyone, regardless of creed, might bury his dead. Even Norwegian Synod ministers who had denied that privilege to those who had left their congregations might find a final resting place there. Expressing doubt that the neighbor was actually the author of the *Skandinaven* letter but had allowed his signature to be affixed to one composed by another, Mo spoke of his regret that an old friendship should be severed

[62] *Unity*, February 16, 1882; Anderson to Bjørnson, February 17, 1882.

168

in such a manner, and ended by appealing for better relations: "You better-thinking men of Lake Hanska, Linden, Madelia, and Butternut Valley congregations — Norwegians, near and far — leave fanaticism and hate and live together in peace and charity." [63]

In March Janson was making plans to wind up his affairs in Minneapolis temporarily so that he could go back to Norway and get his family. Early in the month he received a letter from Jenkin Lloyd Jones asking him to take part in the Western Conference convention, to be held in Cleveland early in May. Somewhat bewildered by American practices, Janson replied:

"What do you mean by 'devotional exercises'? Do you mean only a short prayer, or a prayer and a short sermon? or what? What I wish to do at the meeting is *to read a paper about the Scandinavians and the Scandinavian movement.* Will that be permitted instead of any platform speech? You must think upon, that I am a foreigner and can not move in the English language like a fish in water. Please answer these questions, and I shall then decide what to do at the meeting. I should like rather to be a listener than a speaker on that occasion." [64]

Jones's reply did not wholly satisfy him. When Janson wrote again on March 20, he was still concerned with what kind of topics might be of interest to the convention and asked Jones's opinion on "Do We Christians Always Treat Our Adversaries Fairly?" as a subject. He had questions about how long it took to get to Cleveland from Chicago and where the other ministers were staying, saying he would very much like to have company. Yet, more than that, he was wondering when he was going to be paid, being badly pressed for money. He had sent off his report to the American Unitarian Association sometime before, channeling it through Jones, whom he knew to be a busy man. As he visualized Jones's desk, need took precedence over delicacy:

[63] *Budstikken*, April 11, 1882.
[64] Janson to Jones, March 12, 1882. Italics are Janson's.

"And what shall I think of the Unit. Assoc. in Boston? I have not received a single cent yet, and now we have the 20th of March. What makes me impatient is, that I have not been able to send a cent for the support of my family in Norway, and my wife has been obliged to borrow money. Now she will start for the western part of the country with the children in the last part of April for the purpose of taking farewell with her old father, and she needs money for that journey. And it takes three weeks before a letter reaches her from here. You are sure you have forwarded the report, brother Jones, so that it has not been hidden among your many papers? Excuse my question." [65]

Sometime before his departure from Minneapolis in the spring, Janson received what came to be known as the "salt pork letter." The anonymous sender had mailed it from Lanesboro, Minnesota, addressing it to "Rev. Kristofer Janson," and enclosing a piece of meat. Punning on the abbreviation for "reverend" (in Norwegian *rev* is the word for fox), the writer said that Janson had acquired his rightful title. He was sending the morsel in the hope that it would satisfy the fox who had come to devour the cock on the church steeple, and failing in that, was trying to undermine the church with its claws.

Janson forwarded the letter to friends in Lanesboro. On April 18 a statement appeared in *Budstikken* saying that the friends had only contempt for the sender and hoped that Janson would not think such boorishness characteristic of the Norwegians in that locality. They promised to try to find the culprit, but it was not until the middle of May, when Janson was on his way to Norway, that they openly accused someone. Using ruses, they had written to several persons they regarded as suspect, and compared the handwriting of the replies with that of the anonymous letter. The man they charged was a teacher and a choir member of a Lutheran congregation in the vicinity. Luth Jaeger also examined the letters and found

[65] Janson to Jones, March 20, 1882.

the writing similar, but, characteristically, he offered the accused an opportunity to defend himself in *Budstikken*, and shortly afterward, he did. The man denied any knowledge of the "salt pork letter," but much of his communication was given over to a denunciation of the investigators, saying that they had brought no honor upon themselves by using such a "Jesuitical trick." He was forced to face trial, and although *Budstikken* did not give the final outcome of the case, Janson has stated that the man was forced to leave the community.[66]

Before Janson left, he was assured that his report had, indeed, reached Boston. The *Christian Register*, reporting the monthly meeting of the American Unitarian Association, spoke of the full and striking account received from "a new laborer in a new field, Rev. Kristofer Janson, our missionary to the Scandinavians in the States of the Northwest," who had already gathered five or six little congregations. Since there were only two formally organized churches, the others may have been places where Janson's subscription lists circulated and where he hoped to establish permanent organizations.[67]

En route to Cleveland Janson had stopped off in Madison, where he preached in the Unitarian church, something Anderson regarded as noteworthy, as it indicated Janson's increased confidence in his use of English. He picked up an American flag to be presented as Professor Anderson's gift to Bjørnson when the latter commemorated the twenty-fifth anniversary of the publication of his *Synnøve Solbakken* the following summer.[68]

Whatever fears Janson may have had about appearing before the convention seem to have been groundless. The *Christian Register*, reporting how he conducted the devotional service, said his opening prelude had been "like a bit of Norse poetry, made especially winning by the foreign accent and gentle speech." Janson had told a legend about a

[66] Janson, *Hvad jeg har oplevet*, 251.
[67] *Christian Register*, April 13, 1882.
[68] Anderson to Bjørnson, April 18, 1882.

contest among birds to choose as their king the one that could fly the highest. The eagle was expected to win, but just before it took wing, the smallest bird perched on its back and was borne up higher than the eagle, to become king. God's love was like the flight of the eagle, Janson said, adding that he would like to be like the little bird, looking down upon the world in the light of God's love. *Unity* reported that Janson had delivered two papers, one on tolerance (presumably a development of his idea on treating adversaries fairly), and another on the Scandinavians in America. Both, the editor said, were worthy of the author of *The Spellbound Fiddler,* and remarked that Janson's accented speech added to the attractiveness of his address. "Under any circumstances we should have admired the fine thought and nice diction but with the speaker's gracious smile and quaint pronunciation added thereto they become altogether fascinating." Even the handwritten minutes of what seems to have been a business meeting mention Janson. The secretaries recorded that when the Reverend Grendall Reynolds, secretary of the American Unitarian Association, spoke, he emphasized the work being done among the Scandinavians by Kristofer Janson.[69]

Clearly, Janson had stimulated considerable interest in his work. His paper, "The Scandinavians in America," was published in the *Christian Register* in three installments, beginning June 22, 1882. The first two, written in a lucid, interesting style, were largely background material for the third, which discussed Janson's activities since his arrival in Minneapolis the preceding December. Thus the first part dealt with the poverty that induced most emigrants to leave their homeland, the localities where they had mainly congregated, and their efforts to improve their standard of living. The Scandinavians in America had two enemies, Janson declared, the bottle and the priest. Often the hardships of their life in Norway (those of fishermen, for example) had led them to alcohol.

[69] *Christian Register*, May 11, 1882; *Unity*, May 16, 1882; Western Unitarian Conference, Minutes of the Twenty-eighth Annual Meeting, May 4, 1882, filed in Abraham Lincoln Center, Chicago.

In America the practice of standing treat in saloons encouraged drunkenness. The priests gave their people no outside interests, but held the fear of hell over them. They were not cruel men, but they felt they must put aside human considerations when acting in an official capacity. The immigrants came to this country with great reverence for the Bible and a deep respect for the clergyman's learning. "It will be years before the yoke is broken," Janson prophesied. "The opposition already has its martyrs and I my predecessors." In other words, it was dangerous to contend with the Norwegian Synod.

The second installment of the paper dealt with the division of the Norwegian Lutherans into five synods, the church strife, and the restrictions imposed on parishioners by the Norwegian Synod — matters Janson had discussed in *Unity* in December, 1881. Underlying the third part, Janson's activities, lies a philosophy which today is often spoken of as the Protestant ethic: the assumption that hard work and a careful husbandry of one's resources inevitably bring success. In colorful, specific detail Janson recounted his experiences, beginning with his first lecture and going on to tell how he used the proceeds to hire the largest hall in Minneapolis for his mass meeting. With wry humor he described both the old woman who brandished the catechism and the old man who belatedly realized that the devil was tempting him, and then told of those who had welcomed him and had formed the nucleus of his congregation. He mentioned the number of listeners he had preached to every Sunday, adding that he attracted more men than women. Yet he was confident that he would win the women too, for in his congregations they had the same rights as men. He spoke of his evening readings from literature, where, although no admission was charged, a collection was taken. From this and from the contributions at his Sunday services, he had covered his expenses.

He gave a poignant account of his Brown County congregation. Because the farmers were saddled with heavy mortgages and their crops had been ravaged by grasshoppers, they could pay their minister only seventy dollars a year, but friends of the church had pledged an equal amount. The parishioners had difficulty finding a suitable meeting place. When they met in a small schoolhouse, the crowd overflowed and windows had to be kept open so those standing outside could hear. Sometimes they met in a grove, but that would not be pleasant in winter. They had bought an acre of ground on which they hoped to build a chapel. "But where to get the money?" They would need $1,500 to $2,000.

Janson spoke of his great attachment to this congregation; he had found many highly intelligent people among them. They knew nothing of Unitarianism, but wanted a gospel of love, comfort, and peace. Like the Minneapolis congregation, that of Brown County was known as a "free Christian church." Admitting frankly that he avoided the name "Unitarian," Janson said he did so partly because he did not like sect names, and partly out of discretion, adding, "I must be wise like the serpent." He closed with a direct appeal:

"I see a great and blessed work before me. I cannot fully enough thank the Unitarian Association for its valuable assistance, without which I had been unable to do what I have done. I feel assured the society will not withdraw its assistance until my young congregations can stand on their own feet."

Articles such as this made Janson something of a heroic figure to the American Unitarians and won for him such endearing epithets that were to appear in the *Christian Register* and *Unity* as "the brave singer from the North" and "our courageous poet-preacher." As for Janson, he was indeed grateful for the support he had received: His five months in the Middle West had caused him to find his vocation, a work more challenging and closer to his heart than either the *landsmaal* movement or the folk school. At least, that is what he seems to have implied in a farewell sent to Bjørnson when he was returning to America with his family: "I am now at the beginning of the real work of my manhood." [70]

[70] Janson to Bjørnson, August 13, 1882.

by ARLOW W. ANDERSEN

7   *Knut Hamsun's America*

IN THE 1880's a young Norwegian of great promise came to America. European writers had been sending their heroes and heroines abroad to realize their ambitions for a more expansive life, as Henrik Ibsen did with Lona Hessel in *Pillars of Society*. In the words of Hanna Astrup Larsen, whose analysis of Knut Hamsun's literary works appeared some forty years ago, Hamsun came not merely as an immigrant seeking his fortune. He sought opportunities for leading an independent existence and using his gifts. Having bruised himself on Old World littleness, he looked to the New World for bigger visions and for a saner estimate of a man's worth. Although he was destined to be disappointed, some of the things he sought were there.[1]

In 1920 Knut Hamsun was to receive the Nobel prize for literature. He produced many novels but left no memoirs. Fortunately, his son Tore has provided a remarkably complete account, in Norwegian, of his father. If a man's achievements are in large measure the outcome of his childhood ambitions and experiences, Knut Hamsun may well serve as an example. Originally called Knut Pedersen Hamsund, he was born August 4, 1859, into a tailor's family in Garmostræet, district of

[1] Hanna Astrup Larsen, *Knut Hamsun*, 20 (New York, 1922).

175

Arlow W. Andersen

Vaagaa, Gudbrandsdal. When he was about three the family moved northward to a *gaard* (farming estate) called Hamsund, in Hamarøy in Nordland, not far from the Lofoten Islands. The islands and the fisheries did not interest him, but he loved the woods and the mountains. At the age of nine he was sent away for five years, like a medieval apprentice, to the home of his maternal uncle, Hans Olsen. There he worked in a store and did odd jobs. It was a hard and trying period for the boy, living under the strict discipline of an eccentric relative.[2]

Young Hamsun remembered well a nation-wide revival that eventually reached Nordland. Leading the drive for souls was Pastor Lars Oftedal of Stavanger, depicted by some as a bearded champion from Vestlandet (the West Country). Hans Olsen was gripped, and Knut became the object of his concern. In an issue of *Dagbladet* (Christiania), of 1889, the year before Hans Olsen died, Hamsun expressed his disdain for Oftedal, for his uncle, and for the spirit that they personified. He felt that his childhood had been blighted by their influence. Knut finally fled to his native community in Gudbrandsdal, where he worked in a store for a year and was confirmed in the Lutheran faith. He never was reconciled with his uncle. He learned to grit his teeth, says his son, a lesson that was to be useful in the coming years.[3]

Now about fifteen years of age, Hamsun made his way back to the family home in Hamarøy, where for the next five years, 1874–79, he had various jobs and assisted the local *lensmand* (sheriff). He also had the opportunity to do a bit of teaching. In the sheriff's home he encountered the works of Bjørnstjerne Bjørnson, Kristofer Janson, and others, and did not squander

[2] Tore Hamsun, *Knut Hamsun*, 7–24 (Oslo, 1959). See also Theodore Jorgenson, *History of Norwegian Literature*, 390 (New York, 1933); Larsen, *Knut Hamsun*, 12–15. The name of Christiania was changed to Oslo on January 1, 1925.

[3] Tore Hamsun, *Knut Hamsun*, 24–40. Lars Oftedal founded *Stavanger Aftenblad*, a low-church journal, in 1893. In 1891 he had lost his position as a state-church pastor; Per Thomsen, "Lars Oftedal," in Bernt Hjejle and Håkon Stangerup, eds., *Store norske journalister*, 40–47 (Copenhagen, 1957); Per Thomsen, present editor of *Stavanger Aftenblad*, to the author, February 20, 1964.

this opportunity to read. Nor was young Hamsun content until three of his minor romantic stories were accepted by printers in Tromsø and Bodø.[4]

With financial assistance from a wealthy merchant in Hamarøy, Knut next went southward to Hardanger. There he changed his name to Pedersen, which he thought more Norwegian. Later, in 1885, a printer inadvertently omitted the "d" from Hamsund. The young author thought the change a good one and retained it. His struggle for recognition as a literary light began when he was twenty-one; a Copenhagen publisher rejected a manuscript which he had presented in person, at considerable expense and inconvenience to himself. He returned to Norway and arranged to visit Bjørnson at Aulestad, his estate in Gudbrandsdal. The older bard read the spurned manuscript, then advised Hamsun not to write. As an alternative Bjørnson recommended him to Jens Selmer, foremost actor in Christiania, but the result was a few lessons in public speaking, nothing more. Hamsun did become an orator of distinction. When he once lectured on the Swedish playwright August Strindberg to a rather select audience of six, Johan Enger, editor of *Gjøviks Blad*, recorded it as one of the greatest experiences of his life.[5]

After a miserable winter in Christiania, 1879–80 (the basis of his novel, *Hunger*), Hamsun took to road construction work in eastern Norway, all the while feeling the irresistible pull of America. He had a friend whose mother had turned to Unitarianism, a movement said to have been introduced in Norway by Kristofer Janson. She encouraged Hamsun to prepare for the Unitarian ministry, but he preferred to see America.

[4] Tore Hamsun, *Knut Hamsun*, 44–46.

[5] Jorgenson, *Norwegian Literature*, 393; Tore Hamsun, *Knut Hamsun*, 45, 53–56, 61. Knut Hamsun (as Knut Pedersen Hamsund) published *Et gjensyn* (A Meeting Again) in Bodø in 1878. Later he became simply Knut Pedersen. The name changes are discussed in Harald Naess, "Knut Hamsun and Rasmus Anderson," in Carl F. Bayerschmidt and Erik J. Friis, eds., *Scandinavian Studies: Essays Presented to Henry Goddard Leach*, 269–277 (Seattle, 1965). According to Naess, Bjørnson advised Hamsun to drop the name Pedersen, but Anderson was the one who succeeded in getting him to do so. Hamsun disputed the influence of Anderson, who he thought was trying to dominate him. The change did occur, however, in the United States.

This time she provided the necessary funds. She was instrumental in securing from Bjørnson a letter of introduction addressed to Professor Rasmus B. Anderson of the University of Wisconsin. Thus in 1882, at the age of twenty-three, Hamsun departed for the first of two sojourns in America. Rasmus B. Anderson proved not to be hopeful of this newcomer. The professor of Scandinavian language and literature saw little potential in him as a poet and urged him to seek manual employment. Nor is there any evidence that Anderson encouraged Hamsun to take to lecturing. On one occasion, in 1883, Hamsun did speak in a small Wisconsin community and was greatly disappointed. Only four persons attended. Never had he seen so much drinking in a town. The people of this Norwegian center were devoid of thoughts and feelings.[6]

The years 1882–84, spent partly as a store clerk in Elroy, Wisconsin, and partly working in a lumberyard in Madelia, Minnesota, were boring to the young, impatient aristocrat. But there were brighter days. With the help of a schoolteacher, he improved his English. He heard and met Mark Twain and left the lecture hall favorably impressed with the humorist's natural style and his rapport with the audience. Kristofer Janson called on Hamsun in Madelia and persuaded him to go to Minneapolis to assist with his Unitarian congregation. There he was treated like a son in the Janson home. Mrs. Drude Krog Janson, gifted musically and a devotee of good literature, may have meant more to Hamsun in later life than Kristofer Janson himself. Meanwhile the young man busied himself translating items from English into Norwegian for his host, and with occasional talks in Unitarian meetings, though not specifically on religious topics.[7]

In the summer of 1884 Hamsun was told that he had devel-

[6] Tore Hamsun, *Knut Hamsun*, 62. Jorgenson indicates that the money was furnished by the father of Frøis Frøisland, the editor; *Norwegian Literature*, 394. For Hamsun's literary activities during his first visit to the United States, see John T. Flanagan, "Knut Hamsun's Early Years in the Northwest," in *Minnesota History*, 20:397–412 (December, 1939). See also Hamsun to Anderson, April 4, 1883, quoted in Lloyd Hustvedt, *Rasmus Bjørn Anderson: Pioneer Scholar*, 174 (Northfield, 1966).

[7] Tore Hamsun, *Knut Hamsun*, 73; Hustvedt, *Rasmus Bjørn Anderson*, 175.

oped tuberculosis, and he longed to return to Norway. Unitarian friends came to his aid with travel expenses. So concerned was he en route about his health that he often left the railroad coach, just behind the locomotive, to breathe fresh air, and on the sea, air was no problem. Surprisingly, his health was restored by the time he reached his native land. Probably the doctor's diagnosis had been an error. Hamsun explained, writing Rasmus B. Anderson in 1886, "You were right, Professor. I did not have tuberculosis, only a severe case of bronchitis." [8]

Before leaving for Aurdal in Valdres, Hamsun presented a letter of introduction from Kristofer Janson to Lars Holst, editor of *Dagbladet*. Holst promised to consider any literary contributions. Hamsun spent his days at the Hotel Frydenlund in Valdres. He soon published an article on Mark Twain in *Ny Illustrert Tidende* of Christiania. A meeting with Arne Garborg brought him no more encouragement than the earlier encounter with Bjørnson, although Garborg may have been impressed with Hamsun's style, which, he suggested, resembled that of the Russian novelist, Feodor Dostoevsky. Hamsun replied that he had never read Dostoevsky. He applied to *Aftenposten* (Christiania), edited by Amandus Schibsted, for a staff assignment, and was turned down. Occasionally Holst accepted an article. [9]

The restless Hamsun again visited the United States from 1886 to 1888. Through Holst he had been able to borrow money from a businessman of some culture. After settling down in Chicago he dispatched a long report about the journey which was published in *Dagbladet*. He sent a revealing letter, dated September 20, 1886, to his friend Erik Frydenlund in Valdres. He worked as a laborer for the Chicago streetcar system, he explained, and later he became a conductor on the horse cars. He was through with Schibsted of *Aftenposten*. Hamsun couldn't understand the man: he called him the most

[8] Hustvedt, *Rasmus Bjørn Anderson*, 175.
[9] Tore Hamsun, *Knut Hamsun*, 74–80.

peculiar editor in Christiania. Holst and Thommessen of *Verdens Gang* (Christiania) treated him kindly. When he returned to Norway he would write for their papers, doing his very best. Many years later Krøger Johansen, onetime editor of *Normanna* of Minneapolis, told of Hamsun's experiences as a streetcar conductor. Hamsun, who was nearsighted, miscalled streets in the darkness and had no sense of his whereabouts. So preoccupied was he with his thoughts, and sometimes with reading classics, that he would give the passengers the wrong change. Some of them rode free, thanks to his absent-mindedness. Company inspectors finally caught up with the poet turned conductor.[10]

Out of a job, Hamsun struck upon the idea of appealing in writing to the meat-packing king, Philip Armour, for a loan which he frankly stated he could not promise to repay. He took his simple request to the offices in the stockyards and submitted it to the doorman, with little hope of a favorable response. He could see Armour at his desk, busy with a mountain of papers. The doorman returned promptly with the requested twenty-five dollars. Hamsun, still not recovered from the shock, asked, absently, whether he had gotten the money. "Yes," smiled the man. "What did he say?" asked Hamsun. "He said that your letter was worth it." Hamsun then inquired whether he should go in and express his thanks. The messenger thought not; Armour might be annoyed. Hamsun declared later that he had little recollection of what he had written, but he knew that it was in poor English and that Armour's acceptance of it was an ironical gesture.[11]

With heart somewhat lightened, Hamsun proceeded from Chicago to North Dakota, where he worked on the bonanza farm of Oliver Dalrymple in the Red River Valley. In the fall of 1887 he went once more to his Unitarian friends in Minneapolis. By the spring of 1888 he was ready to return again to Norway, planning to raise the passage money through a fare-

[10] Tore Hamsun, *Knut Hamsun*, 81–84; no date is given for Hamsun's letter to *Dagbladet*. See also Flanagan, in *Minnesota History*, 20:403.
[11] Tore Hamsun, *Knut Hamsun*, 85.

well lecture. He reserved Dania Hall in Minneapolis, and before a packed house of Norwegian Americans delivered an attack upon the vaunted American freedom and upon American materialism, morals, and intellectual life. His sharp comments were to be the basis of a book, to be published after he reached Europe. His listeners were obviously amused, few of them having become rich in the promised land, but they found in Hamsun a spokesman for their own views. The lecture netted forty dollars; it was not enough for the return journey, but again friends came to the rescue.[12]

By a strange coincidence Hamsun met Rasmus B. Anderson aboard the Danish vessel "Thingvalla," to the surprise of both. Hamsun was playing cards at the time, gambling in a small way, with three male companions. Anderson, who had become minister to Denmark, remarked that he had thought Hamsun was dead! "And what became of you?" asked Hamsun. Anderson replied stiffly that he had been serving as his country's chief diplomatic representative in Copenhagen since 1885. Then, observing a black ribbon in Hamsun's lapel, he inquired, "Are you in mourning?" Hamsun explained that he was, not for a relative, but for the Haymarket anarchists. Professor Anderson was taken aback. Hamsun saw nothing further of him nor of Mrs. Anderson during the remainder of the voyage. So perturbed was the American minister over Hamsun's remark that he reported him to the captain as a dangerous person. Upon debarking in Copenhagen he alerted the police, and for several months Hamsun was shadowed day and night.[13]

[12] Tore Hamsun, *Knut Hamsun*, 86, 89. Hanna Astrup Larsen believes that Norwegian Americans were quick to resent any attack upon their adopted country; *Knut Hamsun*, 23. Carl G. O. Hansen attended the lecture; Hansen, *My Minneapolis*, 107 (Minneapolis, 1955). Hamsun tells of his farm experience in "The Prairie," in *Living Age*, 310:549 (August 27, 1921).

[13] Tore Hamsun, *Knut Hamsun*, 89–91. Anderson says he was responsible only for closing the American legation to Hamsun; *Life Story of Rasmus B. Anderson*, 317 (Madison, Wisconsin, 1917); see also Hustvedt, *Rasmus Bjørn Anderson*, 176. Haymarket Square, in Chicago, was the scene of a riot that occurred on May 4, 1886; a bomb thrown by an unknown person killed one man and injured more than sixty. In the ensuing turmoil, six police were killed and many persons injured. Four men were hanged as a result of the crime; Henry David, *The History of the Haymarket Affair*, 194 (New York, 1957).

In Copenhagen, a great cultural center, Hamsun rented a cheap room. Tore Hamsun states that his father had money enough to last only fourteen days with dinner, three weeks without dinner. Knut Hamsun then wrote the first chapters of his novel *Hunger*. There had to be an outlet for publication, so for two days he circled the home of Georg Brandes, the literary critic, hoping for a glimpse of the great man, perhaps even an interview. Eventually he approached him indirectly by calling on his brother Edvard, then editor of *Politikken* of Copenhagen. Hamsun left the manuscript with Edvard Brandes, who remarked to a friend, the Swedish author Axel Lundegaard, that Hamsun's face haunted him indescribably. There was something of Dostoevsky in it, he said, and like a fool he ran to the post office that very evening to send the emaciated man ten crowns. Edvard Brandes arranged to have *Hunger* published anonymously in *Ny Jord* (New Soil) of Copenhagen as a serial, beginning in November, 1888. *Ny Jord* had been carrying Hamsun's article, written in Minneapolis, on Kristofer Janson. Norwegian newspapers began to comment upon *Hunger*, struck by its sensational revelation of human agony and endurance, and they speculated about the identity of the author.[14]

Early in 1889 the student society of the University of Copenhagen invited Hamsun to speak. The lecture was mainly a revision of his farewell address in Minneapolis. P. Gustav Philipsen, a Danish printer, declared excitedly that he would like to publish it in an expanded form. So it developed that *Fra det moderne Amerikas aandsliv* (From the Intellectual Life of Modern America) appeared as a volume of 255 pages in Copenhagen in the spring of 1889. There is evidence, however, that Philipsen lacked enthusiasm for the final product. He felt that Hamsun had gone too far on some points, that he became hypercritical of many things American.[15]

[14] Tore Hamsun, *Knut Hamsun*, 93–95. Hamsun's novel *Sult* came out in New York in 1921 as *Hunger*. It was translated by George Egerton.

[15] Tore Hamsun, *Knut Hamsun*, 96. *Fra det moderne Amerikas aandsliv* (Copenhagen, 1889) was never translated into English, and in later years Hamsun did not wish it disseminated.

Hamsun's critical attitude was not an exceptional one. Other Norwegians had vented their displeasure toward American ways. Not all were so kind in their judgments as Kristofer Janson and Bjørnstjerne Bjørnson. For example, certain Norwegian journals repeatedly dwelt on unfavorable aspects of the United States. G. E. Kjeldseth, editor of *Tromsø Stiftstidende*, who in the early 1880's had published a letter from a correspondent who supported emigration, turned within a few years to discouraging it. On September 30, 1888, he published, besides a warning to Gentiles (non-Mormons) that they might be murdered by Mormons in Utah, a drab description of the boardinghouse life of the overworked American laborer. There appeared also in *Stiftstidende* a full report of a lecture given in Minneapolis by a Swedish-born lawyer, Johan Wilhelm Arctander, a Democrat turned Republican. In 1853, at the age of four, he had gone to live in Skien, Norway, and had emigrated to America in 1870. Economic conditions there were deplorable, he said. For this the low-tariff Democrats were to blame, yet they probably would be re-elected. Europeans should not sail for America; they could not live on universal suffrage alone. His words were repeated throughout Norway. Perhaps his readers there were not aware of his satirical and argumentative personality. At a Minneapolis political meeting in 1884 he had required police protection when he left the hall. He had taunted a Norwegian audience that was predominantly Democratic almost to the point of violence.[16]

Stavanger Amstidende og Adresseavis, edited by L. C. Kielland, Jr., published in two installments a lecture given in Christiania by Arctander, now returned from abroad. He complained of conditions in America as they had been portrayed by a man named Homme. There was more than one

[16] Asbjørn Olavson, "Er emigrationen til skade for vort land?" in *Tromsø Stiftstidende*, August 18, 1888; "Mormonisms vederstyggeligheder avsløret," in *Tromsø Stiftstidende*, Sundays and Thursdays, June 10–July 8, 1888. The latter articles were written by M. G. Montgomery, a Minneapolis clergyman, and translated into Norwegian by Pastor P. C. Tranberg of Chicago. For Arctander's lecture, see *Tromsø Stiftstidende*, September 20, 1888. It is discussed by Hansen in *My Minneapolis*, 140.

class in railroad travel, Arctander stated. Land still available for homesteads was far removed from population centers. Americans lacked a history, hence their literature and art were poorly developed. The theater was disappointing, in spite of its beautiful façade. The commercial angle was stressed. The press engaged in flights of sensationalism. Americans did not read books. At one time woman's rights had been the rage, now it was free love. There were some five hundred competing Christian sects. Preachers did not deliver sermons, as in Norway, but told stories. Norwegians in America celebrated May 17, the Norwegian national holiday, by drinking. Knud Madsen had the office of sheriff in Chicago, giving him the dubious honor of hanging the seven condemned anarchists, said to be guilty of murder in the Haymarket affair.[17]

Christian Friele's *Morgenbladet* (Christiania) joined the chorus of approval about Arctander's revelations. The speaker had mentioned confusion in American lawmaking. When the time allotted for a session ran out, the Senate or House clock was stopped to permit the completion of business. Some days two conflicting laws were under debate. Americans throve on excitement; just then it was temperance agitation. Only the immigrant trains were single class. Scandinavians had little influence in American politics. They had a reputation for drinking and carousing, and for clannishness. In 1889 *Morgenbladet* continued with an account of a shameful scene in the Senate, reminiscent of the Sumner-Brooks episode of prewar days. This time the incident was confined to the Senate committee on Indian affairs; there were dire threats, but nothing more violent occurred than an ear pulling. Chairman Chandler of New York was the victim, Senator Blackburn of Kentucky the aggressor.[18]

[17] *Stavanger Amstidende og Adresseavis*, October 29, November 2, 1888. Only four anarchists actually were hanged. See *ante*, note 13.

[18] *Morgenbladet* (Christiania), October 24, 1888, July 17, 1889. In May, 1856, Senator Charles Sumner of Massachusetts had denounced Andrew P. Butler of South Carolina in an antislavery speech. Subsequently, Preston Brooks, member of the House from South Carolina and a nephew of Butler, beat Sumner unconscious with a cane.

It should be mentioned that many, while entertained by Arctander's pointed remarks, accepted them with more than a grain of salt. Still others, like one immigrant in Minnesota, defended the United States. He complained to the editor of *Vestlands-Posten* about unwarranted allusions to murders in Texas and in New York saloons, far away from his own peaceful abode. Not everyone in America carried a revolver. Too many Norwegian journalists were getting false information from English or German sources. He deplored the scarcity of references to his adopted country in the Norwegian newspapers. Even the scant mention of the Civil War annoyed this patriotic immigrant. Although the American conflict had engaged more men and lasted longer than the Franco-Prussian War, European papers constantly discussed the latter. The correspondent had a good word for American democracy. In 1888, said he, ten million voters went to the polls, enough to cause Plato and political philosophers of succeeding centuries to turn in their graves! [19]

We now turn to Knut Hamsun's extended comments upon American intellectual and cultural manifestations. In fairness, it should be stated that he was only thirty, and extremely outspoken. In his later years he requested that there be no further dissemination of the opinions in *Amerikas aandsliv*. It is useful, however, to survey Norwegian press reactions to his observations, and to discover how seriously his words were accepted. We may assume that America was far from perfect. With that understanding, the outbursts of a young poet, of emotional rather than objective appraisal, may still have value.

In his book, expanding upon the two lectures delivered before the students in Copenhagen in 1889, Hamsun first berated the patriotism of Americans. No sooner did the bewildered European encounter the bustle and informality of the port of New York when he was treated to a parade,

[19] *Vestlands-Posten* (Stavanger), January 28, 1889. The letter, signed "N.R.T." filled three columns.

likely as not of war veterans. Americans showed hostility toward those who disagreed with them. Proud of their inventions, they thought that everything new originated in the United States. They were ignorant of affairs outside their country. The public school, extolled by some as an ideal, limited the study of geography and history strictly to America. In place of state-church influence in the classroom there was a religious orthodoxy that manifested itself in morning prayers, hymn singing, and Bible reading.[20]

Hamsun, sensitive to the treatment of aliens, observed that the Yankees called all Scandinavians Swedes. Congress was considering new immigration restrictions, for no good reason. There was plenty of land, and more laborers were needed. The only foreigners who commanded respect were the British. The power of the money aristocracy was strong, even in American journalism. Newspapers reflected American culture with stark realism. They were cluttered with this and that, including local news and sensational stories. They dealt seriously with politics only every fourth year. Hamsun found them unintelligent and uninteresting.[21]

Conceptions of freedom were not as simon-pure as Norwegian journals represented them to be. Editors in the homeland should see this at first hand. Freedom was lacking in many ways. Let a newspaper print an error about Congress and it was punished. An author who showed signs of European influence was silenced. Emile Zola's works were banned because of their alleged immorality. Little children were working in factories under conditions no better than those of slavery.[22]

In the matter of political theory, the ordinary American thought only of dynamite when he heard the word "anarchism." In the hanging of the Haymarket demonstrators the American-vaunted democracy and freedom proved as auto-

[20] *Amerikas aandsliv*, 1–8.
[21] *Amerikas aandsliv*, 10–18, 48.
[22] *Amerikas aandsliv*, 178.

cratic as any medieval despotism. An author who favored monarchy over republicanism would be run out of the country. To disavow any of George Washington's principles invited exile or execution. American freedom was freedom en masse, not freedom for the individual. The bomb thrower in the Haymarket riot of May 4, 1886, was not identified. But because five policemen were killed and two wounded, five anarchists were condemned to death and two were sentenced to life imprisonment. An eye for an eye! Practical American justice! Albert Parsons wasn't even present at the Haymarket meeting. To cap it all, a monument was raised, not to the spokesmen of the downtrodden, but to the fallen police.[23]

In Hamsun's opinion, no better illustration could be found to describe the American system of justice than the Haymarket case. People mainly of Europe's lowest type (referring no doubt to unenlightened immigrants) condemned to death some of America's most intelligent men, simply because intelligence was not understood by the howling mob. The *Police Gazette* was allowed to go through the mails, but not an anarchist paper. One could escape punishment for murder, political corruption, and swindling, but for proclaiming an unwelcome social philosophy the extreme penalty had to be paid. Yankees considered it smart to get away with a swindle. In the absence of extradition laws between Canada and the United States, crooked bank employees escaped into the dominion. Newspapers played up the successful criminal. Crime was coarse and baseless, seldom having an economic motive. More often the criminal simply wanted luxury in the way of fine clothing or elegant dining.[24]

Speaking of the public schools, Hamsun admitted that because America was a new country, composed of many na-

[23] *Amerikas aandsliv*, 183–187. In fact, seven policemen died, and many more were wounded. Albert Parsons, editor of an anarchist paper, was executed as a result of the riot.
[24] *Amerikas aandsliv*, 187–193.

tionalities, it represented an experiment in democracy on a vast scale. But he concluded that the great republic was a culture borrower nevertheless, and as rootless as were the fathers and grandfathers when they forsook Europe. It would be unnatural for Americans to be an enlightened lot. They had emigrated for economic reasons, and by the time they had achieved a degree of financial security they had lost the incentive to learn. Nor was the quality of education commensurate with the heavy costs of the public school system. The curriculum ignored Europe. The teaching schedule was often disregarded. Teachers told stories, but seldom dwelt long upon the abstract. True, American schools excelled in arithmetic and American history and geography, but arithmetic was turned to selfish and practical use in a materialistic society. Before a Yankee boy was very old, he know how to cheat a streetcar conductor! History dealt mainly with American war heroes. While the schools were not confessional, or related to the church, teachers nevertheless were inclined to draw morals from the subject matter rather than stay with the facts.[25]

In free-swinging style the young Hamsun also let fly, though more mildly, at church life in America, which was very active. Minneapolis had no less than 146 congregations of various denominations. Copenhagen, with about the same population, had only 29. American churches were well equipped, even ornate. Sermons had no more intellectual stimulus than in Norway, but were superior to the Norwegian in their combination of logic, down-to-earth speech, and practical illustrations. On Sunday evenings Hamsun sometimes chose church in preference to the theater. There he found entertainment (without cigar smoke) in the company of beautiful and well-dressed ladies. There was much social pressure to belong to the church and to contribute, and preachers had great influence in the community. But America's moral standard was basically monetary, even for church members.

[25] *Amerikas aandsliv*, 195–206.

In the opinion of Robert G. Ingersoll, the great agnostic and lecturer, religious freedom was limited to those with money.[26]

Hamsun proceeded to air his views on American women, who, he declared, had the power. They could practice free love without punishment or stigma. They could easily obtain divorces. Judges heard their pleas sympathetically and almost invariably believed their tales of woe. Without children or perhaps with one or two unwanted offspring, women had time to sit in church. Mothers preferred not to care for their infants personally, but employed nursemaids.[27]

Hamsun's concluding pages gave Yankee culture a rough going over. The American was familiar with English tunes and with formal etiquette, but basically he was still a creature of the prairies. He never became an aristocrat by temperament. In fact, the Civil War was waged to suppress the Southern aristocracy, not to free the slaves. Hamsun quoted Lepel Griffin in an 1884 issue of the *Fortnightly Review* of London: America was disappointing in its politics, literature, culture, and art, in its natural aspect, its towns, and their people! Hamsun's last words were a pessimistic reference to America's "dark sky." [28]

Among the more thorough reviews of Hamsun's *Fra det moderne Amerikas aandsliv* was an unsigned criticism in *Aftenposten*. It may have been written by Amandus Schibsted, the editor in whom Hamsun expressed so little confidence, or by a special literary editor. The reviewer mingled firmness with gentleness in his skillful appraisal of Hamsun's work. Hamsun's recent novel, *Hunger*, had attracted favorable attention, said he, especially among liberals. It was well constructed, despite some exaggerations. Yet it fell short of being a masterpiece, as some *venstre* (left or liberal) reviewers claimed it was. The present work, considered as a cultural contribution, ranked higher. Its content was original. Even

[26] *Amerikas aandsliv*, 207–217.
[27] *Amerikas aandsliv*, 219–222.
[28] *Amerikas aandsliv*, 228–230.

with several grammatical errors, the style was lively and in places witty and stimulating.

Turning to the core of the book, *Aftenposten* found it gratifying that Hamsun had not become enamored, as so many young people were, of everything new in America. He did not lose himself in wonder and see only the rosy side of things. On the contrary, he was so critical of American society that he gave the impression of downright pessimism.

Some of the faults that Hamsun observed, said the reviewer, could undoubtedly be found in other countries. Perhaps Americans were more interested in the latest murder than in politics, but it could not be denied that this was also true of nations even closer to Norway. It seemed to the commentator that Hamsun was attributing the blame for weaknesses in the American judicial system to a popular misunderstanding of the meaning of justice. But the reviewer believed that the American people did possess a sense of justice. They demonstrated this by lynching murderers and thieves because they lacked confidence in their government. They took the law into their own hands.

It was reasonable for appreciation of art and science to be lacking in a country where the lower classes, both native born and immigrant, played so important a role. It should be recognized, on the other hand, that probably in no other land was so much money given toward scientific experimentation as in America. Hamsun saw none of the brighter side of America and its people. He pictured the shadowy aspects so colorfully that the book made pleasant reading!

Best perhaps was Hamsun's disparagement of the poetry of Walt Whitman, who had a big name in America. Even on this side of the Atlantic, in Norway, there were those foolish enough to admire the man who consistently composed meaningless lines. He attacked Ralph Waldo Emerson, too, although he ranked several steps above the half-demented Whitman. But the reviewer did not follow Hamsun in his critical remarks about Shakespeare, who was taken

190

to task for being out of date in his understanding of human psychology. Hamsun could learn something there. We understand and appreciate Shakespeare better, remarked the reviewer, than Hamsun does.

Hamsun had to beware of one-sidedness. With his active mind and piquant style he was inclined toward extreme polemics. The temptation to make a brilliant comment or to express an original idea seemed to capture him. It might hurt his future authorship. Also, he committed sins against the Norwegian language, its grammar, and its usage. Meaningless words and phrases crept in. Abroad, the author had failed to improve upon his command of the Norwegian, bending himself rather toward learning English. Apparently most of his higher education derived from the study of literary works in English. Nevertheless, it was to be hoped that his next production would not be long in coming. He had made a good debut. Thus closed the review in *Aftenposten*.[29]

In *Verdens Gang* a two-column review of Hamsun under "New Books" carried the initials "G. B." The writer was undoubtedly the illustrious Danish Jew, Georg Brandes, ranked by many second only to Charles Augustin Sainte-Beuve of France as the literary critic of the century. Brandes had read Hamsun's book in proof and had recommended it to a publisher. Hamsun understood that Brandes would introduce the volume, and in a letter to a friend he spoke of this undeserved honor. "I am radical in my book," he confessed.[30]

Amerikas aandsliv drew qualified praise from Georg Brandes. First were a few favorable reactions. Hamsun's book was well written. He expressed hostility toward everything coarse, not being deceived by anything which masqueraded as popular, free, or moral. The book was essentially a protest, laden with satire. Brandes cited some examples. Hamsun hadn't felt at home anywhere in America. A man of his aristocratic nature did not find the right climate of opinion or

[29] *Aftenposten* (Christiania), May 10, 1889.
[30] Knut Hamsun to Erik Frydenlund, quoted without date in Tore Hamsun, *Knut Hamsun*, 101; *Verdens Gang* (Christiania), May 9, 1889.

custom in the free states. He was quick to see the weak side, the ridiculous, and the unrefined.

By reading Hamsun, continued Brandes, one did not get to the source of life in the United States. With his unusual talent, Hamsun distorted. Would that he applied his skill with the same intensity toward understanding! His kind of satire could be written of any land. Hamsun did not mention that in America "no military organization eats the marrow of the people." He was so patriotic that he measured intellectual achievement by the degree to which America understood Norway. In France such ignorance would be greater. One could know a great deal without knowing anything about Norway. But the reviewer's intention was not to attack Hamsun. Rather, Brandes would say to Norwegian readers: "Here is a new and distinguished Norwegian prose writer, a man who thinks independently, who is already important and will become greater."

A review of Hamsun's provocative work appeared in *Drammens Tidende*, a conservative paper then edited by Harald Alfstad. The unidentified reviewer found the book amusing, especially "to us who have doubts about the ability of pressing forward socially with pure democracy." It was even more entertaining "because of the facility with which Hamsun tumbles the Yankees around with his facile pen." But he used shirt-sleeve methods while despising Americans for walking in shirt sleeves on warm days. Hamsun, pharasaical in his attitude toward American Christianity, should have sought the more profound things of life, not the externals. Nevertheless, a talented author had risen on the literary horizon. He would gain a wide circle of readers if he could refrain from disturbing their wonted thought patterns and beliefs.[31]

Social-Demokraten, (Christiania), *Tønsbergs Blad*, and *Dagbladet* also commented upon Hamsun's slanted version of American cultural life. In *Social-Demokraten* an extended

[31] *Drammens Tidende*, June 30, 1889.

review was reprinted from *Dansk Social-Demokrat* of Copenhagen. The anonymous writer suggested that Hamsun deliberately bandied exaggerations about, but he agreed with him in most matters. The book was acceptable, with one important exception. Hamsun overlooked the Socialist party in the United States, a party which had abandoned the self-righteous dance and promised enlightenment under America's "dark sky." Danish-born Carl Jeppesen, editor of Norway's *Social-Demokraten*, took no part in this discussion. His few editorials of 1889 on American affairs were limited to the labor movement, agitation for an eight-hour day, and the economic philosophy of Henry George. Gerhard Gløersen of *Tønsbergs Blad* confined his remarks on Hamsun to a few lines. He had no quarrel with the young author's degrading picture of America. "Very unprejudiced" was his over-all judgment of Hamsun.[32]

Hamsun's presentation of the American scene met with strong rebuttal in *Dagbladet*, but not at the hands of Holst. The worthy opponent was Hans Tambs Lyche, whose life and interests are deftly portrayed by the late Paul Knaplund. Lyche, a graduate of the technical school in Christiania, arrived in Chicago in 1880. Influenced strongly by Unitarianism, with its rational and intellectual appeal, he began theological studies in Meadville, Pennsylvania. Eventually he served congregations in Janesville, Wisconsin, and Warwick, Massachusetts, associating almost exclusively with Americans of Anglo-Saxon heritage. Economic pressure to support a wife and a growing family forced him to return to railroad engineering and land surveying in the West.[33]

In 1892 Lyche returned to Norway, where he still held citizenship. Meanwhile he had written a series of letters to *Dagbladet* in response to Hamsun's unfavorable appraisal of the United States. Unlike Hamsun, Lyche came to ad-

[32] *Social Demokraten* (Christiania), January 17, July 4, 7, 18, 21, 1889; *Tønsbergs Blad*, May 18, 1889.
[33] Paul Knaplund, "Nork talsmann for Amerika," in *Nordmanns-Forbundet*, 57: 119–121 (June, 1964).

mire Emerson and the Boston intelligentsia. He had great
praise for the American press, then antedating William Ran-
dolph Hearst and yellow journalism. The cultured visitor
from Norway looked on American materialism as a natural
consequence of tremendous technological development. Despite America's wealth, it had created a comprehensive educational system and other cultural institutions. Absence of
class distinction and the willingness of Americans to work
together for the common good were also commended.

H. Tambs Lyche's articles of 1891 in *Dagbladet* refuted
Hamsun's *Amerikas aandsliv* at many points. *Dagbladet*
published Lyche's rejoinder in several installments. Lyche
first demonstrated that American women, becoming more enlightened with the years, were playing an increasingly important role in public life. A woman Unitarian minister provided his illustration. For over eight years she had conducted
two services every Sunday, usually to a full auditorium. In
a spacious and well-appointed edifice, where Lyche himself
once spoke, she discussed religious and social questions in a
forthright manner. Even Hamsun, said Lyche, would have
had to admire the audience, composed as it was of men and
women of serious mind and striking appearance. Contrary
to Hamsun's contention that America lacked artistic appreciation, beautiful pictures graced the sanctuary walls. It
was a congregation of sound personalities. They were child-
like souls with compassion for all humankind. Theirs was
no stale religion. They were the people who counted in American enterprise.[34]

In two installments on the history of Plymouth Rock,
Lyche named Boston as the Paris of the New World. It was
more outstanding than Paris in matters of intellect and
morals. Foreigners seemed to think that in America everything was materialistic and prosaic. On the contrary, the
Plymouth colonists had laid the groundwork of a new democratic world civilization. Where the highest culture prevailed,

[34] *Dagbladet,* July 12, 21, 22, 28, August 2, 1891.

the incidence of crime and divorce would be the lowest, as in Massachusetts. Lyche would not claim much for the disrupted American South or for the feuding mountain folk.

In a later article in *Dagbladet* Lyche selected Hamsun's "dark sky" as a point of departure. He described the Glen Echo Chautauqua camp near Washington, D.C., as symbolic of a wholesome adult education movement. Throngs of people congregated in such tent cities to hear noted lecturers speak on a wide range of topics. There was no dark sky, thanks to Yankee energy and Yankee pluck. Hamsun had an opportunity to reply to this encomium. He did not hold Holst responsible for his own views and requested *Morgenbladet* and *Vestlands-Posten* to take notice of that statement. He had once admired Lyche. An early Lyche essay on the Chinese philosopher Lao-Tze had impressed him most favorably. But Hamsun had to inform Norwegian readers that some Chautauqua speakers were unscholarly Civil War generals. There was a Mexican plant, the scent of which was said to induce forgetfulness. Lyche had smelled too long of America and had forsaken his first love, Europe. He had become Americanized. His recent articles were written hastily. Hamsun concluded by appealing to Holst to limit the number of unimportant items from the United States in his paper. There was no need to import news of the recurrent railroad accidents. Europe had enough of its own, and they were of greater reader interest. *Verdens Gang*, he thought, displayed better balance in its coverage of American news.

An examination of Ragnar Vold's excellent inside story of *Dagbladet* suggests that the Holst-Hamsun relationship did not suffer from Hamsun's cavalier remarks about the land across the sea. In 1899 a special Christmas Eve number of the paper carried illustrated stories by Hamsun and others. When *Hunger* was published, *Dagbladet* had exulted, "A new personality and a new style in literature!" A Christmas issue of 1890 represented a liberal position, with contributions from many young authors, including Hamsun. But Bjørnstjerne Bjørnson's star was rising. Hamsun's time had not yet come.[35]

Other Norwegian journals were seemingly indifferent; they carried no reviews of Hamsun. Some printed little news from America in 1889, save reports of murders and lynchings, high prices, lawlessness, or a sensational attempt to navigate Niagara Falls in a barrel. Of more interest to readers were the Johnstown flood, Thomas A. Edison's latest inventions, and the admission to the Union of new states in the Scandinavian Northwest: North and South Dakota, Montana, and Washington. Of course there were America letters. But even newspapers which regularly featured book reviews had nothing to say of Hamsun.[36]

Perhaps the most complete and understanding commentary on *Amerikas aandsliv* was that of the author's son Tore. A rather extended analysis of his remarks may be appropriate. Knut Hamsun wrote bitterly of American culture and customs, said Tore Hamsun, but at a desperate time in his life. Young and immoderate, he apparently fancied exaggeration for the sake of dramatic effect. Philip Armour's gift was not an exception. Knut Hamsun himself spoke of the helpfulness of Americans. He once solicited contributions of books for a Norwegian-American community library and was more than satisfied with the response. Neighbors, he pointed out, would hasten to the aid of a farmer in distress, even build a house for him after a fire. "Until I die," he once said, "I shall value what I learned during my two stays, and I am not without pleasant memories therefrom. It is concerning the entire nation that I speak, and of American life." [37]

Tore Hamsun continued that his father was not comfortable with the majority. He sought and admired the few who

[35] Ragnar Vold, *Dagbladet i tigerstaden* (*Dagbladet* in the Tiger City), 315–321 (Oslo, 1949). The Tiger City was Christiania.
[36] Among these were *Stavanger Amstidende og Adresseavis, Bergensposten, Varden* (Skien), *Den Vestlandske Tidende* (Arendal), and *Fædrelandsvennen* (Kristiansand).
[37] See Tore Hamsun, *Knut Hamsun*, 85–99.

struggled for a cause, and they might be socialists or anarchists. The execution of the Haymarket demonstrators was a blot on the system of American freedom for which an intellectually obtuse democracy was responsible. Americans who shouted for death knew nothing about anarchism as a scientific teaching. It was sufficient for them that the men in the Haymarket affair were accused of bomb throwing; in this instance freedom was no better than medieval despotism. If an author favored monarchy he was considered dangerous.

Hamsun described American literature as poor in talent. Mark Twain was an exception. Bits of Edgar Allan Poe, Nathaniel Hawthorne, and Bret Harte were tolerable. Hamsun attacked Walt Whitman and Ralph Waldo Emerson. As poetic writing, *Leaves of Grass* was discordant. Whitman had poems that were overwhelming in their lack of readability. Emerson was acceptable only if one allowed for his being an American and did not expect too much. The best American artists traveled to Europe for inspiration and technical training. Hamsun scoffed at their designing, using as an example the Washington Monument, which, save for its height of 555 feet, hadn't the slightest artistic appeal. What he appreciated, if restrainedly, was American journalism, which was daring and close to life, and paintings of nature scenes.

According to Tore, his father's intention was not to present an objective analysis of American society and culture, but to employ a consciously subjective approach. *Amerikas aandsliv* was built, not upon a scientific foundation, but upon personal experience. Hamsun's determination was to show the foibles of American democracy, which he believed laid a dead hand upon the country's spiritual being. He wanted to see room for an elite class. There was a lack of noble souls. Hamsun's report was generally well received, in Tore's opinion. Norway's foremost young critic, Carl Nærup, praised it as witty and fresh, devoid of the usual banalities. He was

197

surprised that the book did not meet with greater resentment.

In a letter to Erik Frydenlund in Valdres, Hamsun revealed that he planned to continue with the remainder of his touching novel, *Hunger*. Only part of it had appeared in *Ny Jord*. Spring was affecting his nerves again, he complained. He couldn't stand any distraction, and would strike matches on the underside of a table, out of sight. Bjørnson had invited him to visit him at Aulestad for a year! Hamsun politely declined and returned to Copenhagen, where he knew that he could concentrate upon his work. On Christmas Eve, 1889, he was the guest of Georg Brandes, in a house with Persian rugs! In the spring of 1890 *Hunger* came out in complete form. At thirty-one, Hamsun had arrived. He felt himself, however, to be primarily a poet, not a novelist. He again wrote Frydenlund, saying that he expected a second edition of his rendition of America's intellectual life to be published, to satisfy the demand. He also said that Brandes had told him frankly that *Hunger* was a monotonous piece of writing. Hamsun was offended and assured Brandes that he was mistaken.[38]

It may be pertinent to quote Tore Hamsun on the relationship between his father and Ole Thommessen, editor of *Verdens Gang*. From his youth, Hamsun had been influenced by *Verdens Gang* and Thommessen's journalistic style. The same editor later took him to task, after Hamsun had lectured in Christiania. Bjørnson and Thommessen did not get along either. Bjørnson charged that Thommessen was not so liberal as he claimed to be. Hamsun, too, came to believe Thommessen occasionally acted from dishonest motives.[39]

In *Redaktør Lynge* (Editor Lynge), Hamsun chose Thommessen as his central character. Hamsun was satirical, cold, and determined, according to Tore. When he was writing this novel, he was in poor health and distressing financial

[38] Tore Hamsun, *Knut Hamsun*, 101–105.
[39] Tore Hamsun, *Knut Hamsun*, 127–129.

circumstances. He was so despondent from an attack of influenza that he confided to Frydenlund that his nerves jumped even with the striking of a clock. *Redaktør Lynge* met with a varied response. The Brandes brothers, Edvard and Georg, were not favorable at the time. Thommessen, at whom the novel was directed, referred it to Arne Garborg for review in *Verdens Gang*. Garborg obliged, not by discussing the theme of the work but by concentrating, perhaps wisely, on Hamsun's competent style. Nils Kjær, the gifted young literary critic of *Dagbladet*, hailed this most recent creation of Hamsun's, thereby relieving Lars Holst from passing judgment. The book had a good sale, enabling its author to seek rest in Paris.[40]

The name of Knut Hamsun came to world-wide attention in 1920 when he was awarded the coveted Nobel prize for literature. The occasion prompted many critics, including Americans, to survey Hamsun's life and works. *Markens grøde* (usually translated *Growth of the Soil*, although some prefer "The Earth's Increase" as more accurate), considered his prize-winning novel, inspired special comment. Hamsun was fortunate that thirty years had passed since his scathing commentary on American culture had appeared, though some remembered it. American journals generally assumed a congratulatory tone, while reserving judgment as to the wisdom of the Nobel committee's choice. A few comments will serve to illustrate.

Julius Moritzen, writing for *Bookman*, stated that Hamsun's *Amerikas aandsliv* should "not be taken too seriously, impressionistic as it is and reflecting a mood that harbored some real or imaginary grievance." Yet it contained "much of real merit." If Hamsun failed to understand and appreciate America it was because a true son of the Scandinavian North could not forsake his first love.[41]

[40] Tore Hamsun, *Knut Hamsun*, 130. *Redaktør Lynge* was published in Copenhagen in 1893. It was never issued in English.

[41] Julius Moritzen, "Knut Hamsun in Life and Letters," in *Bookman*, 52: 437–441 (January, 1921).

Edwin Bjørkman, in the *New Republic,* concentrated mainly on *Hunger* rather than *Growth of the Soil* in his survey. His observations were peripheral so far as Hamsun's critique of America was concerned, but they were none the less illuminating. "Hamsun pitted his ambitions," said Bjørkman, "against the indifference of Christiania and then of Chicago. The result was a defeat that seemed the more bitter because it looked like punishment incurred by straying after false gods." He said that Hamsun denounced the very principle of urbanity. He belonged to the country, not the city. For that reason *Redaktor Lynge,* with its setting in the capital, was one of his poorer books. "He returned to the country, so to speak, and tried from there to strike at what he could reach of the ever expanding, ever devouring city. After that the city, like the sea, is always found in the distance." Hamsun despised professional folk for their rootlessness. To him the only true home was a piece of ground owned continuously by successive generations.[42]

Less favorable to the prize award of 1920 were some American newspapers. Two New York journals were quoted by the *Literary Digest.* The *World,* deploring the recognition of Hamsun, declared, "Evidently if Americans are to keep up with the times they must pay more attention to the Scandinavian languages or put the translators to work." The *Evening Post* considered Thomas Hardy more worthy. Only one Englishman, Rudyard Kipling, had as yet won the approval of the Nobel committee, it pointed out. Previous selections had been "authors with a wide continental reputation rather than those most esteemed by their own compatriots." A more generous point of view was expressed by Allen Wilson Porterfield, literary critic for the *Nation,* who said, "The European press is unanimous in its approval."[43]

[42] Edwin Bjørkman, "Knut Hamsun: From Hunger to Harvest," in New *Republic,* 26:195–197 (April 13, 1921).
[43] "The Horse-Car Conductor Who Wins the Nobel Prize," in *Literary Digest,* 67:35 (November 20, 1920); Allen Wilson Porterfield, "Knut Hamsun," in *Nation,* 111:652 (December 8, 1920).

Edwin Bjørkman, in his introduction to the American edition of *Hunger*, said that *Amerikas aandsliv*, "a masterpiece of distorted criticism," as one Norwegian reviewer phrased it, no longer was acceptable to the novelist himself. On the flyleaf of Bjørkman's autographed copy were these words: "A youthful work. It has ceased to represent my opinion of America. May 28, 1903. Knut Hamsun." In the light of this retraction it may be assumed that had Hamsun been older and more cautious in his judgments during his American visits, he might have idealized many an obscure toiler on Norwegian farms in the Middle West, as he did Isak, the hero of his great epic, *Growth of the Soil*. The thought is not an original one. Hanna Astrup Larsen observed in her biography of Hamsun that the fictional Isak whom he placed in Nordland was the hero he had failed to find in the Red River Valley of North Dakota in his youth.[44]

Apparently Hamsun's youthful indiscretion of 1889 did him no permanent damage. Evidence shows that he was popular in his homeland and elsewhere in Europe in the 1920's. In Bjørkman's words, Hamsun's reputation took "deepest roots in Russia, where several editions of his collected works appeared" and where he was called "the equal of Tolstoy and Dostoevsky." Norwegians honored Hamsun in 1929 in a *Festskrift* marking his seventy-fifth birthday. In it a number of literary lights paid tribute, among them John Galsworthy, Thomas Mann, Thomas Masaryk, Maxim Gorky, Stefan Zweig, and H. G. Wells. It was Wells who had remarked, upon reading *Growth of the Soil*, "I do not know how to express the admiration I feel for this wonderful book without seeming to be extravagant. One of the very greatest novels I have ever read."[45]

All in all, Hamsun's bill of particulars, charged to the

[44] Knut Hamsun, *Hunger*, vi, vii (New York, 1921); Larsen, *Knut Hamsun*, 21.

[45] Sigurd Hoel, "Knut Hamsun og Amerika," in *Knut Hamsun: Festskrift til 70 aarsdagen; 4 August 1929*, 84–97 (Oslo, 1929). In 1889, Hoel says, Hamsun wrote as a rebel, in 1928 as a father to an impatient son. See also Einar Skavlan's anniversary study, *Knut Hamsun* (Oslo, 1929).

United States, listed items that not only provoked thought but also searched the soul. The cheerless skies reflected in Hamsun's desolate panorama were attributed to various weaknesses in the fiber and functioning of the American cultural body. The intellectual desert displayed itself in ignorance, mob judgment, mass hysteria, rootlessness, and a general cultural void. American nationalism was a perverted patriotism which insulted the immigrant and rarely sought or acknowledged any good in his European background. Other indictments pertained to political corruption and excessive crime, and to sensational newspaper reporting of them. There was also the pursuit of happiness, sanctioned by the preamble to the Declaration of Independence, encouraging all too often the happiness of pursuit, with the attendant bustle and madness to possess this world's goods. False piety and weak family ties rounded out the list.

If a perusal of a score of Norwegian journals for the year 1889 uncovers no massive response, quantitatively speaking, to Hamsun's diatribe, it at least provides material for appraisal of Norwegian thought not only on Hamsun's views but on America itself. Some editors and critics, with unconcealed glee, found support in Hamsun. In this category were Bætzmann of *Aftenposten*, Alfstad of *Drammens Tidende*, and Gløersen of *Tønsbergs Blad*, whose views ranged from outright amusement to serious doubts about the workability of political democracy. They found pleasure, like the avid readers of Henry L. Mencken during the 1920's, in debunking American practices and institutions. Who would argue that they were entirely in error? Many Americans of today know that in the final quarter of the nineteenth century by and large the best brains of the nation were channeled not into politics but into private enterprise.

Other journalists accepted Hamsun's derogatory attitude more restrainedly and with little satisfaction. They disagreed with him on certain points. Georg Brandes thought Hamsun unappreciative and guilty of blanket criticisms. *Drammens*

Tidende called him hypocritical. Jeppesen, the Social Democrat, agreed with *Dansk Social-Demokrat* in charging Hamsun with exaggeration, while conceding that in most matters Hamsun had the better of the argument. In Lars Holst's *Dagbladet* the young author's standing was not in jeopardy. Moderate critics envisaged a promising if not brilliant future for the creator of the two works, *Hunger* and *Amerikas aandsliv.* Their gripping literary style and penetrating intellectual quality won widespread admiration from experts conversant with the Norwegian language.

A final observation or two will complete this evaluation. Hamsun touched the imperfections of American society and of western civilization as a whole. In *Hunger* he exposed the harshness and indifference of his own capital city, Christiania, where he spent a miserable year in poverty. As Hamsun himself stated, his distortions of the American scene, the rash utterances of a youth still in his twenties, were not lasting impressions. Tore Hamsun was convinced that his father valued his experiences in America and carried many pleasant memories with him. Hamsun's denunciation of the New World was never translated into English. Yet, had an American edition been published, it could surely not have been written off simply as a malicious portrayal. Granted that profundity and balance in judgment were to increase as Hamsun grew older, there were shrewd and penetrating insights interspersed among his explosive words of 1889.

by MARC L. RATNER

8   *The Romantic Spencerian*

ONE OF the strongest influences affecting American thought during the late nineteenth century came from the natural sciences. Discoveries and theories in geology and organic evolution undermined the strong religious beliefs of many, affected the idealistic philosophy of romantic transcendentalism, and encouraged a greater interest in the ethical and social implications of man's place in society.[1] In the work of Hjalmar Hjorth Boyesen, Norwegian-American critic and novelist, we can observe the development of a writer who began in the tradition of the European romantic evolutionist and was influenced by the writings of Charles Darwin and Herbert Spencer toward a new view of evolution. Boyesen was interested in a number of specific social and literary problems, viz., education in a militant or industrial society, heredity and race, woman's place in the new society, political forces, and last, though not in importance, the rise of realism in literature. Because of Boyesen's significance as a critic, interest in his contribution to American culture

[1] Richard Hofstadter, *Social Darwinism in American Thought, 1860–1915* (Philadelphia, 1945). On page 22 Hofstadter says, "Herbert Spencer, who of all men made the most ambitious attempt to systematize the implications of evolution, . . . was far more popular in the United States than he was in his native country."

through his literary and social criticism has increased in the last few years.[2]

At the root of much of Boyesen's thinking was the theory of evolution, which he and many of his contemporaries associated with progress. J. B. Bury distinguished between these two concepts: "Evolution itself, it must be remembered, does not necessarily mean, applied to society, the movement of a man to a desirable goal. It is a neutral, scientific conception, compatible either with optimism or pessimism."[3] The fact is, though, that Darwin often struck a note of optimism in his writings and this led to an association between progress and evolution. He wrote that "natural selection works solely by and for the good of each being" and leads to "progress towards perfection," and he suggested that further development of his theory would lead to a law of progress.[4] Herbert Spencer, however, became the foremost interpreter of the new theory and developed the concept of progress through his extension of the tenets of Darwinian evolution to the fields of sociology and ethics.

Not all that Spencer drew from evolutionary theory was derived from Darwin, for Spencer was also influenced by the classic economists, Malthus and Ricardo. Making use of the analysis by these thinkers of the effects of severe competition on the economic survival of man, Spencer aimed at joining the ideas of physics and biology and then applying them to man's situation, individual and social. Out of his speculations, he developed the ideas of the persistence of force which conserves energy and the evolutionary process wherein all forms of matter progress from simple to complex forms. He wrote in *First Principles*: "Evolution is an integration of matter and concomitant dissipation of motion; during which the matter passes from an indefinite, incoherent homogeneity to a definite, co-

---

[2] The outstanding publication on the subject is Clarence A. Glasrud's *Hjalmar Hjorth Boyesen* (Norwegian-American Historical Association, Northfield, 1963).
[3] J. B. Bury, *The Idea of Progress*, 335 (London, 1920).
[4] Charles Darwin, *The Origin of Species*, 305 (New York, 1884).

herent heterogeneity; and during which the retained motion undergoes a parallel transformation." In the human and social field, the laws of nature, as everywhere, are inescapable and unrelenting, though demonstrating a beneficent necessity seen by Spencer as "equilibration," a state where evolution can end only in the establishment of the greatest perfection and the most complete happiness.[5]

Spencer's appeal to the postwar generation was influential in all areas of thought. The writers and thinkers who found support in his philosophy were often the men who were to lead the rebellion against the genteel tradition that had become for them a faded faith. In designing a sociology based on natural development which formed individual man for a social purpose, Spencer attempted to solve the essential problem of the individual in society by having the authoritarian government give way to a free co-operative society based on man's rationality. But essentially as Parrington believes, the dynamic force of the philosophy lay in its idea of continuous growth, creative purpose, and belief in human perfectibility.[6]

In spite of Boyesen's later adherence to Spencer's ideas, his initial romantic views derived from literary and philosophical sources rather than from economics, physics, and biology. His dedication to Goethe was more than that of the German scholar. He felt that Goethe was the model for all intellectuals and "the most complete type of man in modern history." Boyesen wrote in his *Goethe and Schiller* of Goethe's devotion to systematized science: "His advocacy of Neptunism in geology, the discovery of the intermaxillary bone, which enabled him to anticipate the doctrine of evolution, and his theory of the typical plant, sufficiently prove that he did not question Nature in vain. He was not satisfied with the shallow traditional solutions of everyday problems, but sought to penetrate to the hidden soul which breathed and labored un-

[5] Herbert Spencer, *First Principles*, 396, 549 (London, 1884).
[6] Vernon Parrington, *Main Currents in American Thought*, 3: 197–201 (New York, 1927).

der commonplace facts. He saw the colossal law which operated in the growth of the tiniest blade of grass." [7]

For Boyesen, as for many intellectuals, the ideas of the
romantic evolutionists did not at first radically conflict with
the new concepts of Darwinian evolution and, in fact, as Commager states: "Evolution outmoded rather than nullified the
Enlightenment and Transcendentalism, for though its methods were profoundly different, its conclusions were much the
same." [8]

Like Boyesen, Josiah Royce, in his *Spirit of Modern Philosophy*, credited the German romantics of the post-Napoleonic
era such as Goethe with the new concept of history, the unity
of human life, and the growth of human institutions. It was
this groundwork of the romantic evolutionists in historical
and sociological consequences of evolution which made Darwin's scientific achievement immediately important to society.
Royce, who remained a romantic evolutionist, objected to the
doctrine of evolution that existed in his own time because its
theorists tended to subordinate its original idealism and to
concentrate on the scientific, factual, and empirical aspects of
the theory. Though he was opposed to much of Spencer's
thinking, he expressed a similar view to Boyesen's when he
wrote: "The doctrine of evolution, I assert, is in heart and essence the child of the romantic movement itself. Can the child,
inheriting its mother's depth and longing for wisdom, defend
this inheritance in the vast outer universe of rigid order and
absolute law? That is the true problem of the philosophy of
evolution. I know many who regret the tendency in our day to
apply the doctrine of the transformation of species to humanity, who fear the apparently materialistic results of the discovery that the human mind has grown. For my part there lies
in all this discovery of our day the deeply important presup-
position that the transition from animal to man is in fact
really an evolution, that is, a real history, a process having

[7] *Goethe and Schiller; Their Lives and Works, Including a Commentary on
Goethe's Faust*, 140, 142 (New York, 1879).
[8] H. S. Commager, *The American Mind*, 87 (New York, 1952).

207

significance. If this is in truth the real interpretation of nature, then the romantic philosophy has not dreamed in vain, and the outer order of nature will embody once more the life of a divine Self." [9]

Though Boyesen felt that there was "nowhere any evidence of retrogression on a grand scale in human history," he was unhappy with the social conditions of his time. He once wrote that "the tendency of the future will be towards equalization of material conditions, and legislative discrimination against those who now enjoy undue advantages in the struggle for existence." Indeed, ultimately, because Boyesen could see no change in conditions, he altered his perspective from that of a romantic revolutionary optimist who believed in allowing evolution to proceed undirected to that of a reformer who believed that man should direct the evolutionary process. [10]

Boyesen's expressions on evolution were not limited to his poetry and prose. He was a member of the Nineteenth Century Club, where he occasionally engaged in discussions. This club, founded in 1882 by Courtlandt Palmer, was a popular forum for such speakers as Theodore Roosevelt, George Washington Cable, Moncure Conway, Oliver Wendell Holmes, and many others. Founded as an organization for "free thought," with open debates and intellectual and social tolerance its keynotes, its members wished to be, as Palmer said, a "mirror to reflect the century." The members were mainly New Yorkers with strong leanings toward betterment, opposed to the individualism expressed in the society of the "gilded age," and believing that an "ethical evolution from selfishness to altruism" was the answer to the problems of American society. As to their practical program, Palmer stated that they hoped "to place reform in the hands of the true conservatives of the earth," those who aided and guided social evolution along its natural path. [11]

[9] Josiah Royce, *Spirit of Modern Philosophy*, 291 (Boston, 1892).

[10] *Literary and Social Silhouettes*, 160 (New York, 1894).

[11] Courtlandt Palmer, *The Nineteenth Century Club of New York*, 5, 6, 34 (London, 1887).

In tracing the development of Boyesen's ideas on life and literature, one can see a change taking place in his perspective. He followed a pattern of thinking common in America at the end of the nineteenth century, changing from a conservative point of view toward evolution to a reformist outlook. True to his romantic heritage, Boyesen came to feel that science alone could not answer universal problems.

In his earlier work Boyesen took a conservative approach to social problems in that he was willing to allow natural selection to follow its course without interference from men or artificial agencies. He felt that all would come out well eventually. One can clearly see this optimism in his sonnet series, "Evolution," which appeared in the *Atlantic Monthly* in 1878. In the first of these poems, he envisions the glorious future of man:

> And time, upon my sight vast visions throng
>   Of the imperial destiny of man.
> The life that throbbed in plant and beast ere long
>   Will break still wider orbits in its van,
>   A race of peace-robed conquerors and kings,
> Achieving ever-more diviner things.[12]

Boyesen later tempered this optimistic view of nature's great plan with the belief that man must act more positively against the evils within the body of society. Social evolution must be aided by the reforming action of man. While never deserting his conviction that natural social progress was inherent, he did lay greater emphasis on the responsibility of men to aid and abet this progress. Boyesen emphasized this idea at the conclusion of his *Commentary on the Writings of Henrik Ibsen*, published in 1894, in which he stated: "There is a fatal optimism which professes to believe that evils can be cured by ignoring them — professing not to see them. It is the good, nice, religious people who are most prone to this delusion; and it is these, too, who, apropos of Ibsen, declare that no good can come of dragging moral ugliness into the light of day. I confess there was a time when I was myself

[12] "Evolution," in *Atlantic Monthly*, 41:565–567 (May, 1878).

of that opinion. But an ampler and deeper experience has convinced me that such a view is not only foolish, but exceedingly harmful. It encourages vice by spreading over it a charitable mantle of darkness, like Siegfried's invisible-making 'tarnkappe' in the 'Nibelungen Lay'; and under this impenetrable mantle the foulest things may be done, without entailing social ostracism or any open penalty." [13]

An explication of Boyesen's more optimistic poems on evolutionary progress will help to show, I believe, how he reevaluated and ultimately changed his beliefs. The five sonnets entitled "Evolution" were accepted by William Dean Howells and published in the *Atlantic Monthly* in 1878. Interestingly enough, they also appeared in E. L. Youman's *Popular Science Monthly* in June of that same year. From the point of view of Boyesen's intellectual development, the poems are significant in that they were the first major expression of his sentiments on evolution.

In the first sonnet Boyesen presented the creation of the universe "on pillars sunk in unfathomable deep." The "mighty will" of nature was seen at work as a vast "breath," taking "dizzying aeons" to create a "lichen patch." There was a feeling of world spirit in this sonnet, similar to the concept of the oversoul in Emerson. But Boyesen became more definitely anthropocentric in the second stanza. There he spoke of himself as Man, the culmination, the great result of the evolutionary process. When Boyesen stated that his "lullaby by hoarse Silurian storms was chanted," he likened the earlier forms of life — "plant and bird and beast" — to his infancy as Man and spoke of these developmental forms as part of his own nature. "I grow and blossom as a tree," and again, "and thou, O Sea, stern mother of my soul." This "sacred kinship . . . with all that breathes" is further developed in the third sonnet. There Boyesen spoke of the "iron chain that all creation girds" which "forges its bond unceasing from below." The vestiges of his ancestry can be found in the "song-thrush

[13] *A Commentary on the Writings of Henrik Ibsen*, 316 (New York, 1894).

warblings in my brain" and in the pulsations of "water, stone and plant."

In the fourth sonnet, the vastness of creation and time absorbed Boyesen's thoughts. He was awed by the vestiges of the past seen in fossil life. "A fern-leaf's airy woof" shorn by tempests or "a reptile's claw" of some great beast striding through the tepid tide had left its mark on stone. These links with the past became part of Boyesen: "Come, a fraternal grasp, thou hand of stone! / The flesh that once was thine is now mine own."

In these sonnets Boyesen thus presented the evolutionary cycle, and the traces of this cycle in man and nature. The final sonnet completed the series by examining the future pattern of evolution. From its base beginnings, life took on a sublime aspect. The "mean clay" became the "refulgence grand" of man as "peace-robed conquerors." [14]

Boyesen's scientific approach resembled that of the American philosopher, John Fiske, who wrote that there was "the recognition of the fact that, at the outset, men interpreted the Cosmos in terms of human feeling and volition; while, on the other hand, as the newest result of scientific generalization, we now find them beginning to interpret human feeling and volition in terms obtained from the objective study of the Cosmos." [15] It was in his evolution poems that Boyesen, like Fiske, scrutinized the cosmos; that is, as a true scientist, he viewed the life about him and drew from it his cosmic viewpoint. Thus, rather than examining human feeling and drawing conclusions about the universe, man examines the universe and then sees it in human forms.

Boyesen later sought a primal cause for evolution and through it a religious basis for his belief. The sonnets indicated that Boyesen accepted the Spencerian idea of the unknowable.

The sonnets themselves began with exclamatory phrases which sounded remotely like those in Whitman's poetry, espe-

---

[14] The quotations are from "Evolution," in *Atlantic Monthly*, 41:565–567.
[15] John Fiske, *Outlines of Cosmic Philosophy*, 182 (Boston, 1896).

cially when Boyesen used the first person. But the link is a closer one than that of style. The connection between the transcendental romanticism of Whitman and Emerson and the evolutionary romanticism of Boyesen was a natural consequence of the interest of all three in German Romantic thought. Boyesen's theme here was the unity of men and nature. Instead of a world soul or oversoul, of which man's nature was only part, however, Boyesen held to a more anthropocentric position wherein the soul of man became the final expression of evolutionary development and the world a great man-soul. This was exemplified by Boyesen's vision of the primal cause in anthropomorphic terms as "some mighty will" or a "breath perchance that whirled the mists apace."

A further comparison of the attitudes of Whitman and Boyesen will show their different approaches. Where Whitman wrote of his own embryo:

> For it the nebula cohered to an orb,
> The long slow strata piled to rest it on,
> Vast vegetables gave it sustenance,
> Monstrous sauroids transported it in their mouths
>   and deposited it with care

he was talking of the evolution of his body. But for Whitman the body was only a temporary identity:

> I too had been struck from the float
>   forever held in solution,
> I too had received identity by my body.

The world soul does not evolve; it *is* and always was. The individual body is nothing within the world soul. With Boyesen, however, the body and the *soul* of man, as seen through his generic "I" (like Whitman), had both evolved from lesser forms and would continue to evolve, as the world soul does:

> And through endless changing forms
> Of plant and bird and beast unceasingly
> The toiling ages wrought to fashion me.
> Lo, these strange ancestors have left a breath
> Of their strong souls in mine, defying death
> And change.[16]

[16] Walt Whitman, "Song of Myself," and "Crossing Brooklyn Ferry," in

Boyesen's expressions had anthropomorphic connotations that distinguished the primal cause from the Spencerian concept of "force" or "forces" and thus he emphasized that evolution was not sightless or aimless. Clearly, his position was distinct from that of both the romantic and the scientific evolutionists, though his ideas were a fusion of both.

In the sonnets entitled "Sea" and "Air" in his *Idyls of Norway*, Boyesen expressed similar concepts. The sea became the great nurturing mother of "vast Creation's tree" and the "teeming swarms of life that swim and creep / But half-aroused from primordial sleep." The currents of the sea became the pulsations of death and birth. The poem "Air" is unfortunately as nebulous as its title would indicate, though here again Boyesen used the term "undulation" to describe the wavelike breathing motion of pulsing nature and its elements.[17]

If Boyesen's "Evolution" sonnets showed traces of romantic evolutionism, no small influence was due to Bayard Taylor and especially his verse drama, "Prince Deukalion." There can be no doubt that Boyesen was familiar with the poem: "During the last two years while he was engaged in writing *Prince Deukalion*, he [*Taylor*] never failed to read me in his splendid sonorous voice the last act he had finished and this naturally furnished material for discussions of many social and religious problems. It must be evident to everyone that in this poem he has attempted to define his social and political creed, and the hopeful and sanguine element of his character has there found its most complete expression. He endeavored above all to avoid dogmatism in his statement of his convictions and to make his imagery so ample and expressive that it should hint at the philosophical truth, as a loose and gracefully flowing garment suggests and by its general outlines reveals the forms of the man within." [18]

Writings of Walt Whitman, 1:98, 195 (New York, 1902); Boyesen, in *Atlantic Monthly*, 41:565.

[17] *Idyls of Norway and Other Poems*, 50 (New York, 1882).

[18] "Reminiscences of Bayard Taylor," in *Lippincott's Magazine*, 24:214 (August, 1879).

Marc L. Ratner

Reviewing "Prince Deukalion" in 1879, Boyesen wrote that the theme was "nothing less than the evolution of human thought" from classic times to the future, that it showed that man "no longer blindly obedient to authority" was nearer to nature's heart than ever before, and that the march of evolution towards the future was less hindered than in the past. Attaching great importance to these words of Taylor, "To find in endless growth all good," Boyesen linked them with his own ideas of progress. Taylor's poem was based on the principle that because of the perfection of the Creator's mind he must create ideal creatures. The distance between the ideal man and existent man, however, was enormous; therefore, man must strive for the perfection of the ideal. This was a simplified view of that same romantic concept of transcendental evolutionism that had its root in German idealism.[19]

Boyesen did not, however, accept the romantic belief that perfection existed in the ideal or in a harmony with an all-embracing world soul. He became interested in seeing the evolutionary process function toward a more tangible goal. As time went on, he took a position which laid greater emphasis on the social aspects of evolution, and this change was evident in his "Ode." The poem, whose mood resembles that of Sidney Lanier's "The Symphony" (1875) at certain points, becomes an essay on the concept of evolution.[20]

A comparison of the two poems will show the difference between Boyesen's attitude, as he became more interested in the social aspect of evolution, and those of Lanier and Taylor, which were still influenced by romantic concepts of evolution. Lanier's position was much closer to Bayard Taylor's than to any scientific view, and it is significant that Lanier devoted seven pages in "The English Novel" to "Prince Deukalion." Lanier's "The Symphony," which began with the familiar "O Trade! O Trade! would thou were dead," and continued with declamatory lines against commercialism, was paralleled

[19] "Prince Deukalion," in *Scribner's Monthly*, 17:602–605 (February, 1879).

[20] "Ode," in *Independent*, 35:673 (May 31, 1883); Sidney Lanier, "The Symphony," in *Centennial Edition*, 1:46 (Baltimore, 1945).

by Boyesen's " 'Tis wealth, a curse in blessing's guise / Wealth, leagued, ambitious, keen, insatiate." In both poems the declamatory style was continued with repetitions of the phrases " 'Tis wealth," and "O Trade," followed by vindictive arguments by the poets against the exploitation of the land and the people. But Lanier shifted to more romantic imagery and dabbled in medievalism, while Boyesen turned to evolution and the future. Despite the evils of wealth, said Boyesen, the evolutionary pattern went on:

> Through long revolving cycles, fraught with death,
>   And life unquenchable that triumphed ever,
> An upward impulse throbbed in every breath,
>   A darkly groping quest, a dim endeavor.[21]

But the distinction goes farther than this. Hoping for an ideal society based on harmony and love, Lanier attacked trade for its destruction of spiritual values. Thus, "Man's love ascends / To finer and diviner ends" and the symphony of "music is Love in search of a word." On the other hand, Boyesen saw wealth as the "ruthless Juggernaut"; it "saps the deep foundations of the state" and it "hoodwinks senators and drowns debate / With clink of gold." The hope of man lay in the "darkly groping quest" — "the endless progression of thought and deed / [which] Is the crown and glory of men." There was evolutionary optimism in Boyesen's poem. Despite the partial tone of despair, Boyesen reminded his readers that "evil is a faint and waning moon / Against the strong resistless dawn of good."

In effect, Boyesen remained optimistic about man's future, qualifying his thesis only with the admission that wealth and greed could slow man's progress toward the light.

Possibly Boyesen's abandonment of poetry was the outcome of his belief that it might very well have become "an obsoles-

[21] Sidney Lanier, "The English Novel," in *Centennial Edition*, 4:96–101. Lanier states, page 96, that Taylor's poem "not only is possessed with modernness, but consciously possessed, so that what was implicit in Shelley — and a great deal more — here becomes explicit and formulated." (He here refers to Shelley's "Prometheus Unbound" as a poem of romantic evolutionism.) Basically, that is, the romantic view of man liberated from his chains and evolving toward a larger life.

cent art," or of the realization that he was a poor poet. Whatever the reason, he stopped writing serious poetry in 1888. His
other work in verse consisted mostly of literary ballads, other
narrative poems, and love sonnets with little or no speculative
material in them. In his prose, however, he developed further
toward a social perspective of evolution. For example, *The
Mammon of Unrighteousness* was Boyesen's major work of
fiction and the one most relevant to this matter. In several
ways the novel shows the growth of Boyesen's social and political views on immigration, politics, woman's position in
society, and education — important subjects to Boyesen and
his contemporaries.

The philosophical center of *The Mammon of Unrighteousness* is a conflict between two brothers, both of whom accept
the concept of evolution but whose interpretations differ a
great deal. Aleck, the idealist, is set against his materialistic
brother, Horace. Horace, easily the most articulate person in
the novel, glibly argues evolutionist ideas. He scoffs at Aleck's
devotion to principle and self-sacrifice, especially with regard
to women, but ultimately succumbs to the very creature he
has ridiculed, woman. For, despite his intellectualization about
evolutionary forces, he is not immune to the elemental power
of the female sex. An excerpt from one of Horace's dialogues
(almost monologues) with some of the other characters reveals his ideas:

"'Yes,' said Horace, unflinchingly, 'success is after all only
adaptation to environment. Is it not?'

"'Certainly.'

"'Would you say that the pickerel, who eats all the other
fishes in his lake, is the most estimable fish?' the doctor put
in. . . .

"'Yes, I would. In the conditions under which he lives he
has but a choice between eating or being eaten. I respect him
for taking a clear view of his situation.'"

Aleck's comments on the conversation reveal Boyesen's own

feelings and partial disillusionment with the panaceas of perfectibility through the evolutionary process alone.

"'It is my brother's hobby,' Aleck remarked . . . 'that Providence has played a trick on us in putting us here with the instincts and passions which we imagine have been given to us for our own personal happiness and gratification; when all the while, they subserve only some general purpose, such as the preservation of the race and the welfare of society.'" [22]

Some of the descriptive passages in the novel indicate Boyesen's interest in evolution in nature as well as in society. After describing the ravage of time on Drumhead Ravine, near the town in which most of the novel's action takes place, Boyesen said of the beautiful ferns there: "But like all beautiful things, they perished and in their death became the foundation for new life. The long procession of the ages and their grand alternatives, growth and decay, passed over the face of the rock, froze it and scorched it, stripped it, nay undertook a series of cosmic experiments and its work left it as you see it today." Boyesen's primary interest, however, was in man's evolutionary development. He remained more European in his outlook, and for Boyesen the forces of nature were always secondary to the forces of society in influence on man's growth.

Further examples of Boyesen's shift in point of view appeared in his critical writings. For instance, his handling of the Baucis and Philemon story in his critical analysis of the second part of Goethe's *Faust* illustrates this shift. The story concerns the efforts of Faust to oust an old couple who own and live on a small plot on a hill near the shore. The hill is of great importance to Faust, whom Boyesen sees in this story as a symbol of the progress of the human race. The old couple, Baucis and Philemon, do not wish to move because they are attached to their possessions and their land. They are, in essence, the conservative element in society, skeptical of the current that hurries the world on. They ask only to live

[22] *The Mammon of Unrighteousness*, 165 (New York, 1891).

obscurely, untouched by time. Faust, who wants a tower built, sends Mephistopheles to do the job, thus relying on evil to accomplish progress. Mephistopheles burns the old people's cottage and chapel, and they die of fright.

Boyesen treated the whole episode as symbolic, not a reflection on the character of Faust. He considered Philemon and Baucis "victims of progress," and his attitude in *Goethe and Schiller* was that of the conservative evolutionist. He stated: "This process, cruel though it may be, and superficially considered, unjust to the individual, history is continually repeating. It is the well-established law by which the great body of humanity is steadily renewing itself; all dead and worn-out matter is thrown off and its place is supplied by new and vital tissues. The path of progress . . . is strewn with the corpses of innocent victims who trusted in sentiment rather than in truth, and whose only offense was that they had already long been dead." [23]

Where Faust made his mistake was in handing the assignment to Mephistopheles. Yet Faust, who cursed the violent deed, was responsible for it, said Boyesen, for instead of "trusting in the slow and healthful processes of nature," he resorted to magic and the use of Mephistopheles. What saved Faust from damnation was that "his own life, with all its errors and 'obscure aspirations,' had a steady, upward tendency." [24]

Compare this attitude with Boyesen's later concept of the same incident in *Faust*, expressed in an article entitled "Victims of Progress." Here Baucis and Philemon are not poor and humble folk who want only to be left alone but instead are presented as members of the "ruling class," while Faust is furthering the progress of "the dumb and toiling masses." Boyesen clearly delineated the changes which he saw destined to occur: "The progress of civilization is properly gauged by its gradual elevation of the average of happiness; and this is effected not so much by the increased splendor of the rich, as

[23] *Goethe and Schiller*, 275.
[24] *Goethe and Schiller*, 276, 281.

by the increased comfort of the poor. A gradual rearrangement of economic forces is taking place, tending in this direction." The Philemons of the world hate to see the disappearance of the feudal past, and Boyesen linked them with the romantic thinkers who were attempting to keep the "genteel tradition" alive in literature as well as keeping selfish individualism alive in society.[25]

In this attempt to show the shift in Boyesen's thought from the individual view toward one governed by society and its needs, I have tried to point out various influences on his work, and manifestations of his thoughts as expressed in some of his writings. Although he eventually broke with Spencer's ideas about the manner in which man must interfere in the evolutionary process, the philosopher's assumptions and his belief in progress provided the philosophic basis for much of Boyesen's optimistic beliefs and his literary and social criticism.

Alfred Kazin, writing of Boyesen, considered him a unique instance in America of a Victorian realist.[26] For, like many intellectuals in England, Boyesen was as yet recovering from the shock given his romantic faith by the scientific revolution. As I have shown, he attempted wherever possible to assert his new faith in the slow process of this same scientific evolution by referring to Spencerian and Darwinian views. Most American realists were much less concerned with philosophical and scientific processes than with practical solutions to the problems of society. I have indicated that Boyesen himself was aware that the slow evolutionary process needed active participation by individuals, and though he attacked Nietzsche and was wary of Ibsen, his perspective did change over the years. He remained, comparatively speaking, a moderate in his ideas of social change, and while he never completely shook off his romantic mantle, he came to recognize the need for man to give direction and meaning to evolution.

[25] "Victims of Progress," in *Independent*, 40:612 (May 17, 1888).
[26] Alfred Kazin, *On Native Grounds*, 16 (New York, 1942).

9 *Some Recent Publications*

BOOKS AND PAMPHLETS

ANDER, O. FRITIOF, ed. *In the Trek of the Immigrants: Essays Presented to Carl Wittke.* Rock Island, 1964. 325 p.

This volume, dedicated to the eminent historian of immigration, contains essays by Carlton C. Qualey and Kenneth O. Bjork and discusses the contributions to immigrant history made by Marcus L. Hansen and Theodore C. Blegen. Reviewed in *American Historical Review*, October, 1964.

ANDERSSON, THEODORE M. *The Problem of Icelandic Saga Origins: A Historical Survey.* New Haven, 1964. 190 p.

Variations of opinion from the seventeenth to the twentieth century on the historic value of the Icelandic sagas.

ARDEN, G. EVERETT. *Four Northern Lights: Men Who Shaped Scandinavian Churches.* Minneapolis, 1964. 165 p.

Biographical sketches of clergymen, including Hans Nielsen Hauge.

BAYERSCHMIDT, CARL F., and FRIIS, ERIK J., eds. *Scandinavian Studies.* Seattle, 1965. 458 p.

Essays by several scholars, including Richard Beck, Sverre Arestad, Harold Naess, and Erik J. Friis.

BECK, MAGNUS OLAF. *Becks of Normanna.* San Antonio, Texas, 1964. 198 p.

Family history interwoven with the story of the Norwegian settlement at Normanna, Texas, including a history of Our Saviour's Lutheran Church.

BERG, MADS. *Skolens sangbok.* Oslo, 1964. 351 p.

A school songbook. Several English songs are included.

BRØNDSTED, JOHANNES. *The Vikings.* Baltimore, 1965. 347 p.

Included is a section on Viking expeditions to the Western Hemisphere.

CHUBB, THOMAS CALDECOT. *The Northmen.* Cleveland, 1964. 125 p.

One in a series entitled *Major Cultures of the World,* this book is intended mainly for young people and includes a description of the Viking voyages to Vinland. Reviewed in *American-Scandinavian Review,* Autumn, 1965.

DAHL, BORGHILD. *Finding My Way.* New York, 1962. 121 p.

A companion volume to the author's *I Wanted to See.*

——— *This Precious Year.* New York, 1964. 159 p.

Novel about a Norwegian-American girl in South Dakota during the 1930's. Reviewed in *American-Scandinavian Review,* Summer, 1965.

FORSYTHE, HILDA J. *Grandeur in Simplicity.* New York, 1963. 108 p.

Recollections of the author's farm childhood in Wisconsin and of her Norwegian-born father, Hans E. Nelson.

FOSSUM, GLADYS H. *Rosemaling: History, Instructions, and Designs.* Racine, Wisconsin, 1964. 31 p.

FRIIS, ERIK J., ed. *The Norwegian Club, Inc., 1904–1964.* Brooklyn, 1964. 104 p.

History of Det Norske Selskab and its activities. Reviewed in *American-Scandinavian Review,* Spring, 1965.

GULLIXSON, THADDEUS F. *In the Face of the West Wind.* Minneapolis, 1963. 104 p.

Frontier men and women in difficult times. Reviewed in *Lutheran Standard,* December 29, 1964.

GUNHEIM, OLAV. *Dikt, draum, og rim.* Santa Rosa, California, 1963. 31 p.

Poems, dreams, and rhymes, and an autobiographical sketch.

Hadelendings. *Gamalt fra Hadeland, specialnummer: Hadeland i Amerika.* (January, 1964).

Hadelendings in America, including items on pioneer life, personal sketches, and Hadelandslag (society of people from the Hadeland district), and an America letter dated September 8, 1850. A special number of *Hadeland i Amerika.*

HANSEN, MORTEN. *Norske slektsbøker.* Oslo, 1965. 198 p.

Bibliography of family histories, including those of several Norwegian-American families. Reviewed in *Nordmanns-Forbundet,* November, 1965.

HAUGE, ALFRED. *Cleng Peerson: Landkjenning.* Oslo, 1964. 350 p.

The second volume in the author's trilogy, of which *Hundevakt* (1961) was the first, covers the Sloopers' Atlantic crossing in 1825 and their pioneer years.

——— *Cleng Peerson: Ankerfeste.* Oslo, 1965. 335 p.

The third volume in the author's trilogy includes the Norwegian-American settlements. Reviewed in *Nordmanns-Forbundet,* November, 1965.

221

HAUGEN, EINAR, *ed. Norsk-engelsk ordbok.* Madison and Oslo, 1965. 500 p.

This dictionary combines *nynorsk* and *bokmål* into one alphabet for the first time and gives information on grammar, pronunciation, and English meanings, as well as a history of the language, illustrative sentences, and idioms.

————, and CHAPMAN, KENNETH G. *Spoken Norwegian — Revised.* New York, 1964. 416 p.

INGSTAD, HELGE. *Land under the Polar Star.* New York, 1966. 381 p.

Naomi Walford's translation of *Landet under leidarstjernen* (1959), an account of Ingstad's expedition to Greenland in 1953. Reviewed in *Times Literary Supplement* (London), March 24, 1966.

———— *Øst for den store bre.* Oslo, 1945. 157 p.

East of the big glacier; the author's hunting expedition to eastern Greenland, Eirik Raude country, during the winter of 1932–33. First published in 1935.

———— *Vesterveg til Vinland.* Oslo, 1965. 284 p.

A popular account of the author's five expeditions to North America.

INGVOLDSTAD, ORLANDO. *Rimes for Rusty.* Pasadena, 1964. 21 p.

Short poems on assorted subjects.

JERSTAD, JOHAN. *Fjøtland lesebok.* Oslo, 1964. 429 p.

A reader containing articles and poems about the Fjøtland district in Norway. The book includes America letters, 1878–1949, from New York and the Middle West.

JOHNSON, EINAR OSCAR. Soli Deo Gloria: A Study of the Philosophy and Problems of Higher Education among Norwegian Lutherans in the American Environment, 1860–1960.

A manuscript thesis; a microfilm is filed in the Concordia Historical Institute, St. Louis.

JONES, GWYN. *The Norse Atlantic Saga: Being the Norse Voyages of Discovery and Settlement to Iceland, Greenland, America.* London, 1964. 246 p.

KOHT, HALVDAN. *Driving Forces in History.* Cambridge, Massachusetts, 1964. 217 p.

A translation by Einar Haugen of *Drivmakter i historie* (Oslo, 1959).

LARSEN, HENRY A. *Henry med det store skipet.* Oslo, 1964. 276 p.

Henry with the big ship; an autobiography of a Norwegian-Canadian skipper, first to sail the Northwest Passage in both directions. Reviewed in *Nordmanns-Forbundet,* December, 1964.

LIESTØL, ASLAK. *Runer frå bryggen.* Bergen, 1964. 56 p.

Runes from the quay; a survey of the latest runic research, including the Kensington stone.

LOKKE, CARL L. *Klondike Saga: The Chronicle of a Minnesota Gold Mining Company*. Minneapolis, 1965. 209 p.

A joint publication of the Norwegian-American Historical Association and the University of Minnesota Press.

MAGNUSSON, MAGNUS, and PALSSON, HERMANN. *The Vinland Sagas: The Norse Discovery of America, Grœnlendinga Saga and Eirik's Saga*. Baltimore, 1965. 124 p.

Translation from the Icelandic of the two sagas.

MOWAT, FARLEY. *Westviking*. Boston, 1965. 494 p.

NESDAL, SIVERT. *En misjonœrs erindringer*. Leon, Norway, 1965. 519 p.

Reminiscences of a missionary: the biography of a Norwegian-born Lutheran clergyman.

NORWEGIAN-AMERICAN HISTORICAL ASSOCIATION. *Norwegian-American Studies*, vol. 22. Northfield, 1965.

Contents of this volume are listed individually in the section on articles.

OLESON, TRYGGVI J. *Early Voyages and Northern Approaches, 1000–1632*. London, Toronto, New York, 1964. 211 p.

The first volume in the *Canadian Centenary Series*.

OLMANSON, ALBERT, *ed.* and *tr. Letters of Bernt Olmanson, a Union Soldier in the Civil War, 1861–1865*. St. Peter, 1960. 58 p.

Some sixty letters and a brief biographical sketch.

OXENSTIERNA, ERIC. *The Norsemen*. Greenwich, Connecticut, 1965. 320 p.

This volume, originally published in German under the title *Die Wikinger* and now translated and edited by Catherine Hutter, has a chapter on the discovery of America that includes the Ingstad findings in Newfoundland.

PEYTON, KAREN. *The World So Fair*. Philadelphia, 1963. 233 p.

A novel laid in Duluth that portrays Norwegian immigrant life.

POOL, WILLIAM C. *Bosque Territory: A History of an Agrarian Community*. Kyle, Texas, 1964. 206 p.

History of the Bosque County area in Texas. A chapter is devoted to the Norwegian settlement at Norse.

PREUS, JOHAN CARL KEYSER. *Herman Amberg Preus: A Family History*. Minneapolis, 1966. 164 p.

The H. A. Preus family in America, and its immediate ancestors in Norway.

RØLVAAG, OLE E. *Giants in the Earth*. New York, 1964. 486 p.

Introduction by Einar Haugen.

RUTH, ROY K. *The Vinland Voyages: The Icelanders Discover America and Write the First Canadian History.* Winnipeg, 1965. 111 p.

> Translation of the Aris Book of the Icelanders, the Saga of Erik the Red, and the Saga of the Greenlanders, with a chapter on immigrants from Iceland to Canada since 1855.

SCHNACKENBERG, WALTER C. *The Lamp and the Cross.* Tacoma, Washington, 1965. 183 p.

> History of Pacific Lutheran University.

SEMMINGSEN, INGRID, ed. *Husmanns minner.* Oslo. 1960. 230 p.

> Cotter reminiscences; a study of the Norwegian cotter class, which furnished many of the emigrants to America. Mrs. Semmingsen is the first professor of American history at the University of Oslo. Reviewed by Carlton C. Qualey in *Immigrant Research Digest*, Spring, 1965.

SKELTON, R. A., MARSTON, THOMAS E., and PAINTER, GEORGE D. *The Vinland Map and the Tartar Relation.* New Haven, 1965. 291 p.

> Two documents are published in this volume: A world map of about 1440 that includes Vinland, and an account of the Carpini Mission. The authors give descriptions and histories of the two documents.

STEFANSSON, VILHJALMUR. *Discovery: The Autobiography of Vilhjalmur Stefansson.* New York, 1964. 411 p.

STRAUS, LEONORE THOMAS. *The Tender Stone.* New York, 1964. 100 p.

> Record of a voyage made from America to Norway by the author, the artist daughter of a Norwegian immigrant.

TAVUCHIS, NICHOLAS. *Pastors and Immigrants: The Role of the Religious Elite in the Absorption of Norwegian Immigrants.* The Hague and New York, 1963. 84 p.

> Norwegians in the United States, and the role of the Norwegian Synod.

Western Viking (Seattle), May 15, 1964.

> Seventy-fifth anniversary edition of *Washington Posten* and its successor, *Western Viking*. It contains articles on the history of various Norwegian-American institutions in the Pacific Northwest.

WITTKE, CARL. *We Who Built America: The Saga of the Immigrant.* Cleveland, 1964. 550 p.

> This first general revision of the 1939 edition contains little new material. There are bibliographical notes at the end of each chapter.

ARTICLES

AABREKK, ANTON. Med "Valkyrien" over havet. *Nordmanns-Forbundet,* 58:166 (August–September, 1965).

The last voyage of Norwegian emigrants to America under sail, on the "Valkyrie" in 1873.

AGER, WILLIAM T. Incidents in the Early Life of Knut Hamsun. *American Book Collector*, 15:16–18 (September, 1964).

The author and Hamsun at Elroy, Wisconsin. First published in *Kvartalskrift*, January, 1916.

ARESTAD, SVERRE, *ed*. Pioneering in Montana. *Norwegian-American Studies*, 22:104–143 (1965).

AUSTAD, TORE. Report on Norwegian Studies at University of Chicago. *Vinland* (Chicago), February 4, 1965.

BJORNDAL, MAGNUS. Is There an Engineering Shortage? Or Is It Just a Shortage of Technicians? *Norwegian American Technical Journal*, 31–38 (January, 1965).

A study of American engineering education with a plea for the training of technicians.

BLEGEN, THEODORE C. Frederick J. Turner and the Kensington Puzzle. *Minnesota History*, 39:133–140 (Winter, 1964).

Discussion and transcript of a letter from Frederick J. Turner to Gisle Bothne, February 10, 1910, about the Kensington runestone.

BRAATELEIN, TOMMIE. Outstanding Norwegians. *Pacific Coast Viking* (Montrose, California), May, 1965.

Included are Earl Warren, chief justice of the United States Supreme Court; Ole Bardahl, builder, contractor, and chemist, who produced an oil formula; and Ole Evinrude, inventor of the outboard motor.

BRONNER, HEDIN, and FRANZEN, GØSTA. Scandinavian Studies in Institutions of Learning in the United States: Sixth Report, 1963–64. *Scandinavian Studies*, 36:303–322 (November, 1964).

Business. Det norsk-amerikanske handels-kammer feirer 50 år. *Nordisk Tidende* (Brooklyn), October 21, 1965.

History of the Norwegian American Chamber of Commerce.

Bygdelagene og norskdom. *Decorah-Posten*, November 18, 1965.

Evaluation of the current position of the *bygdelag* among Norwegians in America.

CARTFORD, GERHARD M. Music for Youth in an Emerging Church. *Norwegian-American Studies*, 22:162–177 (1965).

CHRISTENSEN, BERNHARD. Augsburg Seminary and Luther Seminary Reunite. *Luther Theological Seminary Review*, 4–14 (May, 1964).

Church. De grât av glede: Første norske julegudstjeneste i Arizona. *Nordmanns-Forbundet*, 57:36 (February, 1964).

A Norwegian Christmas church service and festival in Tucson, Arizona, the first in that state. Henry O. Jaastad was one of the participants.

CUSTER, FRANK. Across the Years of the Capital Times. *Capital Times* (Madison), December 13, 1965.

A survey of the principles and struggles of the newspaper and its editor, William T. Evjue.

DAHLE, REGINE. A Recollection from the 1890's. *Minnesota Posten* (Minneapolis), June 4, 11, 1964. Translated by Astrid Dahle Awes.

A sketch of pioneer life in northern Minnesota, written by the wife of Pastor Ole Dahle.

DE VRIES, CHARLES. Eielsen Synod Passing from Scene. *Lutheran Ambassador*, 5–7 (March 23, 1965).

The synod now has three pastors and fewer than five hundred members.

DOSEY, HERBERT WALTER. The Brig Sleipner. *Inland Seas*, 20: 215–226 (Fall, 1964).

Account of the 1862 voyage from Bergen to Chicago, and the plaque dedication in 1962.

DRAXTEN, NINA. Kristofer Janson's Lecture Tour, 1879–80. *Norwegian-American Studies*, 22: 18–74 (1965).

EIDE, SVERRE. The N. E. S. History and the Outlook at the 40th Anniversary. *Norwegian American Technical Journal*, 5–9 (January, 1965).

History and prospects of the Norwegian Engineers' Society of New York.

EKMAN, ERNST. The Teaching of Scandinavian History in the United States. *Scandinavian Studies*, 37: 259–270 (August, 1965).

FJELDSAA, RUTH L. Hjelpende hender i Solskinnsstaten. *Nordmanns-Forbundet*, 57: 37 (February, 1964).

Helping hands in the Sunshine State. A historical sketch of the thirty-five-year-old Norsk-Amerikanske Mission Club in Miami, Florida.

FOLKEDAHL, BEULAH. From the Archives. *Norwegian-American Studies*, 22: 236–240 (1965).

———— Marshall Academy: A History. *Wisconsin Magazine of History*, 47: 249–260 (Spring, 1964).

Historical sketch of an academy during 1869–81, the period when Norwegian Lutherans operated the school.

———— Some Recent Publications. *Norwegian-American Studies*, 22: 210–235 (1965).

GRIFFITH, ROBERT. Prelude to Insurgency: Irvine L. Lenroot and the Republican Primary of 1908. *Wisconsin Magazine of History*, 49: 16–28 (Autumn, 1965).

Parts played in the campaign by James O. Davidson, Nils P. Haugen, and Herman L. Ekern.

GVAALE, GUDRUN HOVDE. Cleng Peerson: Alfred Hauges romantrilogi. *Syn og segn*, vol. 71, no. 9, p. 482–492 (1965).

Survey and critique of Alfred Hauge's trilogy of books on Cleng Peerson.

HAMBRO, JOHAN. Cleng Peerson, "Peer Gynt of the Prairies." *Norseman*, no. 3, p. 73–75 (1965).

———— Norsemen in the New World. *Norseman*, no. 6, p. 175–178 (1965).

Survey of Norwegians in America, from Leif Erikson to the arrival of the "Restauration"; it includes individual immigrants before 1825.

HANSEN, ELLA. Norsk pige med drømmen "husjobb i Amerika," uten å kunne tale engelsk forteller om hvordan det gikk. *Nordisk Tidende*, January 9, 1964.

The language difficulties of a Norwegian immigrant in modern America.

Hauge. Alfred Hauge drar på ny ut i Cleng Peersons spor. *Western Viking*, July 2, 1965.

Alfred Hauge, author of a trilogy on Cleng Peerson, travels again in his footsteps.

HAUGEN, EINAR. Discovery of America 500 Years before Columbus, in Norse Sagas. *Nordisk Tidende*, October 8, 1964.

Leif's discovery of America, as revealed in the Icelandic sagas, and an appraisal of its significance.

HEG, JAMES E. Commitment Commemorated. *Sons of Norway Viking*, 62: 126, 155 (May, June, 1965).

A great-grandson of Colonel Hans C. Heg stresses the sense of commitment of Norwegian soldiers in the Civil War.

———— From the Saga of the 15th Wisconsin Regiment, Led by Col. Hans Chr. Heg in the Civil War, 100 Years Ago. *Nordisk Tidende*, April 8, 1965.

Captain Heg of the United States Army sketches the activities of the Fifteenth Wisconsin.

HERTSGAARD, O. I. Barndommens nybyggerliv. *Hallingen*, September, 1965.

Childhood on the North Dakota prairie.

HOLSTAD, RUTH. I Remember Grandma. *Ebenezer*, 30: 24–27 (February, 1963).

Sketch about Mrs. Hans A. Holstad of Northfield.

HVAMSTAD, PER TH. Hadelendingenes "Brua." *Nordmanns-Forbundet*, 58:62 (March–April, 1965).

Hadelandlag's magazine over forty years.

———— Kubberulla. *Bygdebrevet*, second series, no. 11, p. 11 (June 8, 1965).

The *kubberulla*, the Norwegian immigrant's wagon, and its predecessors in Norway.

Immigration. Hele 900,000 nordmenn utvandret på 135 år. *Nordisk Tidende*, November 18, 1965.

Statistics and causes of emigration from Norway, mostly to the United States, since 1825.

INGSTAD, HELGE. Vinland Ruins Prove Vikings Found the New World. *National Geographic*, 126:708–734 (November, 1964).

The author's finds at L'Anse aux Meadow, Newfoundland, and the Viking expeditions that preceded his.

INNVIK, ERLING. Decorah-Posten's historie gjennem 90 aar. *Decorah-Posten*, September 3, 1964.

Decorah-Posten through ninety years.

JORGENSON, THEODORE. Decorah-Posten og norsk literatur. *Decorah-Posten*, September 3, 1964.

Decorah-Posten and Norwegian literature.

KRISTOFFERSEN, HANS. Besøk i Kendall, hvor alle norske nå hviler glemte på kirkegården. *Nordisk Tidende*, November 12, 1964.

All that remain of the 1825 Norwegian settlement in western New York are the Norway Road, the Orsland and Stangland monuments in the cemetery, the Ole Orsland barn, and the Larsson house.

———— Det Norske Selskab i New York som nå fyller 60 år. *Nordisk Tidende*, October 15, 1964.

A historical sketch of a Norwegian society.

———— Jeg sov i ruinene etter Ole Bulls falne slot i Alleghenyfjellene. *Nordisk Tidende*, September 10, 1964.

A history of the Ole Bull settlement in northern Pennsylvania, with a description of the area as it is today.

———— Over en halv million begravet på Potters Field; mange norske navn minner om immigrant-tragedier. *Nordisk Tidende*, July 8, 1965.

Names of forgotten Norwegian immigrants buried in mass graves on Hart's Island, the potter's field of the New York area, since 1869.

LEVORSEN, BARBARA. Our Bread and Meat. *Norwegian-American Studies*, 22:178–197 (1965).

Litterære Samfund. Sekretær Randi Bay's utførlige 30 års — rapport, Januar 21, 1955. *Vinland*, January 14, 1965.

The secretary of Det Litteraere Samfund, Chicago, gives a report of its activities since its inception in 1925.

LOFTHUS, DOROTHY. Deerfield Landmark Sold: Started Out as Hauge Church a Century Ago. *Capital Times*, February 25, 1964.

MYKLEBUST, JOHAN. Emigrantskipet "St. Olaf." *Nordmanns-Forbundet*, 58:7–9 (January, 1965).

Historical sketch of the flagship of the Norwegian America Line, the first such line to carry emigrants to America.

NARVESTAD, CARL T. Bygdelagene i Amerika. *Nordmanns-Forbundet*, 57:144 (July, 1964).

Historical sketch of the Valdres Samband, the pioneer *bygdelag* in America, as it celebrates its sixty-fifth anniversary.

NELSON, MARION JOHN. A Pioneer Artist and His Masterpiece. *Norwegian-American Studies*, 22:3–17 (1965).

NELSON, PEDER H. Hadelands nybyggere. *Nordmanns-Forbundet*, 57:7 (January, 1964).

Hadeland pioneers; a sketch of the Glenwood settlement near Decorah, Iowa.

―――― Hallingerne paa Blooming Prairie, Minnesota. *Hallingen*, March, 1964.

Names, pictures, and biographical sketches of early settlers from Halling in Blooming Prairie.

―――― Hallingerne på Blooming Prairie. *Nordmanns-Forbundet*, 58:119 (June, 1965).

Historical items about the Halling settlement at Blooming Prairie, Minnesota.

―――― Norsk-amerikansk folkelesning. *Nordmanns-Forbundet*, 58:174–176 (August–September, 1965).

Books written by Norwegian Americans in the Norwegian language.

―――― Norsk museum ved Walcott, North Dakota. *Hallingen*, June, 1964.

Mrs. Clarence Christianson's museum and its artifacts.

―――― Torvhus og jordhytter: Fra slitets liv på prærien. *Nordmanns-Forbundet*, 58:33 (February, 1965).

Life on the North Dakota prairie in pioneer days.

Newspapers. Den norske avisdød i Amerika. *Decorah-Posten*, August 26, 1965.

Beulah Folkedahl

The expiration of Norwegian newspapers in America, and the significance of the demise of *Duluth Skandinav.*

Norwegian-American Historical Association. Det norsk-amerikanske historielag fylder 40 aar. *Decorah-Posten,* September 2, 1965.

Evaluation of the book production, over forty years, of the Norwegian-American Historical Association, and a review of *Norwegian-American Studies,* volume 22.

Norwegian language. Harvard-Professor Einar Haugen om dagens norske Amerika, fremtids-prospekter, norsk ved Harvard. *Nordisk Tidende,* September 16, 1965.

The position of Norwegian in America's academic world and the language controversy in Norway; an interview with Niels J. Murer of *Aftenposten.*

Norwegian societies. Den norske fiskeklub. *Nordmanns-Forbundet,* 57:249–251 (December, 1964).

San Francisco's Norwegian fish club through fifty years.

Old People's Home. Det norske gamlehjem i Boston feirer 50-års jubileum. *Nordmanns-Forbundet,* 57:258 (December, 1964).

Home for the aged in Boston celebrates its fiftieth anniversary.

OLSEN, JOHN. Bethelship-Metodistkirke feirer 90 års jubileum den 23. og 24. mai. *Nordisk Tidende,* May 14, 1964.

Bethelship Methodist church in Brooklyn celebrates its ninetieth anniversary. It was organized by Scandinavians on a ship in New York harbor in 1845.

OPSAHL, O. K. Slekten Myhro. *Hallingen,* September, 1965.

A history of the Myhro family, from the early 1700's to 1957.

Paulson family. The Best of Two Worlds. *Bond,* 42:4 (May, 1965).

Description of the Erling Paulson ranch near Dickinson, North Dakota, occupied by the family since 1896.

PETERSEN, EUGENE. Norge Ski Club's historie. *Vinland,* April 9, 1964.

PREUTZ, ALEX E. A Group of Norwegians in Brooklyn at Turn of Century Created "Little Norway" in Rustic Rowland, Penn. *Nordisk Tidende,* June 3, 1965.

QUALEY, CARLTON C., *tr.* and *ed.* Seven America Letters to Valdres. *Norwegian-American Studies,* 22:144–161 (1965).

[RØLVAAG, O. E.] MØRCK, PAAL, *ed.* Amerika-breve fra P. A. Smevik til hans far og bror i Norge. *Vinland,* April 20–December 10, 1964.

America letters from P. A. Smevik to his father and brother in Norway, reprinted from the volume of the same name published in Minneapolis in 1912. Rølvaag occasionally used the pseudonym "Paal Mørck."

ROSHOLT, MALCOLM. Two Men of Old Waupaca. *Norwegian-American Studies*, 22: 75–103 (1965).

Sanderson, Ole A. Fra Iowa til Nebraska i 1880. *Hallingen*, March, 1965.

From Iowa to Nebraska in 1880; included is Sanderson's daybook kept on the journey.

SCHULTZ, VERNON F. Schuetzen Club Annual Shoot Is 73-Year Syttende Mai Tradition. *Capital Times*, May 13, 1965.

Norwegians, Germans, and Swiss in the Black Earth, Wisconsin, area.

SEHL, KARI. Oplevelser i Amerika. *Hallingen*, June, 1965.

Mrs. Torstein Sehl, wife of a merchant in Brocket, North Dakota, tells of experiences in America.

SØYLAND, CARL. Monument over "Utvandringens far." *Nordisk Tidende*, July 1, 1965.

A monument to Cleng Peerson, the "Father of Emigration," was unveiled in Haugesund-Tysvær, Norway.

———— Omkring et 60 års jubileum. *Nordisk Tidende*, October 22, 1964.

Sketch of the Norske Selskap, a club in Brooklyn, with an evaluation of past and current purposes and problems.

———— Påstrømmende tanker ved avisjubileum i Seattle. *Nordisk Tidende*, May 28, 1964.

Historical sketch of *Washington Posten.*

STOEM, HENRIK. Fra Leksvik til S.-Dakota: Amerika-brev fra Henrik Stoem som reiste over havet i 1873. *Bygdebrevet*, series 2, no. 9, p. 18, 30 (May 11, 1965).

From Leksvik to South Dakota: an America letter written in 1950 from Volin, South Dakota, telling of life there from 1873 to 1950.

STOYLEN, SIGVALD. Streiflys over Marcus Thranes liv og omskriftende virke i Amerika. *Nordisk Tidende*, March 4, 11, 1965.

A sketch and evaluation of Marcus Thrane.

THORTVEDT, LEIF. A Journey across Minnesota in 1870. *Gopher Historian*, 29: 15–20 (Spring, 1965).

A trip from Houston to the Red River Valley made by Norwegian immigrants.

TORGRIM, WILLARD. History of Luren Singing Society, Decorah, Iowa. *Sanger-Hilsen*, 54: 10–12 (May–June, 1964).

A few high lights about the oldest organization of its kind in America.

Vinland the Good Emerges from the Mists. *American Heritage*, vol. 16, no. 6, p. 4–11, 99–106 (October, 1965).

Included are essays entitled "The Mapping of Vinland," "Was There a Lasting Colony?" and "Did Columbus or Cabot See the Map?"

VOLLO, I. N. Erindringer og oplevelser. *Hallingen*, September, 1965.

Recollections of a Norwegian Canadian.

WHITEHILL, WALTER MUIR. The Independent Historical Society. *Norwegian-American Studies*, 22:198–209 (1965).

WOIWODE, LARRY. The Deathless Lovers. *New Yorker*, July 10, 1965.

The author's visits with his Norwegian-American grandmother in North Dakota.

BIOGRAPHICAL SKETCHES

BARLIEN, HANS

En merkelig emigrant-skikkelse: Hans Barlien fra Trøndelag. *Nordmanns-Forbundet*, 57:15 (January, 1964).

A remarkable emigrant figure: Hans Barlien from Trøndelag.

BJELLE, OLE LARSON

Fra krambusvend til representanthuset. *Hallingen*, June, 1965.

From store clerk to house of representatives.

BUSCHMANN, AUGUST

August Buschmann traff eventyret i pioner-dager på Alaska-kysten. *Western Viking*, June 5, 1964.

August Buschmann met adventure in pioneer days on the Alaska coast.

GRINAGER, MONS

Per Th. Hvamstad. Hadelending i borgerkrigen. *Nordmanns-Forbundet*, 57:64 (March–April, 1964).

A Hadelander in the Civil War. Grinager was captain in the Fifteenth Wisconsin Regiment.

HAMMER, EINAR

Einar Hammer, Sons of Norway Ex-Official, Dies. *Minnesota Posten*, August 26, 1965.

HAUGEN, KRISTINE

Fru Kristine Haugen død i Stoughton, Wisconsin. *Nordisk Tidende*, September 30, 1965.

Eyvind J. Evans. Penn-Skudd. *Minnesota Posten*, December 23, 1965.

HEKTOEN, LUDVIG

Arne Kildal. Norskættet lege minnes i Amerika. *Nordmanns-Forbundet*, 57:92 (May, 1964).

A Norwegian-American doctor commemorated in America. Hektoen was a prominent Chicago physician.

HOFF, PHILIP

Rolf N. B. Haugen. Philip Hoff: Vermont Governor. *Norseman*, no. 2, p. 49–51 (1965).

HUMPHREY, HUBERT H.

Johan Hambro. Første norsk-amerikanske vice-president. *Nordmanns-Forbundet*, 57:246–248 (December, 1964).

The first Norwegian-American Vice-President.

Hans Kristoffersen. Hva med senator Hubert Humphreys norske bakgrund? *Nordisk Tidende*, September 3, 1964.

Sketch of Humphrey's Norwegian background.

IBSEN, NICOLAI A.

Peder H. Nelson. Henrik Ibsens bror. *Nordmanns-Forbundet*, 57:63 (March–April, 1964).

Henrik Ibsen's brother; Nicolai Ibsen's life in America.

JAASTAD, HENRY

Norwegian Born "Mayor Jaastad," Tucson's Great Friend, 93, Dead. *Nordisk Tidende*, December 30, 1965.

Henry Olson Jaastad, Ex-Mayor, Dies at 93. *Tucson Daily Citizen*, December 21, 1965.

JOHNSON, SIMON

R. Dahle-Melsæther. "Praeriens digter" 90 aar. *Decorah-Posten*, September 24, 1964.

Poet of the prairie, ninety years old.

KNAPHUS, TORLEIF

Noted Utah Sculptor, 63, Dies. *Minnesota Posten*, June 24, 1965.

KNAPLUND, PAUL

Prof.-Emeritus Paul Knaplund, Long-Time UW Historian, Dies. *Capital Times*, April 9, 1964.

KUMLIEN, THURE

Dorothy Peterson. Noted Pioneer Naturalist Lived in Albion Prairie Century Ago. *Capital Times*, April 28, 1964.

LARSEN, HENRY ASBJØRN

Canada to Erect Statue of Norwegian in Vancouver. *Pacific Coast Viking*, May, 1965.

Den berømte norsk-kanadiske kaptein som seilte nordvest passasjen østover og vestover død. *Nordisk Tidende*, November 5, 1964.

The renowned Norwegian-Canadian captain, who sailed the Northwest Passage both eastward and westward, is dead.

Henry Asbjørn Larsen. *Arctic*, 18:67 (March, 1965).

Explorer of the Northwest Passage and superintendent of the Royal Canadian Mounted Police.

LILLEHEI, C. WALTON

Meredith Ann Wilson. Modern American Vikings. *Sons of Norway Viking*, 61:51 (March, 1964).

Lillehei's career in heart surgery.

LYCHE, HANS TAMBS

Paul Knaplund. Norsk talsmann for Amerika. *Nordmanns-Forbundet*, 57:119–121 (June, 1964).

Norwegian spokesman for America; a sketch of a Norwegian-born Unitarian clergyman and journalist.

OLAV, HANS

Ambassadør Hans Olav, 62, død i Oslo; tidligere redaktør av Nordisk Tidende. *Nordisk Tidende*, December 16, 1965.

Former editor died in Oslo.

Carl Søyland. Tidligere redaktør vandret bort. *Nordisk Tidende*, December 23, 1965.

ROMNES, HAAKON INGOLF

Norsk immigrant-sønn president i verdens største firma, A. T. & T. *Nordisk Tidende*, February 4, 1965.

American Telephone and Telegraph Company president.

SINGSTAD, OLE

Ole Eide. Dr. Ole Singstad. *Norwegian American Technical Journal*, 13 (January, 1965).

STRAND, MARTHINIUS

Marthinius Strand død. *Decorah-Posten*, November 4, 1965.

Salt Lake City industrialist and former president of National Ski Association.

THRANE, ROBERT

"Jeg har altid kjent en dragning til dere." *Nordisk Tidende*, October 15, 1964.

"I have always felt drawn to you," referring to Norway. An interview with Robert Thrane in Oslo, with reminiscences of his grandfather, Marcus Thrane.

VEBLEN, THORSTEIN B.

Hjørdis Christiansen. Professor Thorstein B. Veblen. *Decorah-Posten*, August 27, 1964.

Sketch based on Juul Dieserud's account of 1923.

HISTORIES OF CONGREGATIONS

BROOKLYN, NEW YORK

Trinity Lutheran Church. C. O. Pedersen. This World of Ours. *Nordisk Tidende*, September 16–30, 1965.

PRAIRIEVILLE, TEXAS

"Four Mile Lutheran Church, 1964." 114 p. Typescript. Norwegian-American Historical Association archives.

ALBANY, WISCONSIN

Albany Lutheran Church: Centennial 1863–1963. 20 p.

COLFAX, WISCONSIN

Centennial Festival, Holden Lutheran Congregation, June 13–14, 1964. 18 p.

LA CROSSE, WISCONSIN

Our Savior's Evangelical Lutheran Church, 100th Anniversary, 1861–1961. 20 p.

SOLON SPRINGS, WISCONSIN

Our Savior's Lutheran Church, 1914–1964. 12 p.

WOODVILLE, WISCONSIN

Zion Lutheran Church, 75th Anniversary, 1887–1962. 32 p.

by BEULAH FOLKEDAHL

10   *From the Archives*

The J. JØRGEN THOMPSON Papers are a rich source of information about St. Olaf College and Spokane College.

In the Slooper Society files is a letter in English to Ove Rosdale, November 12, 1874, written by LARS ELLICKSON from Santa Fe, where he was in military service with Company G, First Regiment, Illinois Infantry.

"Notes on Norwegian Settlements in Texas," by AXEL ARNESON, is a fourteen-page typescript about frontier hospitality, church and school life, and relations with Indians.

Among the papers of A. O. SERUM, a Halstad, Minnesota, farmer, are articles and letters on crop production, co-operatives, and local history, as well as correspondence with personnel at Augsburg and Augustana seminaries.

An interesting item in the IVER SIMLEY Papers is an auction bill announcing the sale of the family *gaard*, issued by Simley's father just before he emigrated to Black Earth, Wisconsin, in 1869.

A manuscript volume of 167 pages entitled "Days That Are Gone," by A. Sophie Boe, is a detailed story of her father, NILS E. BOE, as a child, a student, a Civil War soldier, husband and father, and as a pastor in Kansas, Michigan, Illinois, Iowa, and Wisconsin.

A history of Aaberg Academy, Devils Lake, North Dakota, was written by PASTOR OLE H. AABERG, founder and president.

Among F. A. Schmidt's correspondents were leading church-men: Claus L. Clausen, O. J. Hatlestad, Kristofer Janson, J. N. Kildahl, U. V. Koren, Laur. Larsen, Th. N. Mohn, B. J. Muus, J. A. Ottesen, H. A. Preus, P. A. Rasmussen, and H. A. Stub.

A manuscript entitled "Amerika feberen begynner, av norsk utvandrings historie 1839" discusses causes and results of migration and includes a letter by Ansten Nattestad of November 6, 1839. It was donated by Sverre H. Ader, Norway.

In the Augsburg College and Seminary Papers is a typescript of the testimony of Sven Oftedal and Ole Paulson in the court record of the United Norwegian Lutheran Church vs. Augsburg Seminary.

Among the Julius B. Baumann Papers are three scrapbooks: "Stottegalskab i Reform," "Norskdom og norsk-am. literatur i Decorah-Posten," and "Over Grænsen."

The "Protocol for Scandinavia Association Board of Directors," 1893–1932, is a primary source on the history of Scandinavia Academy and its successor, Central Wisconsin College.

A typescript of eighteen pages contains biographical material about Viggo Drewsen, chief of the technical research department of the West Virginia Pulp and Paper Company in New York.

Papers of Hans O. Egeberg (1875–1933) relate to his career as employment manager at the Gary Steel Works, Gary, Indiana.

Peter J. Eikeland's manuscript article, "Vanskeligheter for norskundervisninger ved vore høiereskole" (ca. 1923), gives a historic survey of the teaching of Norwegian.

Minnie J. Gasmann of Amherst, Wisconsin, presented a copy of biographical data about Hans Jacob and Johan Gotfred Gasmann, their ancestors and descendants, a translated version.

The Abraham Grimstvedt correspondence presents a bright picture of life in America as it was lived in Dane County, Wissin; Fillmore County, Minnesota; and Decorah and Lake Mills, Iowa, from 1850–75, by his sisters and their husbands.

In the Anders O. Hagen Papers are letters from W. J. L. Frich, U. V. Koren, B. J. Muus, H. A. Preus, and P. A. Rasmussen.

The Einar Haugen and Kristine Haugen Papers include letters from Ole E. Rølvaag, 1920–31.

Beulah Folkedahl

In the J. J. HEIMARK Papers are account books, 1880–1933, of the Moe grocery store, St. Paul.

Descriptions of the Hudson's Bay Company retail stores and stage lines are in the notes taken by Anton Hillesland during his interviews with Swen N. Heskin, farmer and lay preacher in the Goose River settlement in North Dakota.

The HALVOR ROSVALD (Solveson) Papers contain data on Rosvald's expedition to California during the gold rush, in the company of Hans C. Heg.

A paper entitled "Beskrivelse af Holden, Goodhue County, Minnesota, læst ved hundred-aarsfesten den fjerde juli, 1876," read at the celebration honoring the hundredth anniversary of the Declaration of Independence, contains information about first settlers, Indians, crops, prices, local government, and the church.

Family and church histories by OLE A. MYRVIK give an account of pioneer life at Milton, North Dakota.

SOREN A. TYSTAD's history of the Norwegian settlement in Miner County, South Dakota, gives names of pioneers; comments on prairie fires, farming, and the 1880 snowstorm; and discusses the religious life in the settlement.

JOHN N. KILDAHL's letters to his son, John L., offer counsel on pastoral problems as well as items about family affairs.

A manuscript article contains the autobiography of CHRISTIAN LARSON, Winnebago County, Iowa, father of Laurence M. Larson, professor of history at the University of Illinois.

The papers of CLARA (MRS. MARTIN O.) MONSON, consisting of correspondence, family histories, and memoirs, tell much of farm, home, school, and church during pioneer days in Wiota, Lafayette County, Wisconsin.

The Forhandlingsprotokol (record book), 1889–94, of FREMAD, a debating society in Minneola, Minnesota, records the topics of debates, such as capital punishment, power of the press, restricted immigration, the Farmers' Alliance, and the preservation of the Norwegian language in America.

HAGBARTH NIELSEN, California dairyman, has written reminiscences of his mining experiences in Alaska and the Yukon.

The scrapbook of OLE NILSEN, clergyman and writer, contains for the most part items on controversial Lutheran Church subjects, written by Claus L. Clausen, Theo. H. Dahl, Gisle Johnson, U. V. Koren, Laur. Larsen, O. Nilsen, Lars Oftedal, F. A. Schmidt, Georg Sverdrup, and August Weenaas.

A biographical sketch of Andrew Furuseth and data about the "Gjøa," Roald Amundsen's ship, famed for going through the Northwest Passage in 1903–05, are to be found in the RALPH ENGER Papers.

A letter from Peder Ydstie, Minnesota poet, filed in the TOR-KEL OFTELIE Papers, discusses the family life of Kristofer Janson.

The diary of HANS OLSON (Langrud) gives an account of a migration journey the family took in 1870 from Dodgeville, Wisconsin, to Coal Creek, Kansas. Towns on the route of travel and the supply of grass and water for the cattle are the chief topics.

The Sioux Outbreak of 1862 is the subject of a typescript of thirty-nine pages entitled "De Forenede Staters Værste Indianerkrig" by OLE O. ENESTVEDT, a farmer from Sacred Heart, Minnesota.

A nine-page typescript of a biography of MAREN POL (MRS. ANDREAS) PEDERSON, boarding house operator, written by her two granddaughters, recounts the hardships of the sea voyage to the Hawaiian sugar plantations, via Cape Horn, and of making a living in Hawaii and California.

Some salmodicon charts consist of manuscripts of musical scores for a Norwegian one-stringed instrument.

An address given by KENNETH O. BJORK at St. Olaf College on Founders' Day, November 6, 1963, presents the "kingly" ideals of the immigrant founders and guidelines for today's American colleges.

One folder of correspondence in the GERHARD RASMUSSEN Papers deals with the renovation and removal of the Muskego Church from Racine County, Wisconsin, to the campus of Luther Theological Seminary in St. Paul.

HELENA (MRS. GEORG) REIERSEN, in an America letter written in 1860, tells of slavery, railroads, and her husband's commission business in Shreveport, Louisiana.

In an eighty-three-page typescript, "A Hundred Years with Norwegians in the East Bay," SOREN C. ROINESTAD of San Francisco has included sketches of churches, societies, festivals, and leading Norwegian Americans.

Of value in an ULRIK V. KOREN bibliography is Austin K. Rollag's article, "Da Professor Koren kom til Beaver Creek menighet." Rollag was a South Dakota farmer in the Garretson area.

The papers of ZACHARIAS M. TOFTEZON, probably the first white man in the Stanwood, Washington, area, deal with church, health, weather and crops.

Contributors

Professor Carlton C. Qualey, editor of the present volume, is chairman of the department of history in Carleton College, Northfield, Minnesota. He was recently appointed Laird Bell Professor of History.

Dr. Eugene L. Fevold is professor of church history in Luther Theological Seminary, St. Paul. He is the author, with E. Clifford Nelson, of *The Lutheran Church among Norwegian-Americans: A History of the Evangelical Lutheran Church* (Minneapolis, 1960).

Dr. Millard L. Gieske is assistant dean of the graduate school in the University of Minnesota. He has done book reviews for *Minnesota History*, and is presently working on a history of the evolution of the Democratic–Farmer-Labor party in Minnesota.

Miss Nora O. Solum, professor emeritus of English, St. Olaf College, has done a number of Rølvaag translations and was collaborator with Theodore Jorgenson on *O. E. Rølvaag: A Biography* (New York and London, 1939).

Professor C. A. Clausen recently retired as professor of history in St. Olaf College, Northfield. He is the editor of *The Lady with the Pen: Elise Wærenskjold in Texas*, published by the association in 1961, and of various articles and translations in the present series.

Miss Beulah Folkedahl is curator of archives for the Norwegian-American Historical Association. Besides several articles and translations, she has compiled three of the "Some Recent Publications" series for *Norwegian-American Studies*.

Miss Nina Draxten, assistant professor of literature and writing in the general college, University of Minnesota, is engaged in completing her book on Kristofer Janson's years in America.

Dr. Arlow W. Andersen is professor of history in Wisconsin State University, Oshkosh. He is the author of *The Immigrant Takes His Stand: The Norwegian-American Press and Public Affairs, 1847–1872* (Northfield, 1953) and *The Salt of the Earth: A History of Norwegian-Danish Methodism in America* (Nashville, Tennessee, 1962).

Dr. Marc L. Ratner is professor of English in California State College at Hayward. He is the author of a number of critical articles in periodicals and will publish a book on William Styron next year.

NORWEGIAN-AMERICAN HISTORICAL ASSOCIATION

OFFICERS

Publications

STUDIES AND RECORDS

VOLUME I. Minneapolis, 1926. 175 p. Illustrations. Health Conditions and the Practice of Medicine among the Early Norwegian Settlers, 1825–1865, by Knut Gjerset and Ludvig Hektoen; The Norwegian Quakers of 1825, by Henry J. Cadbury; Bishop Jacob Neumann's Word of Admonition to the Peasants, translated and edited by Gunnar J. Malmin; Norwegians in the West in 1844: A Contemporary Account, by Johan R. Reiersen, translated and edited by Theodore C. Blegen; An Emigrant Voyage in the Fifties, by H. Cock-Jensen, translated by Karen Larsen; Reminiscences of a Pioneer Editor, by Carl Fredrik Solberg, edited by Albert O. Barton. Price $3.00

VOLUME II. Northfield, 1927. 137 p. Norwegian Emigrant Songs, translated and edited by Martin B. Ruud; Four Immigrant Shiploads of 1836 and 1837, by Henry J. Cadbury; Immigration As Viewed by a Norwegian-American Farmer in 1869, a letter translated and edited by Jacob Hodnefield; The Norwegian Pioneer in the Field of American Scholarship, by Laurence M. Larson; Norwegian Language and Literature in American Universities, by George T. Flom; Norwegian-American Church History, by George M. Stephenson. Price $3.00

VOLUME III. Northfield, 1928. 133 p. The Disillusionment of an Immigrant: Sjur Jørgensen Haaeim's "Information on Conditions in North America," translated and edited by Gunnar J. Malmin; A Doctrinaire Idealist: Hans Barlien, by D. G. Ristad; Norwegian-American Emigration Societies of the Forties and Fifties, by Albert O. Barton; Emigration As Viewed by a Norwegian Student of Agriculture in 1850: A. Budde's "From a Letter about America," translated by A. Sophie Bøe, with an introduction by Theodore C. Blegen; An Immigration Journey to America in 1854, a letter translated and edited by Henrietta Larson; Chicago As Viewed by a Norwegian Immigrant in 1864, a letter translated and edited by Brynjolf J. Hovde; The Historical Value of Church Records, by J. Magnus Rohne; A Norwegian-American Landnamsman: Ole S. Gjerset, by Knut Gjerset; The Icelandic Communities in America: Culture Backgrounds and Early Settlements, by Thorstina Jackson.   Price $3.00

VOLUME IV. Northfield, 1929. 159 p. A Contribution to the Study of the Adjustment of a Pioneer Pastor to American Conditions: Laur. Larsen, 1857–1880, by Karen Larsen; Report of the Annual Meeting of the Haugean Churches Held at Lisbon, Illinois, in June, 1854, translated and edited by J. Magnus Rohne; The Attitude of the United States toward Norway in the Crisis of 1905, by H. Fred Swansen; Immigration and Social Amelioration, by Joseph Schafer; The Mind of the Scandinavian Immigrant, by George M. Stephenson; Three Civil War Letters from 1862, translated and edited by Brynjolf J. Hovde; The Sinking of the "Atlantic" on Lake Erie, a letter translated and edited by Henrietta Larson; An Account of a Journey to California in 1852, by Tosten Kittelsen Stabæk, translated by Einar Haugen.   Price $3.00

VOLUME V. Northfield, 1930. 152 p. An Early Norwegian Fur Trader of the Canadian Northwest, by Hjalmar R. Holand; Immigrant Women and the American Frontier, three early "America letters" translated and edited by Theodore C. Blegen; From New York to Wisconsin in 1844, by Johan Gasmann, translated and edited by Carlton C. Qualey; Social and Economic Aspects of Pioneering As Illustrated in Goodhue County, Minnesota, by Theodore Nydahl; Norwegian-American Fiction, 1880–1928, by Aagot D. Hoidahl; Bjørnson and the Norwegian-Americans, 1880–81, by Arthur C. Paulson; The Beginnings of St. Olaf College, by I. F. Grose; Some Recent Publications Relating to Norwegian-American History, compiled by Jacob Hodnefield.   Price $3.00

VOLUME VI. Northfield, 1931. 191 p. Illustrations, map. Norwegians in the Selkirk Settlement, by Paul Knaplund; Claus L. Clausen, Pioneer Pastor and Settlement Promoter: Illustrative

Documents, translated and edited by Carlton C. Qualey; Lars Davidson Reque: Pioneer, by Sophie A. Bøe; A Pioneer Pastor's Journey to Dakota in 1861, by Abraham Jacobson, translated by J. N. Jacobson; The Campaign of the Illinois Central Railroad for Norwegian and Swedish Immigrants, by Paul W. Gates; Norwegians at the Indian Forts on the Missouri River during the Seventies, by Einar Haugen; The Convention Riot at Benson Grove, Iowa, in 1876, by Laurence M. Larson; Bjørnson's Reaction to Emigration, by Arne Odd Johnsen; Alexander Corstvet and Anthony M. Rud, Norwegian-American Novelists, by Albert O. Barton; The Norwegian-American Historical Museum, by Knut Gjerset; Norwegian Migration to America before the Civil War, by Brynjolf J. Hovde; Some Recent Publications Relating to Norwegian-American History, II, compiled by Jacob Hodnefield.

Price $3.00

VOLUME VII. Northfield, 1933. 139 p. Illustrations. Social Aspects of Prairie Pioneering: The Reminiscences of a Pioneer Pastor's Wife, by Mrs. R. O. Brandt; The Fraser River Gold Rush: An Immigrant Letter of 1858, translated and edited by C. A. Clausen; O. E. Rølvaag: Norwegian-American, by Einar I. Haugen; Some Recent Publications Relating to Norwegian-American History, III, compiled by Jacob Hodnesfield; A Hunt for Norwegian-American Records, by Carlton C. Qualey; Ole Edvart Rølvaag, 1876–1931: In Memoriam, by Julius E. Olson. Out of print

VOLUME VIII. Northfield, 1934. 176 p. Tellef Grundysen and the Beginnings of Norwegian-American Fiction, by Laurence M. Larson; The Seventeenth of May in Mid-Atlantic: Ole Rynning's Emigrant Song, translated and edited by Theodore C. Blegen and Martin B. Ruud; Johannes Nordboe and Norwegian Immigration: An "America Letter" of 1837, edited by Arne Odd Johnsen; The First Norwegian Migration into Texas: Four "America Letters," translated and edited by Lyder L. Unstad; Norwegian-Americans and Wisconsin Politics in the Forties, by Bayrd Still; The Emigrant Journey in the Fifties, by Karl E. Erickson, edited by Albert O. Barton; The Political Position of *Emigranten* in the Election of 1852: A Documentary Article, by Harold M. Tolo; The Editorial Policy of *Skandinaven*, 1900–1903, by Agnes M. Larson; Some Recent Publications Relating to Norwegian-American History, IV, compiled by Jacob Hodnefield; Fort Thompson in the Eighties: A Communication.   Price $3.00

VOLUME IX. Northfield, 1936. 131 p. Immigration and Puritanism, by Marcus L. Hansen; Svein Nilsson, Pioneer Norwegian-American Historian, by D. G. Ristad; The Sugar Creek Settlement in Iowa, by H. F. Swansen; Pioneer Town Building in the West: An America Letter Written by Frithjof Meidell at Springfield, Illinois, in 1855, translated with a foreword by Clarence A. Clausen; A Typical Norwegian Settlement: Spring Grove, Minnesota, by Carlton C. Qualey; Marcus Thrane in America: Some Unpublished Letters from 1880–1884, translated and edited by Waldemar Westergaard; The Missouri Flood of 1881, by Halvor B. Hustvedt, translated by Katherine Hustvedt; The Collection and Preservation of Sources, by Laurence M. Larson; Some Recent Publications Relating to Norwegian-American History, V, compiled by Jacob Hodnefield.   Price $3.00

VOLUME X. Northfield, 1938. 202 p. Language and Immigration, by Einar I. Haugen; Two Early Norwegian Dramatic Societies in Chicago, by Napier Wilt and Henriette C. Koren Naeseth; A School and Language Controversy in 1858: A Documentary Study, translated and edited by Arthur C. Paulson and Kenneth Bjørk; A Newcomer Looks at American Colleges, translated and edited by Karen Larsen; The Norwegian Quakers of Marshall County, Iowa, by H. F. Swansen; The Main Factors in Rølvaag's Authorship, by Theodore Jorgenson; Magnus Swenson, Inventor and Engineer, by Olaf Hougen; Some Recent Publications Relating to Norwegian-American History, VI, compiled by Jacob Hodnefield.   Price $3.00

VOLUME XI. Northfield, 1940. 183 p. A Doll's House on the Prairie: The First Ibsen Controversy in America, by Arthur C. Paulson and Kenneth Bjørk; Scandinavian Students at Illinois State University, by Henry O. Evjen; Stephen O. Himoe, Civil War Physician, by E. Biddle Heg; A Pioneer Church Library, by H. F. Swansen; Norwegian Emigration to America during the Nineteenth Century, by Ingrid Gaustad Semmingsen; Jørgen Gjerdrum's Letters from America, 1874–75, by Carlton C. Qualey; The Introduction of Domesticated Reindeer into Alaska, by Arthur S. Peterson; The Unknown Rølvaag: Secretary in the Norwegian-American Historical Association, by Kenneth Bjørk; The Sources of the Rølvaag Biography, by Nora O. Solum; Some Recent Publications Relating to Norwegian-American History, VII, compiled by Jacob Hodnefield.   Price $4.00

VOLUME XII. Northfield, 1941. 203 p. Norwegian-American Surnames, by Marjorie M. Kimmerle; Norwegian Folk Narrative in America, by Ella Valborg Rølvaag; A Journey to America in the Fifties, by Clara Jacobson; James Denoon Reymert and the Norwegian Press, by Martin L. Reymert; Recollections of a Norwegian Pioneer in Texas, by Knudt Olson Hastvedt, translated and edited by C. A. Clausen; Norwegian Clubs in Chicago, by Birger Osland; Buslett's Editorship of *Normannen* from 1894 to 1896, by Evelyn Nilsen; Ole Edvart Rølvaag, by John Heitmann; Ole Evinrude and the Outboard Motor, by Kenneth Bjørk; Some Recent Publications Relating to Norwegian-American History, VIII, compiled by Jacob Hodnefield.   Price $4.00

VOLUME XIII. Northfield, 1943. 203 p. Pioneers in Dakota Territory, 1879-89, edited by Henry H. Bakken; An Official Report on Norwegian and Swedish Immigration, 1870, by A. Lewenhaupt, with a foreword by Theodore C. Blegen; Memories from Little Iowa Parsonage, by Caroline Mathilde Koren Naeseth, translated and edited by Henriette C. K. Naeseth; A Norwegian Schoolmaster Looks at America, an America letter translated and edited by C. A. Clausen; A Singing Church, by Paul Maurice Glasoe; A Norwegian Settlement in Missouri, by A. N. Rygg; Carl G. Barth, 1860–1939: A Sketch, by Florence M. Manning; Pioneering on the Pacific Coast, by John Storseth, with a foreword by Einar Haugen; Materials in the National Archives Relating to the Scandinavian Countries; The Norwegians in America, by Halvdan Koht; Some Recent Publications Relating to Norwegian-American History, IX, compiled by Jacob Hodnefield; Notes and Documents: Norway, Maine, by Halvdan Koht.   Price $4.00

VOLUME XIV. Northfield, 1944. 264 p. A Migration of Skills, by Kenneth Bjørk; An Immigrant Exploration of the Middle West in 1839, a letter by Johannes Johansen and Søren Bache, translated by the Verdandi Study Club; An Immigrant Shipload of 1840, by C. A. Clausen; Behind the Scenes of Emigration: A Series of Letters from the 1840's, by Johan R. Reiersen, translated by Carl O. Paulson and the Verdandi Study Club, edited by Theodore C. Blegen; The Ballad of Oleana: A Verse Translation, by Theodore C. Blegen; Knud Langeland: Pioneer Editor, by Arlow W. Andersen; Memories from Perry Parsonage, by Clara Jacobson; When America Called for Immigrants, by Halvdan Koht; The Norwegian Lutheran Academies, by B. H. Narveson; Pioneering on the Technical Front: A Story Told in America Letters, by Kenneth Bjørk; Some Recent Publications Relating to Norwegian-American History, X, by Jacob Hodnefield; Notes and Documents: Karel Hansen Toll, by A. N. Rygg.   Price $4.00

VOLUME XV. Northfield, 1949. 238 p. A Norwegian-American Pioneer Ballad, by Einar Haugen; Our Vanguard: A Pioneer Play in Three Acts, with Prologue and Epilogue, by Aileen Berger Buetow; An Immigrant's Advice on America: Some Letters of Søren Bache, translated and edited by C. A. Clausen; Lincoln and the Union: A Study of the Editorials of *Emigranten and Fædrelandet*, by Arlow W. Andersen; Thorstein Veblen and St. Olaf College: A Group of Letters by Thorbjørn N. Mohn, edited by Kenneth Bjork; Kristian Prestgard: An Appreciation, by Henriette C. K. Naeseth; Julius B. Baumann: A Biographical Sketch, by John Heitmann; Erik L. Petersen, by Jacob Hodnefield; Scandinavia, Wisconsin, by Alfred O. Erickson; Some Recent Publications Relating to Norwegian-American History, XI, by Jacob Hodnefield; Notes and Documents: Norway, Maine, by Walter W. Wright.
Price $4.00

VOLUME XVI. Northfield, 1950. 218 p. Hvistendahl's Mission to San Francisco, 1870–75, by Kenneth Bjork; Oregon and Washington Territory in the 1870's As Seen through the Eyes of a Pioneer Pastor, by Nora O. Solum; From the Prairie to Puget Sound, by O. B. Iverson, edited by Sverre Arestad; Life in the Klondike and Alaska Gold Fields, letters translated and edited by C. A. Clausen; From the Klondike to the Kougarok, by Carl L. Lokke; Some Recent Publications Relating to Norwegian-American History, XII, compiled by Jacob Hodnefield.   Price $4.00

VOLUME XVII. Northfield, 1952. 185 p. The Struggle over Norwegian, by Einar Haugen; Brother Ebben in His Native Country, by Oystein Ore; Norwegian Gold Seekers in the Rockies, by Kenneth Bjork; Søren Jaabæk, Americanizer in Norway: A Study in Cultural Exchange, by Franklin D. Scott; First Sagas in a New World: A Study of the Beginnings of Norwegian-American Literature, by Gerald H. Thorson; Controlled Scholarship and Productive Nationalism, by Franklin D. Scott; The Second Twenty-five Years, by Theodore C. Blegen; Some Recent Publications Relating to Norwegian-American History, XIII, by Jacob Hodnefield.

Price $4.00

VOLUME XVIII. Northfield, 1954. 252 p. Maps. Norwegian Migration to America, by Einar Haugen; Rasmus B. Anderson, Pioneer and Crusader, by Paul Knaplund; Early Norwegian Settlement in the Rockies, by Kenneth Bjork; A Little More Light on the Kendall Colony, by Richard Canuteson; Segregation and Assimilation of Norwegian Settlements in Wisconsin, by Peter A. Munch; The Novels of Peer Stømme, by Gerald Thorson; Norwegian-American *Bygdelags* and Their Publications, by Jacob Hodnefield; Some Recent Publications Relating to Norwegian-American History, XIV, by Jacob Hodnefield. Price $4.00

VOLUME XIX. Northfield, 1956. 218 p. The Immigrant Image of America, by Theodore C. Blegen; Boyesen and the Norwegian Immigration, by Clarence A. Glasrud; Norwegian Forerunners among the Early Mormons, by William Mulder; "Snowshoe" Thompson: Fact and Legend, by Kenneth Bjork; Norwegian-Danish Methodism on the Pacific Coast, by Arlow William Andersen; A Quest for Norwegian Folk Art in America, by Tora Bøhn; The Trials of an Immigrant: The Journal of Ole K. Trovatten, translated and edited by Clarence A. Clausen; Norwegian Emigrants with University Training, 1830–1880, by Oystein Ore; Some Recent Publications Relating to Norwegian-American History, XV, compiled by Clarence A. Clausen. Price $4.00

VOLUME XX. Northfield, 1959. 246 p. Ibsen in America, by Einar Haugen; Still More Light on the Kendall Colony: A Unique Slooper Letter, by Mario S. De Pillis; A Texas Manifesto: A Letter from Mrs. Elise Wærenskjold, translated and edited by Clarence A. Clausen; History and Sociology, by Peter A. Munch; Beating to Windward, by Otto M. Bratrud, edited by Sverre Arestad; Pioneering in Alaska, by Knute L. Gravem; Marcus Thrane in Christiania: Some Unpublished Letters from 1850–51, translated and edited by Waldemar Westergaard; A Centenary of Norwegian Studies in American Institutions of Learning, by Hedin Bronner; Elizabeth Fedde's Dairy, 1883–88, translated and edited by Beulah Folkedahl; The Content of Studies and Records, Volumes 1–20, compiled by Helen Thane Katz; "With Great Price," by John M. Gaus; Some Recent Publications Relating to Norwegian-American History, XVI, compiled by Clarence A. Clausen.

Price $4.00

VOLUME XXI (*Norwegian-American Studies*). Northfield, 1962. 311 p. Theodore C. Blegen, by Carlton C. Qualey; The Scandinavian Immigrant Writer in America, by Dorothy Burton Skårdal; Questing for Gold and Furs in Alaska, edited by Sverre Arestad; Norwegians Become Americans, translated and edited by Beulah Folkedahl; Cleng Peerson and the Communitarian Background of Norwegian Immigration, by Mario S. De Pillis; Early Years in Dakota, by Barbara Levorsen; A Pioneer Diary from Wisconsin, by Malcolm Rosholt; A Covenant Folk, with Scandinavian Colorings, by Kenneth O. Bjork; Reiersen's Texas, translated and edited by Derwood Johnson; J. R. Reiersen's "Indiscretions," by Einar Haugen; Some Recent Publications, compiled by Beulah Folkedahl; From the archives, by Beulah Folkedahl.   Price $4.00

VOLUME XXII. Northfield, 1965. 264 p. Illustrations. A Pioneer Artist and His Masterpiece, by Marion John Nelson; Kristofer Janson's Lecture Tour, 1879–80, by Nina Draxten; Two Men of Old Waupaca, by Malcolm Rosholt; Pioneering in Montana, edited by Sverre Arestad; Seven America Letters to Valdres, translated and edited by Carlton C. Qualey; Music for Youth in an Emerging Church, by Gerhard M. Cartford; Our Bread and Meat, by Barbara Levorsen; The Independent Historical Society, by Walter Muir Whitehill; Some Recent Publications, compiled by Beulah Folkedahl; From the Archives, by Beulah Folkedahl.   Price $4.00

VOLUME XXIII. Northfield, 1967. 256 p. The Norwegian Immigrant and His Church, by Eugene L. Fevold; Some Civil War Letters of Knute Nelson, edited by Millard L. Gieske; An Immigrant Boy on the Frontier, by Simon Johnson, translated with an introduction by Nora O. Solum; The Gasmann Brothers Write Home, translated and edited by C. A. Clausen; Knud Knudsen and His America Book, by Beulah Folkedahl; Kristofer Janson's Beginning Ministry, by Nina Draxten; Knut Hamsun's America, by Arlow W. Andersen; The Romantic Spencerian, by Marc L. Ratner; Some Recent Publications, compiled by Beulah Folkedahl; From the Archives, by Beulah Folkedahl.　　Price $4.00

TRAVEL AND DESCRIPTION SERIES

VOLUME I. *Ole Rynning's True Account of America.* Translated and edited by Theodore C. Blegen. Minneapolis, 1926. 100 p. Historical introduction; original text of Rynning's book about America as published in Norway in 1838; and a complete English translation.　　Price $1.50

VOLUME II. *Peter Testman's Account of His Experiences in North America.* Translated and edited by Theodore C. Blegen. Northfield, 1927. 60 p. Historical introduction; facsimile of Testman's account of America as published in Norway in 1839; and a complete English translation.　　Price $1.50

VOLUME III. *America in the Forties: The Letters of Ole Munch Ræder.* Translated and edited by Gunnar J. Malmin. Published for the Norwegian-American Historical Association by the University of Minnesota Press, Minneapolis, 1929. 244 p. Historical introduction, frontispiece, index. A series of informal travel letters written 1847–48 by a Norwegian scholar who was sent by his government to America to make a study of the jury system. Price $2.50

VOLUME IV. *Frontier Parsonage: The Letters of Olaus Fredrik Duus, Norwegian Pastor in Wisconsin, 1855–1858.* Translated by the Verdandi Study Club of Minneapolis and edited by Theodore C. Blegen. Northfield, 1947. 120 p. Historical introduction, index.　　Price $3.50

VOLUME V. *Frontier Mother: The Letters of Gro Svendsen.* Translated and edited by Pauline Farseth and Theodore C. Blegen.

253

Northfield, 1950. 153 p. Historical introduction, frontispiece, index. Out of print

VOLUME VI. *The Lady with the Pen: Elise Wærenskjold in Texas.* Translated by the Verdandi Study Club of Minneapolis and edited by C. A. Clausen; foreword by Theodore C. Blegen. Northfield, 1961. 183 p. Historical introduction, illustrations, index. Price $4.00

VOLUME VII. *Klondike Saga: The Chronicle of a Minnesota Gold Mining Company.* By Carl L. Lokke. Preface by Kenneth O. Bjork; foreword by Senator Ernest Gruening. Published for the Norwegian-American Historical Association by the University of Minnesota Press, Minneapolis, 1965. 211 p. Illustrations, maps, appendixes, index. Available from bookstores and from the University of Minnesota Press. Price $5.50

SPECIAL PUBLICATIONS

Norwegian Sailors on the Great Lakes: A Study in the History of American Inland Transportation. By Knut Gjerset. Northfield, 1928. 211 p. Illustrations, index. Out of print

Norwegian Migration to America, 1825–1860. By Theodore C. Blegen. Northfield, 1931. 413 p. Illustrations, maps, appendix, index. Price $6.00

Norwegian Sailors in American Waters: A Study in the History of Maritime Activity on the Eastern Seaboard. By Knut Gjerset. Northfield, 1933. 271 p. Illustrations, index. Price $4.00

The Civil War Letters of Colonel Hans Christian Heg. Edited by Theodore C. Blegen. Northfield, 1936. 260 p. Historical introduction, illustrations, index. Price $4.00

Laur. Larsen: Pioneer College President. By Karen Larsen. Northfield, 1936. 358 p. Illustrations, bibliographical note, index. Out of print

The Changing West and Other Essays. By Laurence M. Larson. Northfield, 1937. 180 p. Illustrations, index. Price $4.50

Norwegian Settlement in the United States. By Carlton C. Qualey. Northfield, 1939. 285 p. Illustrations, maps, appendix, bibliography, index. Price $5.00

The Log Book of a Young Immigrant. By Laurence M. Larson. Northfield, 1939. 318 p. Illustrations, selected list of Larson's writings, index. Price $5.00

Norwegian Migration to America: The American Transition. By Theodore C. Blegen. Northfield, 1940. 655 p. Illustrations, appendix, index. Price $7.00

A Long Pull from Stavanger: The Reminiscences of a Norwegian Immigrant. By Birger Osland. Northfield, 1945. 263 p. Portrait, index. Price $4.00

Saga in Steel and Concrete: Norwegian Engineers in America. By Kenneth Bjork. Northfield, 1947. 504 p. Illustrations, index. Price $6.00

Grass of the Earth: Immigrant Life in the Dakota Country. By Aagot Raaen. Northfield, 1950. 238 p. Index. Out of print

A Chronicle of Old Muskego: The Diary of Søren Bache, 1839–1847. Translated and edited by Clarence A. Clausen and Andreas Elviken. Northfield, 1951. 237 p. Historical introduction, portrait, appendix, index. Price $4.50

The Immigrant Takes His Stand: The Norwegian-American Press and Public Affairs, 1847–1872. By Arlow William Andersen. Northfield, 1953. 176 p. Bibliography, index. Price $4.00

The Diary of Elisabeth Koren, 1853–1855. Translated and edited by David T. Nelson. Northfield, 1955. 381 p. Historical introduction, illustrations, index. Price $5.00

West of the Great Divide: Norwegian Migration to the Pacific Coast, 1847–1893. By Kenneth O. Bjork. Northfield, 1958. 671 p. Illustrations, maps, index. Price $8.00

PUBLICATIONS

AUTHORS SERIES

VOLUME I. *Hjalmar Hjorth Boyesen.* By Clarence A. Glasrud. Northfield, 1963. 245 p. Illustrations, bibliography, index.

Price $5.50

VOLUME II. *Rasmus Bjørn Anderson: Pioneer Scholar.* By Lloyd Hustvedt, Northfield, 1966. 381 p. Illustrations, bibliography, index. Price $6.75